HOW COME?

Every Kid's SCIENCE QUESTIONS Explained

BY **KATHY WOLLARD**

ILLUSTRATED BY **DEBRA SOLOMON**

WORKMAN PUBLISHING · NEW YORK

To Evan and Aaron.
And to Debra Solomon, who's always brought the delightful zaniness to *How Come?*
—KW

For my brilliant Mom.
—DJS

Library of Congress Cataloging-in-Publication Data is available.

ISBN 978-0-7611-7978-8

Workman books are available at special discounts when purchased in bulk for premiums and sales promotions as
well as for fund-raising or educational use. Special editions of book excerpts can also be created to specification.
For details, contact the Special Sales Director at the address below or send an email to specialmarkets@workman.com.

Cover and interior design by Ariana Abud

Workman Publishing Company, Inc.
225 Varick Street
New York, NY 10014-4381
workman.com

Printed in China

First printing December 2014

10 9 8 7 6 5 4 3 2 1

CONTENTS

THE GREAT BEYOND 106

HOME PLANET 150

ALL ABOUT ME (AND YOU) 323

INTRODUCTION

All of the amazing questions in this book were asked by real kids (and a few adults). They mailed and emailed thousands of them to *Newsday*'s How Come? newspaper column from all over the world: from Brooklyn, New York, to Bangalore, India. Questions poured in from Australia and Brazil, Indonesia and Canada, from Oman and the U.K. All of these curious kids helped make the book you're holding in your hand.

In 1993, the first *How Come?* book was published in the U.S., and since then it has been translated and published in 11 countries. Kids everywhere want to know why the sky is blue, why we see shimmering patches of water on a summer road, and why we can't feel the Earth turning. Science is a way for us to tease out the answers—to get the universe to reveal its secrets.

Since science is always making new—and often startling—discoveries, the answers evolve and change. This new *How Come?* has the latest scoop. Here you'll find the most up-to-date (and often surprising) explanations for those enduring mysteries, which every discovery makes brand-new again. (You won't believe the reason why our fingers wrinkle underwater! See page 324.) And as you skip around the book, you'll see that completely different things—like raindrops and soap bubbles, or moving elevators and spinning planets—actually have everything in common. —Kathy Wollard

Measure FOR Measure
20 pounds of *How Come?* mail = 9 kg

You'll see this little box throughout the book. It's a handy reference to the metric conversions for the measurements mentioned in the entry. The metric system—kilograms and kilometers instead of pounds and miles—is used by scientists (and almost everyone else) almost everywhere on Earth.

EVERY QUESTION IS A GOOD QUESTION!

Is there something you're wondering about? Send all your questions to:
howcome@how-come.net,
and they may be answered in the
How Come? newspaper column.

TRICKS OF LIGHT AND SOUND

Light is made of tiny bundles of energy, particles called photons. Photons zip along at an astonishing 186,000 miles a second in a vacuum (such as space). Although light is a particle, it also acts like a wave. Our eyes can only see light in a certain range of wavelengths—those of visible light, the kind we see coming from the Sun, or a lamp.

Ultraviolet light, X-rays, and gamma rays are also kinds of light—but with photons too energetic (and with too short a wavelength) for human eyes to see. Likewise, infrared light, microwaves, and radio waves are too low-energy (and with too long a wavelength) for us to see. Many other animals, however, like birds and bumblebees, can see light in some frequencies we can't. Visible

light comes in a rainbow of colors; white light is these colors combined. Put a prism in a beam of bright sunlight, and the light will split into its colors, or wavelengths: red, orange, yellow, green, blue, indigo, and finally violet, the shortest wavelength of the visible spectrum.

The rainbow is revealed because the prism bends the light of each wavelength a little more or less than the next, so each emerges on its own. A second prism to catch the rainbow light, placed upside down, will recombine the colors—making one white beam again.

Unlike light, sound waves need material to travel through: gas (the air around us), liquid (say, seawater), or solids (like a wooden door). In fact, with sound, the medium *is* the message: Sound is no more or no less than a passing vibration in matter. Sound waves moving through the air, gas molecules bunching up and then spreading out, travel at about 1,100 feet per second (about 340 m/s). That's why we see the bright flash of lightning in the distance, but hear its low rumble several seconds later.

Why is the sky blue?

Bored with Blue?...Suggestions for the summer sky

What about plaids...

or animal prints...

...how about mile-long paisleys crawling through a sea of stripes?

The sunlight that lights up the daytime sky is white. So why isn't the sky a brilliant white? In order for the sky to look blue, something must be happening to the light as it passes through Earth's atmosphere.

When white light streams in from the Sun, it zips from the near vacuum of space into the gassy atmosphere blanketing our planet. While Earth's air contains traces of many gases, from carbon dioxide to argon, nitrogen (at 78 percent) and oxygen (21 percent) make up most of the atmosphere. And when photons of sunlight encounter the gas molecules of Earth's air, they are changed by the encounter.

Where does the blue come from? Actually, the blue was in sunlight all along. White light is made of a concealed rainbow of colors, revealed when a beam of sunlight passes through a prism. Then we see the familiar rainbow spectrum: red, orange, yellow, green, blue, indigo, violet. Each color is a different energy and wavelength.

The air's gases tease these colors out of white light. Some sunlight simply zips through the empty spaces between gas molecules, reaching the ground intact. But light that has a run-in with gas molecules is absorbed, split into its true colors, and then scattered every which way.

How does it work? A gas molecule's member atoms

get excited by the photons (particles) of light, and re-emit photons in distinct wavelengths—from red to yellow to violet. The light then heads on toward the ground or is sent out sideways into the sky. Depending on the angle, some light even zooms back into space.

And here's how the sky turns blue: The shorter-wavelength blue-to-violet end of the sunlight spectrum is scattered much more than the reds and yellows. So we see blue light from every direction in the sky, overpowering fainter red, yellow, and orange.

Interestingly, violet light is scattered by gas molecules even more strongly than blue. So why don't we see a sky awash in purples? According to physicist Jearl Walker of Cleveland State University, there are two explanations: The violet part of sunlight is dimmer than the blue, and human eyes are less sensitive to shorter-wavelength violet.

It may be a different story for others living on Earth. Since the eyes of animals are sensitive to different wavelengths of light, it's likely that many animals perceive Earth's sky in different hues. Honeybees, for example, can see all the way into the spectrum's invisible-to-us ultraviolet. To a bee, the sky may be tinted purple.

For us humans, during the daytime, the blue stands out, intensified by the black backdrop of space behind the sunlit atmosphere. But where does the blue go at night? While the Sun is below the horizon, Earth's sky is still

Other animals, whose eyes have different color receptors, may see a differently colored sky.

just as full of gas, scattering the light that remains. According to Walker, the night sky is indeed still blue. But the blue is simply too dim for our eyes and brain to perceive. However, a camera set for a long exposure—collecting light for several minutes to several hours—can reveal the deep, true blue of a starry night.

Why does the sky turn colors at sunset?

On a sunny day, the sky is blue, the clouds white, and the Sun a normal, if a bit boring, yellowish-white. But at sunset, white clouds and blue sky turn pink and orange and purple, and the Sun glows orange red. This stunning change is brought to you mainly by whizzing gas molecules, along with other tiny particles drifting in the sky.

Here's how it works. The light that is produced inside the Sun is white light. But white light contains within it many colors—all the colors of the rainbow. A prism splits white light into its true colors like a comb separating hair into its strands. White light enters the prism; bands of red, orange, yellow, green, blue, indigo, and violet light stream out the other side.

As sunlight encounters the atmosphere's gas molecules (like nitrogen and oxygen), it is broken up into its colors, then scattered every which way. Longer-wavelength light, like red, is scattered less. Shorter-wavelength light—blue and violet—is scattered more, flooding the sky.

At sunset and sunrise, with the Sun near the horizon, its rays traveling nearly parallel to the ground, sunlight must travel a longer path through a thicker blanket of air before it reaches our eyes. Even more of the blue end of the spectrum is scattered out of the light beam and into the sky. And we see the Sun's face redden.

Clouds reflect the reddened light too, creating a tapestry of oranges, reds, and pinks. Just after the Sun sets, purple patches may develop in the sky. Some scientists think the purple is a color overlap: intense red light from near the horizon mixing with blue light

Fast Fact

When volcanoes erupt, dust and ash particles and droplets of sulfuric acid are lofted high into the sky. After the sun sets, these "clouds" 12 to 18 miles high can scatter yellow light, creating crimson twilight afterglows.

Sunsets: basking in the sun's... long red hair

from higher in the sky.

As the Sun sets, light streaming through our west-facing windows turns a deep gold, and bright oranges and reds streak the sky. But when the Sun rises, the light that first floods through our east-facing windows may be a beautiful blue as the sky begins to light, often followed by a rosy pink as the Sun makes its appearance.

How come? Dust and pollutants are near their peak at sunset, after a day's activity by human beings—digging in the ground, constructing buildings, operating machinery, driving cars. The tiniest of these particles, comparable in size to gas molecules, also scatter blues out of sunbeams—making the Sun's face appear extra-red. Larger particles reflect and scatter warmer colors, adding red shades to the sky.

The air at sunset is also usually much warmer than the air at sunrise, since the Earth cools overnight, radiating heat into space. And hotter air is more turbulent than cooler air. At dawn, scientists say, the lower atmosphere is calmer, cooler, and cleaner. Daytime's dust has settled. Air molecules still scatter blues out of the streaming sunlight. But since there are fewer tiny particles to add to the scattering, the rising sun may appear less red than the setting sun. And clouds in the dawn sky may wear more delicate tints of pink, yellow, and peach.

Why is the color of a flame yellow-orange?

Bright yellow flames on the birthday candles studding an iced cake. Dusky blue flames circling the burner of a gas stove. Dancing yellow-orange flames crackling over wood in the fireplace, with flashes of red, green, and blue. Fire comes in a rainbow of colors, some rarely seen outside a science lab.

Flame color depends on two things: the temperature of the flame and the material being burned.

Anyone who's watched a burner on an old-style electric stove knows that color can change with temperature. Turn the burner on HIGH to warm a pot of soup, and the cool black coils slowly begin to glow. A bit of dark red creeps in, gradually changing to a bright orange-red, meaning hot-hot-hot.

While electric stove coils can get very hot, the burner is not *really* burning—it's not on fire. It's just getting

very hot. If those coils were a chunk of steel heated to even higher temperatures in a blast furnace, the color would progress to a brilliant yellowish-white.

But the colors of a burning candle flame also depend, at least in part, on temperature.

Fires need oxygen. (If you put a jar over a candle, the flame will die out.) When a candle is burning, the middle of the flame isn't getting much oxygen. So it looks darker. But the outside and top of the flame, which get lots of air, burn bright.

As the wick burns and the wax melts, bits of carbon fly up. These teeny pieces of carbon, heated, glow like hot coals in a grill—or like the coils of your electric stove. But since a typical candle flame is hotter than the burner on an electric stove—more than 2,500°F (1,371°C)—it glows yellow instead of red. This is what makes candle flames mostly yellow. Near the burning wick, in the actual reaction or combustion zone, the flame is hottest of all— and therefore blue.

A gas stove runs on natural gas or propane, which burn purely and cleanly, with little or no soot to glow yellow. So a gas stove has a blue flame. (Solid yellow flames mean something's wrong; call the gas company.)

Spill a little salt into a blue gas flame, and it will also flare yellow. Why? Heated in a flame, the sodium in table salt emits bright yellow light.

Different metals and metallic salts emit different wavelengths (colors) of light when heated in a flame. Electrons in the chemical get excited and gain energy, rather like corn popping in a microwave. When the electrons return to their normal energy levels, they release the excess energy as photons of light. While sodium atoms give off yellow

Fast Fact

Minerals like calcium, sodium, and copper, heated to high temperatures, give exploding fireworks their brilliant colors.

light, different forms of copper emit higher-energy green or blue-green light.

A wood fire, which usually burns at a lower temperature than a candle, is often a warmer orange-yellow. Calcium salts, phosphorus, and other elements in wood or in materials thrown on the fire add their own signature colors—like red and blue-green—to the crackling flames.

Scientists can even use a flame test to identify some chemicals. Potassium iodide sprinkled into a Bunsen burner will make the flame violet; barium will turn it green.

How are shadows formed?

In *Peter Pan* by J. M. Barrie, Peter loses his shadow when Nana the dog grabs it as Peter escapes out a window. Finding the shadow, Nana's owner, Mrs. Darling, rolls it up and puts it in a drawer for safekeeping.

Real shadows are more ephemeral. Try to grab a shadow, and your hand will simply pass into its shade. Try to jump on your own shadow, and it jumps with you, ever connected to your feet.

A shadow appears when an object stands in the way of light. The less light that can pass through an object, the more solid its shadow. So a translucent beach ball casts a faint shadow, while your body casts a solid, dark shadow.

On a sunny day, a shadow is a patch of night. But any light source can make a shadow—the Sun, a lamp, a flashlight, the silvery Moon. Try making your own shadows using an unshaded lamp, your hand, and a plain white wall. You'll discover that if you move your hand closer to the wall, the shadow becomes more sharply defined. Or if you move the lamp close to your hand, your

> Try making your own shadows using an unshaded lamp, your hand, and a plain white wall.

shadow becomes fuzzier. Move the lamp away, and the shadow becomes sharper again.

Finally, the larger the light, the fuzzier the shadow. When a lightbulb wears a lampshade, the shade creates, in effect, a bigger, more diffuse light source. Which is why a lampshade makes for a blurrier shadow than a bare lightbulb.

The Sun is enormous (a million Earths could fit inside it), but it is also enormously distant (nearly 93 million miles away, or 149,600,000 km). So the Sun appears as a rather small light source in the sky. Which is why the combination of the Sun, you, and the sidewalk makes such great shadows.

The Sun is very bright but very far away, you are very solid, and the sidewalk is very near.

Even the sharpest shadow is a bit blurry around the edges. Outdoors, this out-of-focus quality is a result of the Sun being larger than a point in the sky. Light streams from countless points on the Sun's disk, each ray traveling on its own course and creating a shadow of its own. The rays of light diffract (bend slightly) around your body's edges, creating an interference pattern of darkness and light, and a shadow with fuzzy edges. If light were to come from one shrunk-down perfect point, there would be one sharp, clean shadow.

On an overcast day, with the Sun hidden behind clouds, the whole sky acts as a diffuse light source—like an enormous lampshade. Your body still casts a shadow. But your shadow is so hugely spread out and fuzzy that you can't see it at all.

SHADOW PLAY

To make your Sun-made shadow bigger or smaller, simply venture outdoors several times from early morning until noon. Your shadow will be longer when the Sun is low in the sky, shorter when the Sun is higher. With the Sun directly overhead, shadows dwindle to nothing. You'll cast the longest, skinniest shadow near sunrise or sunset.

Me And My Light Source...

Hey, there you are!

Where you going?

Bye-bye!

Where do rainbows come from?

William Wordsworth, an English poet who published his first sonnet in 1787, wrote:

> *My heart leaps up when I behold*
> *A rainbow in the sky . . .*

Something about seeing a rainbow gives us a shivery feeling. The bands of color, dipping down from the sky, are so beautiful and rare.

People once thought rainbows were signs from the gods. It's not surprising. A rainbow appears in the sky, seemingly out of nowhere. Then, just as mysteriously, it vanishes.

Today, we know something about how rainbows are made, but that should not make us appreciate them any less. Scientists who unravel rainbow mysteries use math. They say that even the math that explains a rainbow is special and lovely (although it's also very complicated).

The colors of a regular rainbow always come in the same order: first red, then orange, yellow, green, blue, indigo, and violet. Red is the brightest band of color, running along the top of the bow. Then come the others, each paler than the last. Violet, the inner band, is dimmest and hardest to see of all.

What are rainbows made from? The recipe is simple: droplets of water in the air, light, and someone to look up at just the right moment.

It's not enough, however, for the Sun to come out during a shower. A rainbow is a kind of trick of light, and the conditions must be just right for us to see one. Sunlight must be streaming from behind us, so the Sun must be low on the horizon. And in front of us, of course, there must be a curtain of falling raindrops.

How does it work? A beam of sunlight, making its long journey from space, plunges into the heart of

> Raindrops can act like tiny prisms, splitting white light into a spectrum of colors.

a raindrop. When a ray of sunlight pierces the drop, it begins to bend. That's because the light is passing into water, which is much denser (its molecules more closely packed) than thin air.

White light is really a blend of hidden colors—red, orange, yellow, green, blue, indigo, violet (think Roy G. Biv). And as a light beam enters a drop, each color, or wavelength, bends (refracts) a little more or less, like sunlight passing through a glass prism. The result? The white sunbeam splits apart into beautiful rays of color, each going off on its own direction inside the drop.

Inside the raindrop, the colored rays collide with the mirrorlike raindrop wall, bend again, and shoot back out of the drop. Making their escape,

Fast Fact

You don't always need raindrops to make rainbows. Light can be refracted by fog or by a spray of water from a garden hose.

the colored rays bend again as they move from denser water into open air. The sunlight had originally come from behind you. Now the altered light, in its true colors, is shooting back at you.

While all raindrops in the sky refract sunlight, we're only able to see the light coming from drops at a certain viewing angle. From this "rainbow band" of drops, our eyes receive different colors from drops in different positions in the sky.

Since red and orange wavelengths are bent the most, we see these colors courtesy of higher drops.

Blue and violet are less sharply bent, so we get these colors from lower drops. Yellow and green are provided by the drops in the middle of the band. And you see an arc of colors, stretching across the sky.

Because they are tricks of light, rainbows aren't "things" in the sky, like birds or clouds. Each person present sees a different rainbow (or, if lucky, double rainbow) made from the light rays streaming in from behind and the raindrops in front. The rainbow you see is yours alone.

DOUBLE RAINBOWS

Once in a while, you may have the rare pleasure of seeing two rainbows appear at once. The second rainbow is larger, but pale, and hard to see. And unlike the bright "primary" rainbow, the secondary rainbow has its colors reversed: The outer band is violet, the inner band red.

What causes a secondary rainbow to materialize? The second bow appears when light rays enter near the bottom of each raindrop, and then reflect from the inside wall of a raindrop twice (instead of once) before exiting. When these twice-reflected rays emerge from many different raindrops, we see a second rainbow, paler and wider, above the first.

Why are the second bow's colors reversed? Doubly bent red light from the very highest drops ends up traveling over our heads. So we see violet light, bent to our eyes from lower raindrops, as the first band of light, followed by indigo, blue, green, yellow, orange, and then red from lower drops.

Between the two rainbows, the sky appears dim. Why? Since there is extra light below the primary bow—and more light above the mirror-image secondary bow—the sky between the two looks dark by comparison.

The slice of sky sandwiched between rainbows is called Alexander's Dark Band. It was named after Alexander of Aphrodisias, an ancient Greek philosopher who wrote about the puzzling dark patch some 1,800 years ago.

Why do things look darker when they're wet?

Refraction at Work!

I only look wet because I am wet.

Ever take a swim in the ocean, and notice that your hair and your swimsuit both look darker? As you walk back to your beach chair, you notice your wet feet leave dark footprints in the sand. As you dry off, your towel darkens, too.

But it's not just seawater that does the trick. Pelting raindrops can turn your plain white shirt into a polka-dotted mess. Rinse off the sidewalk with a hose, and you'll see the white cement turn gray. You can even use the narrow stream of a hose to write your name on the driveway.

Many porous objects—paper, fabric, tree bark, soil, hair—darken as they are doused in (clear) water. How come?

When light strikes a dry material, some is reflected straight back. Some is absorbed. And some is scattered every which way from the irregular surface. (Think of the rough surface of sand, the shingled surface of each hair, the woven surface of fabric.) When a material looks darker than normal, it means that less than the usual amount of light is rebounding back.

Take fabric. Cotton fabric is a weave of natural fibers, the gaps between fibers filled with air. When light strikes the dry surface of a cotton shirt, it is refracted (it bends) at the interface between fibers and trapped air. Much of the light simply scatters back out from the surface of the material.

But when the fabric is struck by raindrops, water seeps in and fills the air gaps. The irregular surface, which scatters light when dry, is

> Many porous objects—from paper and cloth to soil and hair—darken when doused in water.

smoothed by the film of water. Since water is denser than air, its "refractive index," or the amount it bends light, is closer to that of the cotton fabric. So at the shirt's wet spots, light has smoother sailing: More light penetrates into the fabric, instead of scattering from the surface. That means less light reaching our eyes. And so the wet parts of the fabric appear

darker than the surrounding dry material.

Likewise, hair soaks up water in the shower or ocean, temporarily plumping and smoothing the surface of each strand. According to physicists, light is absorbed by the water layer and repeatedly reflects within it. So instead of scattering off the hair's surface, more light is effectively trapped inside. And hair (even gray hair) appears darker.

When water drenches a road, its effect on light can

It ain't fair when underwear becomes outerwear...

FROM DARK TO LIGHT

When hair or concrete gets wet, we notice only the darkening. But a wet fabric can also become more transparent. As more light penetrates the material traveling in straighter lines, more exits through the other side. If you happen to be wearing this wet material, the light will bounce off your skin and right back out. Which is why getting soaking wet in the rain can be such an embarrassing situation.

make driving doubly dicey. At night, in dry conditions, light from your car's headlights hits the road, reflecting and scattering from the surface. The light that reaches your eyes allows you to see both the road surface itself and the lines marking lanes and shoulder.

But when it rains, a thin layer of water coats the surface of the asphalt. Instead of striking the road itself, some of the light from your headlights reflects back from the water's surface, creating a (confusing) mirror effect.

Meanwhile, light that does penetrate down to the road's surface must travel back out through the water layer. And at the water's surface, instead of exiting into the air, some of that light is simply reflected back down to the road. The result: The light that does reach your eyes from the road's surface is significantly dimmed, and dividing lines become much harder to see.

Why do our eyes turn red in flash photos?

When an animal's eyes glow green or yellow in the headlights, it's a sign of good night vision. A special layer of cells in the back of the eye reflects light back like a mirror. Some of that light is reabsorbed by the eye, letting a deer, raccoon, or opossum see better in the dark.

But human eye-glow doesn't lead to anything but weird-looking birthday photos—Mom, Dad, and little Billy leaning over the candle-studded cake, all with gleaming red eyes. If a camera steals your soul, perhaps a flashbulb replaces it with something demonic.

Actually, the creepy red-eye effect is due to something a lot more benign—those

The ingredients for the red-eye effect: a dim room, a camera with a flash, and a person looking straight into the lens.

pesky blood vessels in the back of the eye.

The ingredients for the red-eye effect are simple: a dark night or dim room, a camera with a flash, and a person willing to look straight into the lens (or better yet, at the flash itself).

When the flash goes off, light streams through the pupil, the eye's adjustable porthole. The eye's lens focuses the light on the light-collecting retina in the rear, which is fed by a crisscrossing network of blood vessels. When the burst of white light hits the vessels, they absorb light from the blue-green end of the spectrum, but reflect back red. Ruby-red light shoots back out through the eye and into the camera lens. Presto: the possessed effect.

In a dim room, our pupils are already open wide. And because of the way our eyes' iris muscles must bunch up to contract the pupils, they don't shut quickly. So when the flashbulb goes off, the pupil doesn't have time to shrink much—and the bright, focused light shoots straight through. Outdoors in the daytime, pupils are already at their most constricted, so a flash photo won't show red eyes.

Light blue or gray eyes often glow most crimson in photos, since pale irises have less pigment to block light.

Many cameras reduce the red-eye effect by setting off several quick flashes before actually taking the picture. That way, the pupils have time to constrict before the final flash.

To avoid red-eye, try taking pictures with more room light and no flash. In a camera with an adjustable flash, point the bulb at a white ceiling or wall rather than at the people you're photographing. You can also use photo-processing software to reduce the red in the final photograph.

How can X-rays take pictures of your bones?

Remember Superman's X-ray vision? His eyes shot X-rays at a door; the beams bored through, and he could see what his enemies were up to on the other side. Only doors made of lead could foil Superman.

Lead is a good shield against X-rays. That's why we wear heavy lead aprons at the dentist's office. But Superman's X-ray eyes came from the imagination of his creator. Eyes can't shoot beams of light. Our eyes see when light from other sources, like the Sun, is reflected back from an object.

However, X-rays are indeed a kind of light—a kind that is invisible to us. X-ray light has a lot more energy than visible light. That's how it can penetrate wooden doors—or skin and muscle.

X-rays and ordinary visible light are just part of the electromagnetic spectrum—light of varying wavelengths, frequencies, and energies. There's the "visible" light our eyes are equipped to see (the light of a glowing lightbulb or the Sun). Ultraviolet light, more energetic than the ordinary violet we can see, is perfectly visible to some other animals, like bees. On a summer afternoon, as UV light invisibly tans our skin, a nearby bumblebee may be attracted to an ultraviolet design on a flower.

Meanwhile, all around us, other kinds of light fill the air, such as low-energy radio waves. Microwaves—less energtic than those in a microwave oven—stream from cell towers. Occasionally zooming by are higher-energy X-rays and gamma rays, penetrating Earth's atmosphere from the Sun and distant stars.

The energy of photons of visible blue light is about 3.1 electron volts (eV). But X-ray photons carry about 100 to 100,000 eV. Like weakly tossed balls, most photons of visible light bounce off skin. But X-ray photons are so energetic—the fastballs of the electromagnetic spectrum—that they tear right through watery skin cells.

Mineral-rich bones and teeth are much denser than skin. Instead of sailing through, X-ray photons are stopped in their tracks and absorbed. The result: an image on film showing a broken bone or decayed tooth.

Even in the restricted doses used in medical imaging, X-rays could injure DNA at the heart of cells. During an X-ray of teeth, a lead apron can keep these super-energetic photons from penetrating other parts of the body.

Why lead? Lead is an inexpensive metal that's soft enough to cut easily, but extremely dense. Density is the amount of matter packed into a space; lead is about 11 times as dense as the same volume of water. Each tiny atom of ordinary lead has 164 protons and electrons.

(Compare that to oxygen's measly 16, or hydrogen's 2.)

A beam of light, which can slip through the empty spaces in flimsier materials, encounters many more atomic particles in lead. A lead apron contains a sheet about 1/100th to 1/50th inch thick (0.03 to 0.05 cm). The higher-energy the X-rays, the thicker the lead required to stop them.

Your Bones at the Beach

Why do oily puddles on the driveway have rainbow colors?

What do a clear (clean) soap bubble and a dark (dirty) oil spill have in common? Their floaty rainbow colors are the result of waves of light, getting in each other's way.

White light from the Sun contains a hidden rainbow of colors, each color a different wavelength. You can see this rainbow when light passes through a prism, and its colors spill out onto the wall. Thin layers on a surface, such as a film of oil or soap on water, can also tease the rainbow out of white light, creating an iridescent sheen.

How? When light strikes an oily puddle or soap bubble, some rays immediately bounce off the outside surface. But others penetrate into the thin film before reemerging. Since these rays travel a slightly longer path, they are slightly out of sync with the others when they emerge at the surface.

Now, imagine waves on the ocean. If two waves meet and match up, peak to peak, the

resulting wave will be strongly reinforced. But if the peak of one wave meets up with the trough (low point) of another, the two cancel each other out.

Something similar happens with light waves. Scientists call this process interference. When the peaks of light waves exactly (or almost) coincide, the light brightens. But if one wave's crest matches up with another's trough, the two cancel each other out, making a dim or dark spot. So when light waves combine and interfere at the surface of a thin layer, colors are reinforced—or canceled. For example, a yellow wave peak matching up with a purplish-pink peak produces red.

When a crest matches to a trough and colors get canceled, we see their "complementary colors," their color opposites. So when red waves are canceled, blue-green hues emerge. Where blues are canceled,

EVERYWHERE A RAINBOW

Interference happens in more than oil slicks and soap bubbles. It's why you see a gleaming rainbow in the surface of a DVD. Shimmery, iridescent colors appear in everything from pearls to peacock feathers, beetles to butterfly wings—on any object that has a thin film to redirect light.

Ordinary color, such as the red of a robin's chest, or the orange of a monarch butterfly's wings, comes from pigments. The pigment melanin, for example, gives our skin, hair, and eyes their color. And in autumn, anthocyanin pigments color leaves red and purple.

But it's the structure of an object that produces a rainbow effect.

Take butterfly wings. Their standard colors come from pigments. Their iridescent colors appear because of wing structure. How? Butterfly wings contain very thin layers of chitin—the hard material that makes shells for insects and shellfish—separated by air. So each thin layer is like the thin film in an oil slick, and each layer makes light iridesce. Multiple layers produce spectacular effects making butterfly wings shine far more brilliantly than a roadside pool of oil.

yellows bloom. The result, in an oil slick or soap bubble, is an assortment of brilliant, swirling colors.

The exact colors you see depend on your own viewing angle, and on the depth of the thin film (say, oil). Scientists can actually determine a film's thickness by the colors that

pattern its surface, since they reveal what happened to the emerging light.

As a soap bubble evaporates, the colors change more than those on a puddle. Gravity pulls water toward the bottom, thinning the top wall and making colors shift and swirl.

Why do we see an imaginary patch of water on the road ahead?

Ah, summertime. Season of cookouts, fireworks, road trips, and mirages . . . like that cool, shimmering pool of water on the highway ahead on a scorching-hot, drought-dry day.

Mirages can be even more spectacular in Earth's coldest regions. Take a trip to the Arctic, and if conditions are just right, you may see an upside-down iceberg, seemingly hanging in the air above the sea.

A mirage is created by light's bendy encounters with air molecules. Take the mundane mini-mirage of a patch of water on a (dry) blacktop road. Asphalt is very good at soaking up heat from the Sun, and heat rising from the hot road warms the air above it.

As sunlight streams down through the sky, it passes from a layer of cooler, thicker air into the thinner, hotter air just above the road. Thinner air means fewer gas molecules for light to encounter. So as the leading edge of a light wave enters the hot air, its way is clearer, and it speeds up.

However, the rest of the light wave, still traveling through thicker air, lags a bit. This makes a kind of kink in the wave. The bent (refracted) light wave is now traveling along the road, its bottom in hot air and its top in cooler. The resulting drag causes the wave to bend again—sending the beam of light up, toward your eyes. And you see water.

How come? Part of the light that reaches your eyes is carrying an image of the sky. Since hot air is full of movement, the image shimmers. Presto: a patch of "water" on the road ahead. But as you drive nearer, the image seems to move down the road, vanishing and reappearing, always out of reach.

Such a mirage is called an inferior image, because the mirage appears below the real pictured object (in this case, the sky). But there are

Fast Fact

Since mirages are as (optically) real as rainbows and rings around the Moon, we can even photograph these tricks of light.

also superior mirages, casting images up from the ground. This can often happen on a lake or ocean, where a cool, thick layer of air often hangs under a heated layer. In this case, light rays bouncing off water or expanses of ice may bend up into the sky and then back down to us.

In 1643, a priest named Angelucci described an incredible vision he had seen while looking across the Straits of Messina between Sicily and Italy. At first, he said, the sea stretched out calmly to the horizon. But as he watched, a dark line of mountains suddenly rose up out of the water.

In front of the mountains, thousands of dirty white columns sprang up from nowhere. Soon, the columns shrank, and finally curved over into Roman arches. Then, in a kind of grand finale, giant castles, studded with windows and towers, grew on top of the arches.

What the priest saw was a kind of towering, complicated mirage called a *fata morgana*. *Fata* means "fairy" in Italian.

In legend, Morgan le Fay was King Arthur's sister. Her special talent: creating castles that hung suspended in the air.

The mountains, columns, and castles that appeared before Father Angelucci were really shimmering slices of the sea, cast up in a hodgepodge of angles. Such fantastic images can be created even out of a flat, calm sea, as light bending this

way and that throws pieces of the ocean into the sky.

Besides ghostly mountain ranges, real mountains and city skyscrapers can appear out of place and upside down. And sunlight striking a boat hidden below the horizon can bend as it travels through the atmosphere, making the boat appear as if it's in the water ahead—or even sailing through the clouds.

A Water Mirage is called an "Inferior Image" Because...

It's not a swimming pool?

It's running away?

Or, because you see it below the real image?

How come words appear backward in a mirror?

ALICE IN AND OUT AND THROUGH THE LOOKING GLASS

Oh the opposite arm is raised.

hmmm... still the opposite arm.

Hey! I think I saw a rabbit!

In Lewis Carroll's *Through the Looking Glass*, Alice (of *Alice's Adventures in Wonderland* fame) discovered that a mirror was a doorway to a parallel universe, where everything is reversed—and anything might happen. While mirrors aren't really an entry to another world, they are very curious objects.

A mirror seems to reverse left and right—making newspaper headlines and T-shirt slogans read backward, and flipping the image of your face and

A mirror reflects back what we present to it. When we turn a headline around to face the mirror, it is reflected back, letter for letter, left to right: backward.

body. But a mirror doesn't flip top and bottom—we don't appear in a full-length mirror with our head at the bottom, feet and floor at the top.

How come?

A flat mirror reflects the light bouncing from whatever we hold up to it— whether a newspaper or our own adorable faces— in straight lines. So the left side of your face appears on the left side of the mirror, the right side on the right. The top of your head is at the top of the mirror.

A mirror reflects back what we present to it. When we turn a newspaper headline around to face the mirror, it reflects it back, letter for letter, left to right: backward. If the headline were on a transparent piece of glass, and you turned it around to face the mirror, you'd see that it reads backward through the glass, too. (Try this with the logo on a drinking glass.)

(Some say the key to the mirror mystery is that mirrors reverse "in" and "out," which is why, when you point at a mirror, your reflection points back at you.)

If you really want to, you can see your true image—your face in the world—by using two mirrors. Set the mirrors at a right angle, like two walls meeting in the corner. When you look at your face in the corner— your true face—you may be shocked at what you see.

Despite photos and home videos, few of us have really seen—up close, in real time— what we look like to others. Everyone's face is a little off-kilter in some way—one side of the nose a bit different from the other, eyebrows not exactly matched. Looking in a regular mirror for years, we don't notice these small imbalances.

But looking at your true image makes every quirk evident. Moles and freckles are reversed; your smile is slightly crooked. And perhaps the most unsettling thing: Your hair is parted on the other side.

If you can stop looking at your new mirror self, hold up a newspaper . . . and read the headlines.

Why do wheels appear to spin backward?

Mikey the movie...

Mikey reaches warp speed entering the kitchen.

His mom appears in the doorway...

And the spokes of Mikey's wheels appear to go backward...

We've all seen it in movies or old TV westerns—as the stagecoach (or train) picks up speed, its fast-moving wheels appear to switch direction, slowly turning backward. We also occasionally see the phenomenon in real life, with spinning car tires and whirling ceiling fans. Scientists call it the Wagon-Wheel Effect.

What causes the "backward" effect? The answer, it turns out, depends on whether the effect you see is on film, in a fluorescent-lit room, on the freeway at night, or in daylight.

There's no argument about what's happening when we're watching, say, a train engine on film. A movie camera that uses film takes many snapshots per second of the scene unfolding in front of it, adding up to thousands of individual images on a long strip of film. Because the pictures are taken in quick succession, there's little motion lost between each one.

When you view the finished movie, snapshots of the action flash by on the screen. As they do, your brain keeps the previous image in mind as you see the next one. The action appears continuous—just as it was in real life.

But when a filmed wheel rotates at just the right speed, the backward effect occurs. How? If one snapshot is taken with a spoke in the 6:00 position, the same spoke may have sped around to 5:59 when the next snapshot is taken. And the next shot may be of the spoke frozen at the 5:58 position.

When your eyes and brain put the motion together, the wheel seems to slowly turn backward. The illusion is a kind of camera strobing—as in a dance club, when flashing strobe lights freeze dancers in a series of positions. The same thing can happen when we use a digital camera, which records a series of images, at 25 to 50 frames a second. A similar illusion can even occur in real life, in a room lit by fluorescent lights at night.

According to neuroscientist David Eagleman, older fluorescent lights cycle on and off 60 times a second, and the strobe-light effect can make a ceiling fan appear to turn backward. The flickering sodium-vapor lights on a freeway at night can have the same effect, he says, on our perception of spinning car wheels.

But what about the backward effect in broad daylight? Some scientists think that the brain/eye system may process visual information in individual units—like a movie camera's individual snapshots of motion.

However, Eagleman believes that this "snap-shotting" view of the brain is wrong. He has done experiments showing that the daylight backward effect is real, but can be explained by the way the brain interprets motion from the right and left.

When the brain sees a pattern moving from the right to the left, Eagleman says, more of its leftward than rightward motion detectors are activated. But in a kind of brain neuron rivalry, the rightward detectors win out now and then, and a moving pattern appears to reverse itself.

To see the real-world effect for yourself, Eagleman suggests staring at your home ceiling fan. During the daytime, with all artificial lighting off, turn the fan on at a slow speed. Then make yourself comfy—say, on the couch—because seeing the illusion can take eight minutes or more. With patience, he says, you should eventually see the fan running backward for a few seconds.

When a fire engine goes by, why does the siren's sound change?

Early Doppler research moved at a snail's pace...

Have you ever stood on a city sidewalk and heard the distant wail of an approaching fire engine? As the fire truck comes into view, the sound of its siren becomes louder and more frantic, the wail higher and higher pitched. Then, as it passes, the opposite effect occurs: The sound of the siren drops in pitch, getting lower and lower as the vehicle vanishes into distant traffic.

But the fire truck's driver

hears no such change; to him, the siren that he flipped on 20 blocks ago has sounded at a steady pitch. Just as with the shifting whistle of a passing train, or the roar of a jet plane taking off into the sky, what you hear depends on your vantage point.

We can thank the Doppler shift for the built-in sound effects of noisy objects on the move. An Austrian physicist and mathematician named Christian Doppler was one of the first to do experiments on the strange effect. In 1845, Doppler coaxed a group of trumpet players to board an open train car, to demonstrate the effect in action. As the musicians began to play, the train engine moved the car back and forth along the track. Meanwhile, a second group of musicians stood still by the track, carefully

> By measuring the Doppler shift of light from faraway stars, scientists discovered the universe is expanding.

noting the trumpets' constantly changing pitch.

How does it work? As, say, a whistling train rushes toward a railroad crossing, the sound waves coming from its whistle are squashed together. This creates waves of higher frequency, so we hear a higher-pitched sound. But as the train passes us, the sound waves spread out behind it, rather like the smoke coming from a coal-fired engine's smokestack. Result: We now hear a lower-frequency, deeper sound.

But the whistle, the train, and the people aboard it are all moving together. Since the passengers and crew hear the sound from a constant distance, the pitch of the whistle remains the same for them.

The Doppler effect works on other kinds of waves, too, including electromagnetic radiation—everything from radio waves to X-rays to visible light.

Take visible light waves. If our fire engine were emitting a bright yellow light from its front and back, the frequency of the light waves would change as the engine approached and then sped into the distance. At ordinary, everyday speeds, we wouldn't notice a color change. But if our imaginary fire truck could speed up to an enormous velocity—a large fraction of the speed of light (186,000 miles per second or 299,792,458 m/s exactly)— we would notice a startling difference.

The driver would see a steady yellow light beaming out on the road in front of him. But to sidewalk onlookers, the light waves would become compressed as the fire engine came nearer. And they would see the light change from yellow to higher-frequency blue.

As the engine passed, observers would watch the light on the back shift from blue back to yellow, as the light waves spread out again. Finally, they would glimpse the light from the fire engine as a receding speck of low-frequency red, disappearing on the horizon.

By the 1920s, astronomers like Edwin Hubble had realized that light from distant galaxies is similarly shifted toward the red end of the spectrum, indicating that they, too, are speeding away from us. By measuring the shift of the light from these faraway stars, scientists verified that the galaxies are rushing away from each other, the light of their stars spreading out like the sound waves of receding trains. Scientists had used the familiar Doppler effect to discover something amazing: The universe itself

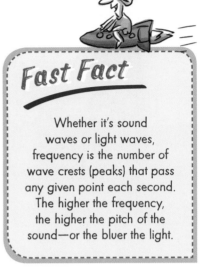

Fast Fact

Whether it's sound waves or light waves, frequency is the number of wave crests (peaks) that pass any given point each second. The higher the frequency, the higher the pitch of the sound—or the bluer the light.

is expanding, the galaxies moving apart like polka dots on the surface of an inflating balloon.

How come we can hear the sound of the ocean in a big seashell?

Ocean in a Seashell

He hears crashing waves, Seagulls, and Elvis.

When you hold a large seashell to your ear, you can hear a distant roaring sound. It's as if the great rumble and crash of the ocean waves is somehow trapped within the shell. So when you bring a seashell home from the beach, it keeps the memory of the sea alive.

But even if you don't have a seashell handy, and it's too cold to go to the beach, you can always hear the ocean. Just pick up an empty coffee mug, and hold it to your ear, tilted slightly away. Ah, there it is—the gentle, echoing roar of the waves.

That's right, you don't need a big conch shell to listen to the sea. In fact, many objects around the house can function as your ocean listening portal. Even a coffee-stained mug, one that's never left Midtown Manhattan.

As lovely as the idea is, it's not really the ocean you're hearing when you put your ear to a big seashell (or coffee cup). So what, exactly, are you hearing? Some will tell you it's the sound of your own blood, rushing through the vessels in your ear. The seashell, pressed to your head, simply amplifies the sound. The hard walls of the shell then bounce it back to your eardrum. And you feel relaxed, as if you've actually dug your toes into sun-warmed sand.

But scientists note that the "ocean" sound in a shell doesn't get any louder when your blood is really rushing in your ear—say, just after hard exercise. In fact, they suggest listening to a shell in a soundproof booth. While your own blood continues to pulse through your ear, the sound of the sea abruptly vanishes.

So where does the roar come from? Even a quiet room is filled with sounds, many so faint that we can't hear them. A big seashell amplifies these sounds, bouncing them back to us in a rush of noise—that sounds a lot like ocean waves.

The trick is resonance. If you've ever swung on a swing, you'll have noticed that if you pump your legs in just the right rhythm, the swing will go higher and faster. Why? When your rhythm exactly matches the natural rhythm (frequency) of the swing, its own back-and-forth motion is amplified.

Thanks to resonance, you get the fun of a wilder ride.

Resonance can even shatter glass. When a musical note matching the glass's own natural frequency makes it vibrate violently, the glass will break.

Which brings us back to shells. The chambers and twisting, turning walls of a large conch shell will resonate to many different natural frequencies. So as sounds from a room enter the shell, some set up extra-strong vibrations here and there. The sounds that match the shell's own frequencies resonate, becoming louder.

Bouncing off the shell's hard echo-chamber walls, the strengthened sounds combine, emerging as a kind of roar that rises and falls. Presto: instant ocean.

Why do fingernails (and sometimes chalk) sound so awful on a blackboard?

There's an official name for the horrible sounds that emanate from a blackboard: chalk squeal. Scientists say that the explanation involves both friction and resonance.

Chalk squeal and—shudder—fingernail screech occur when frictional forces aren't constant as chalk meets board. Friction is the force that puts on the brakes on an object in motion. Scientists

define friction as "the force between two solid surfaces that resists sliding." The main cause of friction is an overly friendly relationship between the atoms of two surfaces (like the bottom of a heavy

THE WORST SOUNDS

A 2006 survey in the United Kingdom rated fingernails on a blackboard second among Great Britain's least favorite sounds. Number one: children screaming. Also irritating: car alarms, dentists' drills, ring tones, and dripping faucets.

Interestingly, many of the 20 most irritating noises involve the stick-slip phenomenon, including a knife on a plate, a squeaky door, a chair scraping the floor, and someone (excruciatingly) learning to play the violin.

What is it about the noises generated by sticking and slipping objects that is so loathsome? A 1980s experiment at Northwestern University had volunteers rate different sounds, including a metal drawer being opened and Styrofoam rubbing on Styrofoam. The sounds were wince-worthy even when high-pitched tones were filtered out. It turns out that it's the middle-to-low tones of stick-slipping that make us shudder most.

Using sound modeling, the Northwestern researchers found that the most detested noises had a sound profile similar to the alarm cries of macaque monkeys. Perhaps, they speculate, such sounds may trigger some deep-seated reaction that helped us survive, once upon a time. So if the screech of a train's brakes makes you cringe, you may have a lot of ancestral company.

of times each second. Since each jump covers such a tiny distance, we don't see gaps in the letters written on the board.

But each time the chalk sticks, it emits a burst of noise, which gets louder if the chalk is pressed harder. Researchers say the screech occurs because—where chalk meets board—the constantly varying frictional forces excite the natural resonances of the chalk. The chalk's vibrations are reinforced (they resonate), becoming stronger. So as the chalk stutters across the blackboard, it makes a squealing sound. The slipping and sticking also occurs when you drag your fingernails down a blackboard, which usually tops the list of sounds that make us flinch.

bookcase and the floor). At the spots where two such objects make contact—called junctions—their atoms have formed bonds. When we drag chalk across a blackboard at certain angles and with enough pressure, it sticks to the board, slips, jumps to a new spot, and then sticks again. Scientists call it the stick-slip phenomenon. The chalk may stick and slip hundreds

Why do we sound better singing in the shower?

Even if your family groans when you sing along to the car radio, even if you didn't make the cut for the choir, and even if you got asked to be the drummer rather than the lead vocalist in your friends' garage band, you sound exactly like your favorite pop (or opera) star in the shower. How come? And why do we enjoy singing in the shower to begin with?

First, there's the psychology and brain chemistry of shower crooning. In the shower, we are behind closed doors (bathroom and shower), water blasting. Under the comforting blanket of hot water and steam, we feel relaxed and unselfconscious. The splashing water also produces negative ions, which are thought to make us happier. And so we are inclined to burst into song, confident that no one can really hear us, anyway.

But we probably wouldn't keep on singing if we didn't sound so mysteriously good. We can thank shower acoustics for putting us in the running to be the next Bathroom Idol.

Scientists say that a shower stall acts a bit like an electronic sound mixer, naturally improving the quality of your singing voice. How it works: The hard tile or glass in most showers absorbs very little sound, bouncing most sound waves right back. (Ordinary ceramic tile reflects about 98 percent of the sound striking it.) As the sound ricochets back and forth between walls in the confined space, your voice is effectively amplified. Presto: instant vocal power.

Meanwhile, the shower also acts like a bass booster. A cavelike space such as a shower stall has its own special amplifying frequencies. Sounds that happen to match those frequencies will resonate. In an ordinary, smallish shower, the resonating frequencies fall in the lower range of the human voice. So when you sing low notes, the shower obligingly amplifies those sounds, like turning up the bass on a stereo.

Finally, there's a touch of reverberation. As sound

Best Place to Record a Song...
(don't try this at home)

This is a song about a dog — who is always hungryyyyyy!

waves bounce around the shower stall, some travel longer paths before entering your ears. This stretches out the sound, like an electric organ played in reverb mode. And the prolonged, echoing notes make your voice sound richer to you.

Reverberation also makes you sound like you're in tune, even when you're really not. As your voice bounces between the walls (and through the spray of water, where sound waves temporarily accelerate), the sound gets a bit blurry. The fuzziness smoothes out variations in singing pitch, rather like a karaoke machine.

Of course, you're not really hearing your true singing voice. But to feel like a pop star for 15 minutes in the morning, shower in a smooth-tiled stall with a glass door for the best reflections. And for the most impressive bass boost, make sure your shower is on the small side. Bigger-size spaces have their strongest resonant frequencies below the range of human hearing.

How come a glass rings if you run your wet finger around the rim?

Like absentmindedly drumming on a tabletop, idly running a finger around the rim of a glass can make a kind of music—an otherworldly, ghostly music.

Sound waves are the result of vibrations coursing through a material, whether that material is metal, wood, or glass. That's why when we strike a tuning fork, which produces a similar ringing sound, we can actually see and feel the tuning fork shaking. The sound reaches our ears because the tuning fork's vibrations make the air around it vibrate. Waves of air molecules strike our eardrums, causing them to

A set of glasses filled to different levels can create a chorus of notes.

vibrate, too.

When you run your wet finger around the rim of a wineglass or crystal goblet, it's a lot like tapping the glass repeatedly with a spoon. You are making the glass vibrate. An object like a wineglass also has its own special resonant frequency, or natural frequency of vibration. When

your rubbing finger causes the glass to vibrate near its resonant frequency, the glass will vibrate more strongly.

Why must your finger be wet? Scientists say that there will be too much friction between a dry finger and glass, causing it to stick too often on its way around the rim. An oily finger (or a greasy rim) will cause a fingertip to slip around too easily, causing little vibration. Like a bow on a violin string, a wet finger creates a good stick:slip ratio, making the glass vibrate strongly. The result is an unearthly ringing sound.

Glasses vibrate at

different frequencies, depending on their material (regular glass or crystal), size, shape, and thickness. Their unique sound also depends on how much liquid they contain. So by adding more or less water, you can change the musical note that a glass produces. A set of glasses, filled to different levels, can create a chorus of notes, making a complete musical instrument—a kind of glass harp.

Statesman and inventor Benjamin Franklin invented the compact glass armonica in 1761. He worked with a glassblower to create varying sizes of bowls, each tuned to a particular note, no water required. The bowls nested on a revolving spindle, making them easy to reach; the operator/musician used a foot pedal to spin the bowls. Franklin's wife was awakened one night by the armonica's ethereal music drifting down from the attic, and thought she had died and was hearing the music of angels.

Fast Fact

Musical glasses were played in concerts in Europe by the late 1600s, and the "glass harp" remained popular into the 1800s. Three Scottish musicians, for example, played a set of 120 glasses, which ranged in size from a thimble to a 3-gallon jug (that's about 11 liters).

Why does the wind whistle, howl, and moan?

Noises for When the Wind is Howling Your Way...

eeeeee!

oh-oh-oh!

Vooooooo!

The umbrella eater...   The hat grabber...   ...The wind sock maker.

What would a haunted house be without a dark and stormy night—and a high, moaning wind? Likewise, the wind needs the drafty old house—and the tossing trees around it—to create its spooky sound effects.

Telephone wires. The eaves of a house. Pine branches. When the wind wants to whistle or howl, it needs instruments to play—obstacles in its way.

Depending on the rush of the wind, and the shape of what it's rushing over, wind may moan, scream, or sing. As the wind speed rises and falls, so does the frequency of the sound produced.

The sounds we hear come courtesy of sound waves, vibrations traveling through air (or another medium, like water). Air bunches up and spreads out again, in waves of varying pressure.

So when a door suddenly

blows shut downstairs, it makes waves. Propagating through the air at about 1,100 feet per second, the sound waves quickly reach your eardrums. Startled, you go downstairs to close the windows.

When you do, you notice that the wind's whistling pitch changes as you pull the window shut. That's because the windy repertoire constantly shifts, as air streams across, under, and through the world's cracks and crevices.

Imagine a high wind blowing through telephone wires. As it skims across the top and bottom of a wire, the wind becomes unstable. If wind were visible, you would see the thin, cylinder-shaped wire shedding mini-whirlwinds of air as the wind blows past it.

These eddies in the wind in turn set up patterns of changing pressure in the air ahead of the wire. When

---

Differently shaped obstacles in a wind's path produce different sounds, like musical instruments.

---

the sound waves created by the tumbling air reach our ears, we hear whistling. As the wind blows faster, the frequency of the sound gets higher. Wind really starts screaming through wires when its speed reaches at least 25 miles per hour.

Just as with variously shaped musical instruments, differently shaped obstacles in a wind's path produce distinct sounds. Wind blowing through pine trees, their cylindrical needles setting air aswirl, has been compared to the sound of the sea.

Houses also create wind music, especially the eerie kind. Like a person blowing forcefully across the mouth of a jug, wind gusting over the chimney of an enclosed fireplace speaks in a low-pitched, hollow moan.

Winds whine at small cracks or holes in a building. And a strong wind can wail as it blows down eaves and against a house's sharp edges and corners. As air spills off the edges of a roof, some of the waves created reflect back into the streaming wind. This produces whirling vortexes of air, which strike, and then spin off, the roof edge. The result is a complex, ever-shifting sound wave pattern, which we hear as howling.

Measure FOR Measure
1,100 feet per second = 335 m/s
25 miles per hour = 40.2 km/h

UNSEEN FORCES, INVISIBLE PARTICLES

Everything—you, this book, the stars—is made of atoms. The simplest atom, hydrogen, is only about one 250 millionth of an inch across. (Think of how wide 1/16th inch on a ruler is. Now instead of 16, imagine dividing the inch into 250 million teensy parts.) In each tiny atom, whizzing electrons orbit a bundle of protons and neutrons, rather like planets orbit a star. (The simplest atom, hydrogen, has just one proton and one electron.) Each atom is held together by the electromagnetic force, one of four basic forces in the universe. Negatively charged electrons are very attracted to positively charged protons. (The same electromagnetic force makes lightning zigzag down through the sky.) Gravity, the attraction of matter to matter, is the force that keeps planets in orbit, and makes your shoe drop to the floor when it falls off your foot. We notice gravity more than electromagnetism, but the electrical force is by far the stronger—1,000,000,000,000,000,000, 000,000,000,000,000,000,000 (one duodecillion) times as powerful.

But in the tiny world of an atom's center, an even more powerful force, called the strong force, binds protons and neutrons into a tight clump. A fourth force, the weak force, plays a role when one kind of quark (the particle that makes up protons and neutrons) changes into another.

Find out how we get shocked by doorknobs in winter, why a yo-yo comes back, how a stone can skip across a pond, and why we can see through glass.

How did scientists figure out that matter is made of atoms if they couldn't see them?

Even though we can't see atoms with the naked eye, the idea of their existence has been around for thousands of years. In the fifth century BC, the ancient Greek philosopher and scientist Democritus proposed the idea that if you keep dividing matter into smaller parts, you'll eventually reach the smallest possible amount of the material: one atom.

Democritus, it turns out, was right. One atom's worth of calcium is the least amount of calcium in a glass of milk. One atom's worth

Protons and neutrons are made up of even smaller particles, called quarks.

of gold is the tiniest piece of gold in a wedding band. And one atom's worth of sodium is the teeniest particle of sodium in your saltshaker.

But while atoms are impossibly small, they are also more than 99 percent

empty space. If the Sun were the nucleus of an atom, the electrons in the atom's outermost orbits would be more than 10 billion miles away—nearly three times the distance of Pluto.

Although Democritus couldn't prove that atoms actually existed, the idea came up again and again over the centuries. Why? Because it helped explain what scientists were seeing in experiments. In the early 1800s, the British chemist John Dalton found that when two substances combine in a chemical

reaction, their weights, as in a food recipe, come in fixed proportions. This suggested that there were identical, equal-weight atoms of one substance linking up with different weight atoms of another substance.

Measure FOR Measure
10 billion miles = 16 billion km
4 to 16 billionths of an inch =
    0.1016 to 0.4064 nanometers

Atoms, Dalton thought, were tiny round balls. But later experiments convinced scientists that each atom, whether of calcium, mercury, or any other element, were made of even teensier common parts.

In the early 1900s, scientist Ernest Rutherford devised experiments that showed what an atom must be like on the inside.

Scientists shot high-speed, positively charged particles from radioactive radon at a very thin gold foil. Some of the particles whizzed right through. Others mysteriously veered off to the sides. Some even ricocheted back at the experimenters. Rutherford said it was like firing a heavy mortar shell at tissue paper, and having it bounce back and hit you.

Why didn't all the positively charged particles simply pass through the foil? The scientists realized that many must have been electrically repelled. Rutherford's experiment helped prove that atoms contain a nucleus made of positively charged particles—so-called protons.

Experiments later proved that electrically neutral particles, or neutrons, are also packed into atoms' centers. Whizzing around the nucleus, at a (relatively) great distance, are negatively charged particles. These negative electrons "swarm" around the nucleus, attracted to the positive protons like bees to nectar.

"SEEING" ATOMS—AND PUSHING THEM AROUND

While scientists have long known that atoms exist, they were frustrated because they couldn't actually see them. Now, scientists can call up images of actual atoms on a computer screen, and move the real atoms around on a surface, by using a scanning tunneling microscope (STM).

It's impossible to see atoms using ordinary microscopes, because atoms are so tiny—about 4 to 16 billionths of an inch across. A hair on your arm is a million times wider than an atom. Nor can we use visible light to illuminate an atom—a wavelength of ordinary light is about 2,000 to 5,000 times wider than the atom itself.

But an STM is not something you look through. It's a computerized tool with a conducting tip that can be moved ever so carefully just above a material's surface. As the tip moves, electrons jump across the gap between the tip and the surface, creating a tiny electric current.

This current changes as the distance between the tip and the surface changes. A surface that looks smooth is actually bumpy at the atomic level. The tip passes over individual atoms, which are like hills on the surface. The computer maps the surface of the material, creating an image of its atoms. Voilà: We can "see" atoms.

Scientists also use STMs to manipulate atoms. First, they cool atoms to about −453°F (−269.4°C). (That's nearly as cold as "absolute zero" [−273.15°C], when particles virtually stop moving). Using the STM tip as you would use a magnet to move a pin—without actually touching it—scientists have nudged atoms into patterns that spelled words. The words are a kind of atomic Braille, which can only be read by using an STM.

Why are bubbles round?

We've all admired bubbles—especially soap bubbles, with their perfectly round shape and shimmery colors. One British scientist, Sir Charles Vernon Boys (aka C. V. Boys), was so intrigued that in 1890, he published a 200-page book titled *Soap-Bubbles, Their Colours and the Forces Which Mould Them.*

Boys called bubbles "magnificent objects," and pointed out that the force that holds bubbles together is present in all liquids—you can't pour tea, turn off a dripping tap, or wade in a pond without encountering it.

Imagine filling a balloon with water. The rubbery skin of the balloon stretches and stretches as more water is added. It can only stretch so far, however, until it bursts.

Now think about a drop of water. Picture a drop collecting at the end of a faucet. It hangs, growing bigger and bigger. Finally, after it has reached a certain size, it falls off. Why, Boys asked, does the water hang at the end of the faucet at all? It is as if, he said, the water were hanging in a little elastic bag, like the balloon. Then, it's as if the elastic bag breaks or tears away when it fills with too much water.

There isn't really a bag around a water drop. But something, Boys said, must be holding the drop together in much the same way as an invisible skin would.

This "something"— a property of water and other liquids—is called surface tension. Take water. Water molecules under the surface are strongly attracted to each other. Surface water molecules, however, are not attracted to the air molecules above them. They are only attracted downward and inward, toward the rest of the water. This "surface tension" creates the effect of a skin on the water.

Surface tension allows us to blow soap bubbles.

The "skin" keeps the water hanging on the end of the faucet—until finally, it gets so heavy it breaks off.

Different liquids have "skins" that are stronger or weaker, Boys pointed out.

Alcohol, for example, has a weaker surface tension than water and doesn't form drops as well. But liquid mercury, which skids across the floor in beads from a broken glass thermometer, has six times the surface tension of water.

Surface tension also holds soap bubbles together. When you dip a wand into a soapy solution and then pull it out, you see a thin film stretched across the wand. Blow into it, and surface tension makes the soapy film stretch like an elastic skin. The film closes around the air, and the bubble pops out and floats away.

Because of the elastic "skin" of a bubble, the air inside a soap bubble is under pressure—like the air inside a balloon. The strength of the pressure depends on how tightly the bubble is curved. The tighter the curve, the smaller the bubble, and the more force on the air within. Boys did experiments that showed that air, rushing out of a popped soap bubble like air jetting out of a balloon, can blow out a candle flame.

But why is the bubble round? The answer is that the surface tension causes the liquid film to pull itself into the most compact shape possible. The most compact shape in nature is a ball (and not a rectangle, for instance). The air inside is held in by the same force all around the bubble. (At least until the fragile bubble bursts.)

Still, Boys noted, with effort bubbles can be made that are not perfectly round. For example, if you take a soap bubble between two rings and tug on either side, you can pull the bubble into the shape of a cylinder. The bigger such non-round bubbles get, the more unstable they are. A long cylinder will soon develop a "waist" and break apart—into two spherical bubbles.

How come soda pop fizzes?

AN ODE TO CARBON DIOXIDE...

You're the fizz in my soda...
We're free!

You're the bubbles on my tongue...
YUCK! Liverwurst!

You're the whoosh from the pop-top, You're the burp when I'm done!
URP!

Carbon dioxide is a gas-of-all-trades. Yeast releases the gas as it feasts on sugars in dough, making bread expand into a springy loaf. Solid carbon dioxide—otherwise known as "dry ice"—keeps food and medicines icy cold, and supplies spooky special effects on Halloween. And plants absorb carbon dioxide from the air, use energy from sunlight to split it into carbon and oxygen, and make carbohydrates. (We breathe in the leftover oxygen, without which we couldn't live.)

But in a sillier job, carbon dioxide also makes soft drinks fizzy. It's the gas that put the "carbon" in "carbonation."

Soft drink makers inject zillions of carbon dioxide molecules into each bottle or can, then seal it up tight.

Unlike water, which turns to steam at 212°F (100°C), carbon dioxide normally boils into a gas at a chilly −109°F (−78°C). Yet an unopened bottle of pop is almost bubble-free. That's because high pressure forces the carbon dioxide into the liquid around it. When you open the bottle, you reduce the pressure. You can see gas bubble up in the soda and rise to the surface, where carbon dioxide invisibly takes flight.

To see how much carbon dioxide, or CO_2, is in your bottle of soda, try this experiment: Pull a small balloon over the lid of an unopened bottle and down onto the neck. Then unscrew the lid through the balloon. You should see the balloon start to inflate.

The first rush of CO_2 will come from the airspace between the surface of the soda and the lid. When the pocket of CO_2 escapes—with a pop and a hiss—dissolved gas in the soda begins to form bubbles, rise, and escape into the air, too. Over the next several hours, the CO_2 will continue to slowly bubble up and rise into the balloon, inflating it. You can make the balloon inflate faster by gently shaking the bottle.

Soft drink makers add carbon dioxide mainly for taste and "mouth feel." Carbon dioxide gives soda pop its bright, bubbly "party" taste. Some of the dissolved CO_2 reacts with water to form carbonic acid, adding an edge to the drink's sweetness. As a side benefit, carbonation inhibits the growth of bacteria. Leave out the CO_2, and soda is just flavored water without the "pop."

Shaking a soda before opening it adds drama (and mess) to the carbon dioxide prison break. According to physicist Jearl Walker of Cleveland State University, the act of shaking alters the environment inside the can. Remember that layer of gas at the top of the can, sandwiched between the lid and the liquid soda? Vigorous shaking forces the gas from

Fast Fact

A can of soda at room temperature has an internal pressure of about 55 pounds per square inch.

the airspace into the liquid below, where it takes the form of gas-filled bubbles.

Open the can immediately after shaking, and the pressure inside drops dramatically. Carbon dioxide gas dissolved in the soda swiftly moves into the bubbles created by the shaking. Walker says that the bubbles can grow so big so quickly that they actually push the liquid out ahead of them as they rush toward the exit. The result: a soda overflow, your Coke furiously foaming over the sides of its container.

Why do we get zapped by doorknobs in winter?

Have you avoided wearing a hat on a sub-zero day, afraid of the bad-hair aftermath? After scuffing across the carpet in your slippers, have you approached doorknobs warily? Do you pull masses of stuck-together socks out of the dryer? Does rustling your blanket at night in winter produce tiny, crackling sparks?

The culprit, of course, is static electricity, the same phenomenon behind brilliant flashes of lightning in July. The zaps

Static electricity occurs when objects become temporarily charged.

that hurt and sparks that fly in dry rooms are just proof that opposites attract. In this case, the opposites aren't Valentine sweethearts, but electrical charges.

It all comes down to the atoms that make up everything, from combs to doorknobs to our hands. Each tiny atom is normally electrically neutral. Positively charged protons at the center are balanced by an equal number of negatively charged electrons, moving in a kind of cloud around the nucleus.

Losing an electron or two will suddenly make an atom positively charged; gaining one or more extra electrons will mean a negative charge. A positively charged atom is an electron magnet. Likewise, an atom with too many electrons is all primed to unload its extra electron passengers. And sparks sometimes fly when atoms rebalance themselves.

Which explains what happens when you shuffle across a dry carpet, only to get zapped by a doorknob. Your body picks up extra electrons, giving you a slight negative charge. Touch a metal doorknob (a good conductor), and you'll get a tiny, sparking shock, as excess electrons flee your fingertips in a mini-current.

Even when so-called static electricity doesn't hurt, it's still annoying. Pull off a knit hat on a frigid winter day, and hair and hat rubbing

Fast Fact

In a list of materials that easily *lose* electrons, becoming positively charged, dry skin, hair, and fur are near the top. So are glass, nylon, and wool. Materials that easily *gain* electrons, becoming negatively charged, include PVC plastic, silicon, and Teflon. While everyday static electricity is annoying, it's also useful. For example, electrical attraction is what makes plastic wrap cling to glass bowls.

Static Do...

together dislodges electrons, charging both. The result: Hair follows hat, clinging dramatically, a few crackles thrown in as mini-sparks fly. But since like charges repel each other, your positively charged strands separate from one another, producing that Bride-of-Frankenstein fright-wig look.

Static electricity is worse in winter because both indoor and outdoor air are extra-dry. Humid air helps carry extra electrons off you more quickly; you don't build up much of a charge—so you don't get static shocks.

ELECTRIC WATER

If dryness increases static electricity, how come we can get a shock from running water? The water itself isn't charged; it's electrically neutral. However, positive charges in the water molecules are attracted to stray negative charges on your fingers (extra electrons you picked up from walking across the carpet). So as you move your fingers toward the water, its positive charges move toward you. And *ZAP*—you feel a tiny shock.

See the attraction in action: Turn on the faucet to a thin trickle. Then run a plastic comb (about 10 times) through your dry hair. Bring the now-charged comb to within an inch of the flowing water. Presto: The stream should mysteriously bend toward the comb.

Electric Water!

Polly want First Aid!

Babies hate it! So do dogs... And parrots!

How come we can see through glass?

We can't see through a wood log, a piece of aluminum, or a chunk of cheese. But we can see through plain glass. That's one reason we make windows out of glass, rather than oak, tinfoil, or cheddar.

Visible light zips unhindered through the vacuum of space. But when light strikes solids, it suddenly encounters molecule after molecule, set in a rigid structure. Depending on its frequency, light may or may not make it through. We can't see through a solid wood door. Yet some solids, such as glass, look as clear as air. Put a glass window in the door, and sunlight pours through, lighting the indoors. How come?

It all comes down to how photons (particles) of light interact with atoms in a material. All matter is made of atoms, tiny particles with a nucleus and a swarm of teensy electrons. Atoms are connected in groups called molecules. In a solid,

---

Glass molecules reflect some visible light back, which is why you can see the glassy surface. But most visible light makes it through, and out the other side.

---

molecules are very attracted to each other—they are bound together, giving a solid (like a wooden block) its definite shape. However, even in a solid, molecules still vibrate and even rotate.

When light strikes the molecules of a solid, some of it is absorbed, and some of its energy ends up staying in the solid, as heat. (Think of a rock, heating in the summer sun.) Much of the light, however, is reflected: sent back out the way it came. So you see the solid object (that big rock on the ground), but you can't see through it.

But if a sheet of clear glass is lying on the ground, you can see the grass underneath. In fact, glass can be so transparent that

STATES OF MATTER

In a solid, the molecules are *very* attracted to each other—they really stick together. That's why solids have definite shapes (a block of wood, a blade of grass, a bar of soap). But even though the molecules in a solid hold tight to each other, they are always vibrating a little. (Nothing in nature stands completely still.)

In a liquid, the molecules are still attracted, but held more loosely together. They slip and slide past each other. That's why a liquid flows, and how it can spread out to fit its container.

But in a gas, molecules fly off in all directions, zipping around at high speeds. (The average speed of a nitrogen molecule in air is 1,500 miles per hour [2,414 km/h].) And there's a lot of extra empty space between molecules. You can walk right through a gas like air, and not even notice it's there.

At the everyday air pressure on the surface of the Earth, water is a solid—ice—at or below 32°F. Between 32°F and 212°F (100°C), water is a liquid. At and above 212°F, water is an invisible water vapor.

people and other animals occasionally walk, fly, or run right into plate glass windows or doors.

Glass is a peculiar kind of solid. Glass molecules absorb most photons of light, but then emit photons of light traveling on in the same direction as the original photons.

To understand how it works, we need to know more about atoms.

An atom is normally in its "ground state," with its orbiting electrons held close to the nucleus at their lowest possible energy level. There is also a maximum amount of energy electrons can possess and still remain part of an atom. Between these ground-state and "ionizing" energy levels, electrons can orbit in intermediate energy states.

But here's the trick: Each kind of atom—oxygen, sodium, etc.—has its own rigidly defined energy levels for its electrons (sort of like the click-through settings on a three-way lamp), with no in-between settings allowed. So, an electron can orbit, say, at energy level 4 or 5, but not at 4.2 or 5.1.

Electrons can both absorb and emit photons of light. Photons are just tiny, measurable packets of electromagnetic energy. So an electron gets a boost to a new energy level by absorbing a photon. And it drops an energy level by losing a photon.

Electrons in the atoms of glass molecules absorb most high-energy ultraviolet photons from sunlight, since the particular energy of UV photons is just right for the

electrons to get an allowed boost. (The absorption of most incoming UV light is why it's hard to get a suntan through a glass car window.) And glass molecules begin jiggling and bumping as they absorb the infrared radiation in sunlight. (Which is why that same car window can get so hot to the touch.)

The ordinary visible light in sunlight doesn't have the right energy to be neatly absorbed by the energy-hungry electrons in glass. So glass molecules reflect some of the visible light back—which is why you can see the surface of a window, as well as a reflection of yourself in it. But most visible light makes it all the way through and out the other side. Which is why glass is transparent.

According to Louis Bloomfield, a University of Virginia physicist, electrons in the glass in effect "play" with the photons for an instant and then let them continue on their way. The photons are briefly absorbed and then spat out again in light's run-in with atom after atom in the glass. So even though we can see straight through glass, there is actually a lot going on inside.

Why is it so hard to shake the last drops of water out of a glass?

Pour a glass of water into the sink, and the water streams effortlessly out, emptying the glass. Oops, wait: Some of the water isn't cooperating. Tiny drops cling to the sides and bottom, stubbornly refusing to accompany their friends down the drain.

Is it fear of the unknown? ("Where does that dark drain lead to?") Or have some water droplets figured out how to outsmart gravity? Actually, it's a kind of electrical attraction.

Water molecules in liquid form slide past each other, like people moving in a crowd. That's what makes liquids shape-shifters, able to flow into nooks and crannies of a container. But in solid ice, water molecules sit frozen in a crystal lattice, vibrating in place.

But while molecules move more freely in liquid form, they are still electrically attracted to each other. Why? Each H_2O molecule is shaped rather like a triangle, with an oxygen atom at one end and two hydrogen atoms at the other. Since the oxygen atom is bigger, it has more (positively charged) protons in its nucleus. And since opposites attract, it draws (negative) electrons from the hydrogen atoms toward itself. Result: The oxygen end of a water molecule has a slight negative charge; the hydrogen end is weakly positive.

So even in a flowy liquid, water molecules form bonds: The hydrogen end of each molecule is attracted to the oxygen end of other H_2O molecules. This "hydrogen

H_2O molecules are *very* attracted to molecules in glass.

bonding" holds water molecules together in a loose mass. Since the molecules in a liquid share some attraction, liquids—like solids, but unlike gases—also have surfaces.

But at the surface, water molecules aren't all that attracted to gas molecules in the air above. Their attraction is "downward," to other water molecules filling the glass, and to their fellow H_2O molecules on the surface. This makes the surface, a patchwork of highly bonded molecules, resemble the thin skin of a balloon.

(Such "surface tension" is why some very lightweight insects can walk across a pond without breaking through.)

Surface tension is also what pulls parcels of water into rounded drops. Attracted to other water molecules, but not to surrounding air molecules, small amounts of water form springy balls.

Result? Turn a glass of water upside down and most of the water pours right out, pulled by gravity. But smaller groupings of water molecules form drops on the glass's surface. What holds them in place? Water molecules, it turns out, are *very* attracted to molecules in glass.

Shake the glass, and weightier drops fall out, gravity tugging them earthward. The smallest, lightest drops cling on, their own surface molecules and the glass's locked in an electrical embrace. In fact, water is so fond of glass that rather than converging into drops, it can also spread out, wetting the glass. Try to shake it out, and it may race around the rim of the glass, holding on tight.

How come oil and water don't mix?

If you've ever taken a bottle of Italian dressing out of the refrigerator, poured bath oil into a bathtub full of water, or watched an oil slick float menacingly toward a beach on television, you know it's true: Oil and water keep to themselves. It takes a lot of shaking to get oil and vinegar (which is mostly water) to mix at all. And even then, you'd better pour fast—the oil is busily migrating up to the surface the second you stop.

Do oil and water have a long-standing feud that started when the universe was young? Not exactly. It's just that oil and water are opposites—polar opposites, in fact.

Oil and water don't mix because of how their

molecules are constructed. Molecules are atoms bonded together in a group. Because of the way their atoms are arranged, some molecules have opposite poles, rather like the north and south poles of a magnet. But in a polar molecule, the poles are electrical, not magnetic.

Water molecules are polar. A water molecule is shaped like a V, with an oxygen atom at the bottom point of the V and a hydrogen atom on each of the two ends. The bottom of the molecule has a negative electrical charge, while the top carries a positive charge.

In nonpolar molecules, the electrical charges aren't separated, so the molecules don't have opposite positive and negative ends.

Polar molecules are found with other polar molecules, and nonpolar molecules with other nonpolar molecules. Like some kids in a school lunchroom, broken up into cliques and sitting at different tables, they just don't socialize.

Which brings us back to oil and water. Oil and water don't mix because oil is nonpolar and water is polar. But alcohol and water mix seamlessly, since they're both polar. Scientists say that alcohol and water are "miscible," while oil and water are "immiscible."

Since positive and negative charges are attracted, the negative area of a polar molecule attracts the positive area on another polar molecule. So it's natural for polar molecules to be drawn to each other and to mix it up in a solution. And since polar molecules tend to stick together, the ones that are nonpolar, like those in oil, can't easily mix in.

A simple rule to figuring out what will mix and what won't is: "Like dissolves like." So it's easy to mix alcohol and water and fairly easy to mix sugar and water (since sugar molecules are weakly polar). It's also easy to mix olive oil and corn oil, or even safflower oil and motor oil.

One unexpected result of this rule: If you mix 1 quart (0.95 l) of water with 1 quart of alcohol, the mixture will add up to less than 2 quarts (1.9 l). Why? The molecules mix so well that some empty spaces in the liquids fill in with molecules, compacting the mixture.

Since some liquids don't mix, toy companies can make those ocean-in-a-bottle toys that use oil, water, and other liquids to make rolling waves full of suspended glitter. On the other hand, a toxic chemical could lurk in water and be so perfectly mixed in—since it's polar—that we wouldn't know it was there if we didn't run lab tests.

Why is water so slippery, even without any soap?

We expect to zip down a waterslide, helpfully pulled by gravity. What's not so fun: slipping in an invisible puddle on the kitchen floor, flip-flopped feet flying in opposite directions.

Ouch.

Of course, adding to the slippery situation is the fact that water is clear, and often nearly invisible. Which is why building lobbies and bridges post that familiar warning: SLIPPERY WHEN WET.

How can plain water be such a menace? What a layer of water does to a road or floor is the same thing it does to those twisty slides at water parks: It reduces friction. And with friction dampened, thrills (and spills) follow.

Scientists say friction is a force that acts in the opposite direction to the motion of an object. So when there's more friction between two objects, movement gets more difficult. When one surface rubs against another surface—shoe soles on a floor, car tires on an asphalt road—their nooks and crannies catch. And that produces a kind of dragging effect.

Walk across a dry, rough-hewn barn floor, and it's unlikely that you'll go sliding. Friction even slows the progress of your feet across a tile floor. But spill some water, and those ceramic tiles turn into the equivalent of an icy pond . . . lurking in front of your kitchen sink. Take a step and suddenly, you're gliding on a liquid film, reducing your shoe's contact with the floor's helpful-for-walking surface flaws.

While a film of water between two surfaces reduces friction, liquid water is slippery all on its own. A sloshy liquid is, after all, a collection of molecules slip-sliding past each other. So you can dip your hands into a sink full of liquid water. But try the same thing with a block of ice, and you'll just bump against the chilly surface. In water's solid state, its molecules are mostly fixed in place, in a kind of crystal lattice.

Ice, of course, is its own brand of slippery. Toss an ice cube and it will slide across the kitchen floor, creating a slippery hazard (and a short-lived cat toy).

In the past, scientists thought the slipperiness of ice was caused by pressure or friction creating a liquid layer on its surface. For example, an ice skater's weight on a frozen pond would create pressure on the ice, forcing its top layer to condense and melt. Meanwhile, friction between the skates' blades and the ice would heat the top layer. The result: more melting, creating a glide-worthy liquid film.

But researchers have found that even without any applied pressure or friction, ice is already slippery. How? Studies show that ice's surface molecules constantly vibrate up and down, rather than stay frozen in their crystal lattice. This vertical vibration creates what scientists call a "liquid-like" layer on the icy

BUTTER SLIDES AND CORN OIL CHUTES

On roads, rainwater stirs up oily residues, increasing the slip factor. Oils and grease are friction reducers, which is why they're used to lubricate moving parts in cars, bikes, and other machinery. But not many people would plunk down an all-day admission to a Grease Park, donning bathing suits to careen down the Giant Butter Slide, or speed through the Corn Oil Chute. Water, however, provides just the right amount of lubrication to keep your body zipping along a fiberglass slide.

surface, reducing friction to a minimum. So an ice cube, just plucked from the freezer, can zip across the kitchen floor at breakneck speed.

Why does water dance across a hot frying pan?

It's an old-favorite method to test whether a pan is hot enough—ready, say, to pour in the pancake batter. Heat a frying pan or pancake griddle for a few minutes, then sprinkle in some water. If the drops sizzle and disappear, the pan isn't ready. Wait a minute, then try again. If the drops bead up like water splashed on wax paper and bounce madly around the pan, it's pancake time.

If we'd never seen the skittering water with our own eyes, we might assume just the opposite would happen: At higher temperatures, the water would evaporate faster. Instead, a hotter skillet seems to make water coalesce into tight little

> Like a genie on a flying carpet, each drop levitates on its film of steam, flying around the surface of the pan.

beads, which then skip across the surface as if running across hot coals.

This peculiar behavior of water on a heated metal surface even has a name. It's called the Leidenfrost effect, but it has nothing to do with frost and everything to do with heat. Johann Gottlob Leidenfrost, a medical doctor in 18th-century Germany, was the first scientist to officially study hot, bouncy water. He observed how water behaved when dropped onto a red-hot iron spoon, measuring how long each drop lasted. Then he wrote up his study in a short work titled *A Tract About Some Qualities of Common Water*.

When a pan's temperature is below 212°F (100°C), water's boiling point, a drop just spreads out and gradually evaporates. As the pan temperature rises to 212°F, a tossed-in drop quickly sizzles away. But get the pan really hot, and presto: rolling balls of water.

So why does water last longer on a surface that is

much hotter than its boiling point? It turns out that when water contacts scorching metal, it makes its own insulating layer. How? When water is sprinkled onto a hot frying pan, the bottom of each drop immediately evaporates, forming a layer of vapor. Like a genie on a flying carpet, each drop levitates on its film of steam, flying around the pan's surface for many seconds.

The transition to long-lasting drops occurs at or around the Leidenfrost point, or a temperature of about 428°F (220°C) for water. When drops ride on their steam carpet, they are held about 0.1 to 0.2 millimeter above the hot metal surface. This keeps the drop cooler, so it can dart across the pan for up to a minute without disappearing.

The hover effect persists as long as water continues to vaporize from the bottom, until the drop finally vanishes. Heat the pan much past 428°F, and the graceful dance ends, since sprinkled-in water evaporates too quickly.

Fast Fact

The Leidenfrost effect also applies to other liquids. The boiling point of liquid nitrogen at ordinary air pressure is about −320°F (−196°C). So when liquid nitrogen spills from its tank in a warm room, it skitters in drops across the floor, riding a vapor layer like water in a hot frying pan.

H₂O's Got Talent!

Soft Shoe!

Frantic Shoe!

Flyin' Shoes

Below 212°F

Above 212°F

At 428°F

When you drop a stone into a lake, why does it make ripples?

When you watch watery circles spread out from the spot where a stone has sunk and disappeared, you are witnessing one of the basic mechanisms of the universe—waves. It's a very wavy world.

Imagine you're at the beach. As you play in the ocean, waves push against you and wash over you, as wind makes water build up and then subside. Meanwhile, breezy waves pass through the grasses on a nearby sand dune, and ripples appear in the sand itself.

You hear the shrieks and laughter of the other beachgoers as sound waves travel through the air and hit your eardrums. The summer sun beats down on your back, in waves of electromagnetic radiation. Some of these waves, the ordinary visible light waves, simply bounce

A wave coursing through water or other matter— a mechanical wave— isn't a thing itself, but a passing disturbance.

off. Those that reach your friend's eyes enable her to see you.

The higher-energy light waves—the ultraviolet— actually push into your skin, causing it to make more protective melanin. Your skin gets darker and may burn. Every so often, a very high-energy wave—a gamma or cosmic ray from the depths of space—penetrates the atmosphere and passes straight through your body.

Human society runs in waves, too. History repeats itself in a series of waves, war alternating with peace, long skirts alternating with short, yo-yo sales going up, down, and up again. Emotionally, we are also up and down and up again. Meanwhile, over eons, continents slam together and then drift apart, over and over, nature's cyclical solving of Earth's jigsaw puzzle.

Of course, just thinking about all these waves is generating electrical waves inside your brain.

A wave coursing through water or other matter—a mechanical wave—isn't a thing itself, but a passing disturbance. When wind causes a wave to pass through a wheat field and reach the edge, the wheat doesn't go running across the road. The wave is an undulation passing from row to row, like a rumor passed from person to person.

Likewise, when you drop a rock into a pond, the water doesn't speed away from the stone. Instead, a disturbance travels through the water, causing it to rhythmically rise

and fall in place. (A duck, ripple-riding, will bob up and down.)

Here's how it works: The stone pushes a circular volume of water down into a trough as it sinks. Around the hole, a ring of water crests in reaction. That causes an even larger ring of water to sink, and so on. Presto: spreading concentric circles.

Throw a second stone in nearby, and two sets of circles

will overlap. In some places, the crests or troughs of the waves may coincide, making bigger waves. In other places, a crest will coincide with a trough, canceling out both waves. There, the water will be still.

Without a source of energy, waves lose energy and fade away. So be prepared with a pile of rocks to keep a pond in ripples.

How can a stone skip across a pond?

Toss a stone across a pond and, like magic, it bounces along the surface like a ball on a trampoline. The British call it playing Ducks and Drakes, with one bounce a duck, the next a drake, leaving ripples in their wake like the real thing.

Human beings have probably been playing this game for as long as there were bodies of water and small objects to throw. In about AD 166, a writer in ancient Rome mentioned children skipping shells across the surface of the sea.

Anyone who's ever

tried bouncing a rock across a pond soon realizes there are rules. The stone's shape and size matter, as does the throw. Toss a rock slowly and at a large angle and it will promptly sink.

The best skipping stones are flattish, neither too heavy nor too light. Calm water works better than a wind-ruffled surface. And throwing technique is crucial.

Think of a skipping stone as a skimming water-skier, scientists suggest. The stone and the skier both feel an upward force from the water. And this force increases with the skimming object's speed.

So a stone with greater initial velocity will be more likely to skip across the surface. Toss the stone

nearly parallel to the water, and be sure to put a spin on it: A spinning stone's forward motion is actually stabilized as it flies through the air. When it hits the water, the stone's spin keeps it balanced. So instead of its motion degrading into a crazy somersault, the stone neatly skips along the surface.

With each small bounce, a tossed rock loses energy, experiences frictional drag from the water, and is also tugged down by gravity. So after a number of (slowing) skips, the stone sinks below the surface. The official world record for most skips has steadily increased, from 38 in 1992 to 40 in 2002 to 51 in 2007.

How small are air molecules?

If you could grab a single, random air molecule, odds are you'd find a squirming nitrogen molecule in your palm. Okay, maybe not *squirming*. But even as you read this, about 78 percent of the air surrounding your head—and the rest of you— is made of nitrogen.

Leaving aside air's varying water content, good old oxygen makes up about 21 percent more, or about one out of every five air molecules. Result: By volume, nitrogen and oxygen make up 99 percent of dry air.

Most of the remaining one percent is a gas called argon.

Next comes carbon dioxide, at about 0.04 percent. Even fewer and farther between are molecules of neon (as in old-style sign lighting), helium (think floaty birthday balloons), methane (swamp gas!), krypton, hydrogen, nitrous oxide (so-called laughing gas), xenon, ozone, and more, including iodine and ammonia.

Air molecules aren't lazily floating, like dandelion puffballs. Instead, they zip around us, at speeds from 700 to more than 3,000 miles per hour. The gas molecules, from the common to the exotic, are fairly evenly mixed in the air (although much of the ozone is concentrated in a thin layer about 15 miles up). While air molecules come in different varieties, they have one thing in common: All are impossibly tiny.

Molecules are bunches of atoms, rather like bunches of grapes. The more atoms glommed together, the bigger the molecule. (A water molecule has two hydrogen atoms and one oxygen atom. Large molecules, like DNA, are made of tens of millions.)

A nitrogen molecule, for example, is made up of just two nitrogen atoms. Likewise, an oxygen molecule contains two oxygen atoms. Each individual air molecule measures from one billionth to a few hundred-millionths of an inch across.

(On a ruler, each inch is divided into 16 parts. Now imagine dividing an inch into a billion eensy parts. No wonder we can't see air molecules stream in and out through our nose.)

But while we can't see them with our naked eyes, we can visualize how small the molecules are, in our mind's eye. Scientists Gerald Feinberg and Robert Shapiro, in *Life Beyond Earth*, suggested comparing an air molecule to a salt crystal.

Spill a little salt on a table, and separate out one tiny grain. Now, like Alice in Wonderland, imagine yourself shrinking down, down, down. As you shrink,

Fast Fact

There are 440 quintillion gas molecules in one cubic inch of air at sea level.

the salt crystal grows in front of your eyes, first to the size of a baby's block, and then to the size of a house.

Keep shrinking, until the salt crystal towers above you, stretching into the air like a skyscraper. As you get smaller and smaller, watch the top disappear from view.

Shrinking accomplished, glance around. A gumball-size object suddenly zooms near your head. Reach out and grab it. Rattling around in the palm of your hand: a stray air molecule. While above you looms the salt crystal—a hundred Empire State Buildings high.

Measure FOR Measure

700 to 3,000 miles per hour = 1,127 to 4,828 km/h

15 miles = 24 km

1 billionth of an inch = 0.0254 nanometers

1 cubic inch = 16.4 cm³

Does air weigh anything?

You don't notice the air unless there's a breeze. But countless trillions of gas molecules are constantly banging against your head and stomach and arms and legs. A typical nitrogen molecule, for example, zooms around at about 1,030 miles per hour at room temperature.

These energetic gas molecules are clutched to Earth by our planet's gravity; otherwise, they would simply escape to space. (Some escape anyway, especially the lightest ones, flying off the top edge of the atmosphere toward parts unknown.)

Earth's air is around 78 percent nitrogen molecules. Another 21 percent is oxygen molecules, and the rest other gases. Other planets have their own special recipes of gases enveloping them like shrouds.

Scientists weigh air by measuring how much it presses against objects on

Earth. At any average spot on Earth's surface, the air is pressing against each tiny square inch of you with about 14.7 pounds of force. (Pick up a dumbbell that weighs 15 pounds and you'll see that the air packs a significant force.)

The higher you go, however, the thinner the air gets. At 18,000 feet, way up a mountain, the air is pressing with only about 7.4 pounds of force. However, don't rejoice at the weight off your shoulders—this also means that you are breathing in only half the air molecules you normally do. That's what causes the dizziness, shortness of breath, and nausea of altitude sickness.

Life on Earth evolved to live comfortably with the air weighing down just the amount it does on or near the surface of the planet. Some ocean animals and plants evolved to withstand much higher pressures, deep under the combined weight of the atmosphere and the ocean.

Other planets, of course, have atmospheres with different weights—or virtually no atmosphere at all. Mercury, for example, has a wispy, barely-there atmosphere made mainly of sodium gas.

But just next door, on Venus, it's a vastly different story. Venus is enveloped by a suffocatingly thick layer of carbon dioxide gas. Attempting to stroll across a rocky plain on Venus would be like trying to walk across a swimming pool underwater. Drop a penny through Venus's air, and it would flutter slowly to the ground, as if it were falling through liquid. The weight of the air would be literally crushing—more than 1,300 pounds pressing on each square inch of you.

Jupiter, a gaseous world in the outer solar system, has an atmosphere that would press on you with an elephantlike force of nearly 1,500 pounds per square inch.

By contrast, Martian air, which is also mainly carbon dioxide molecules, is very thin. If you were standing on the rusty surface of Mars, the atmosphere would press down on each square inch of you with only about 1 pound of force.

Measure FOR Measure

1,030 miles per hour = 1,658 km/h
15 pounds = 6.8 kg
18,000 feet = 5,486 m

What makes popcorn pop?

Popcorn Pops the Question...

Won't we be disgusting covered with cream and sugar?

Who decided to eat the noisiest food in the world at the movies?

How did the king of snacks become organic packing material?

Thousands of years before popcorn appeared in multiplexes, people in North and Central America were eating it *and* wearing it, as puffy necklaces. Food chemists think that the first use of wild corn was as popped kernels. The corn probably revealed its inflatable goodness when it was tossed into a fire. Corn poppers, made out of fired clay, came next.

Of the five basic kinds of cultivated corn, only one pops. Think of a kernel of popcorn as a tiny version of an old-fashioned pressure cooker. Its unusually hard shell is the lid. But unlike a real pressure cooker, a popcorn kernel has no safety valve.

About 13.5 percent of a piece of popcorn is water held in the endosperm, the starch inside the kernel. Compared to regular corn, popcorn has a much tougher shell (hull), and contains more of a kind of translucent starch that expands smoothly when heated.

So when popcorn meets heat, and a kernel's temperature rises to 212°F, water trapped inside reaches the boiling point. And as in a furiously boiling teakettle, the water begins to change from liquid to gas.

A teakettle's steam escapes through the spout, rising into the kitchen air. But the steam in a heating popcorn kernel is trapped inside. The extra-hard hull acts like a tightly sealed lid, pushing the steam into the kernel's granules of starch. Invaded by steam, the granules expand into jellylike globs.

The popcorn's hull is so strong that temperatures in

> A popcorn hull is so strong that the temperature in the kernel can reach 347°F before steam breaks through.

the kernel can soar well above the water's boiling point, to about 347°F, before steam breaks through. Chemists say the inner pressure increases to nine times that of Earth's atmosphere before the hull finally explodes, torn apart by expanding steam and superheated water.

Freed from their vegetable prison, the steam and hot water carry the inner white starch with them. The kernel turns itself inside out, swelling to 40 times its original size. The cauliflower shape of a "popped" kernel,

scientists say, comes courtesy of the starch granules, which expand like bubbles.

The best kernels have a hull whose cellulose molecules are arranged in a tight, orderly, crystalline structure. The result: Steam is trapped until the kernel explodes with full force.

After the explosion comes the eating. And a study at Scranton University found that popcorn is surprisingly nutritious, containing up to 300 milligrams of plant polyphenols in an average 4-cup serving. (A cup of strawberries contains about 270 mg.) Studies show that these compounds may help protect against cancer, heart disease, diabetes, and diseases of the nervous system. Most of popcorn's polyphenols are in the hull—which also packs the most fiber.

Measure FOR Measure
212°F = 100°C
347°F = 175°C
I cup = 0.24 l
4 cups = 0.95 l

How does a compass work?

Before there was a Global Positioning System (GPS) receiver in every car (or in the backpacks of wayward hikers), there was the magnetic compass. In fact, before there were cars and nylon backpacks, explorers and sailors and pirates used their trusty compasses to find their way around the big, featureless ocean. Even on a cloudy night, with no stars to guide you, a small piece of magnetized metal, mounted so that it could swing freely, told you which way was north.

What's so special about north? If you know where north is, you know it all. Face north, and south will be behind you, east on your right, and west on your left.

Rotate a handheld compass, and the needle, strangely, doesn't turn with it. Feeling an attraction we're unaware of, the floating metal needle moves on its own, like the pointer on a spooky movie

Ouija board. The needle seems drawn toward some distant beacon, feeling the pull even through walls.

But the needle on a compass isn't made of just any old metal. Instead, it's a metal that's been magnetized. This slender, lightweight magnet has its own north and south poles, which are attracted to the opposite poles of other magnets. Meanwhile, the magnet is free to pivot in any direction.

Luckily for lost travelers (especially before GPS tracking in cell phones and cars), the planet we travel on is itself a magnet. Pocket compasses respond to Earth's magnetism by lining up in its magnetic field. So even on a cloudy night, with no stars to guide him, a sailor adrift in a dark sea can find "north"— and thus south, east, and west.

(The Earth's field reverses itself every 500,000 years or so, but for now, Earth's "south" pole is in the north, its "north" pole in the south. Which is why a magnetized needle's north pole, attracted to its opposite, will point north. About 800,000 years ago, compass needles would have pointed south.)

Human beings have used compasses to navigate for more than 2,000 years. The earliest compasses were made of wood, topped with a bit of lodestone, a naturally magnetic iron ore. Floated on water or other liquid, the wooden compass was free to move, the lodestone turning until it aligned itself with the Earth's field.

Scientists think that the Earth's magnetic field is generated by looping electric currents in our planet's (superhot) liquid metal core. Imagine a bar magnet stuck vertically through the center of the Earth, its invisible field arcing out into space like a horizontal figure 8. Although we don't notice it, magnetized objects feel its pull.

But while the Earth is large, its magnetic field is rather feeble. Our planetary magnet is thousands of times weaker than the magnets on your refrigerator, which can keep class photos and shopping lists clasped to the metal door (or grab a stray paper clip if it comes too near).

The Earth's magnetic field varies across the planet, but it's strongest at the poles. Magnetic strength is usually measured in gauss or tesla units. At its weakest, in parts of South America, the Earth's field strength is about 0.3 gauss (30 microteslas). Near the north and south magnetic poles, the strength increases to about 0.65 gauss (65 microteslas). By contrast, that small, cow-shaped magnet on your refrigerator may be 50 gauss (5,000 microteslas) strong. So it's no wonder that the Earth's weak magnetism can't make paper clips migrate en masse to the poles.

When we spin a bucket of water around, why doesn't the water spill out?

When the Centripetal Bathtub Stops...

It's a mega-mess time!

It's no-more-fun time!

It's Scrape-the-kid-off-the-wall time.

Swing a bucket of water up, over, and around with enough energy, and not one drop falls out. Why does the water stay inside an upside-down pail? For clues, think about clothes clinging to the sides of the washer in the spin cycle, or even Earth speeding around the Sun at 67,000 miles per hour (108,000 km/h).

When you swing a bucket of water over your head, down, and around again, you are exerting a centripetal (toward the center) force on the bucket. You are forcing an object in motion—the bucket—to take a circular path. Meanwhile, the force of gravity is tugging the pail and its contents down, toward the Earth.

Swing the bucket fast, and the water, trying to fly out, presses against the bottom of the pail. As the bucket swings through the top of the circle, the water's up and out motion more than balances the "down" force of gravity toward the Earth. So none spills.

What if you don't swing the pail fast enough, or stop halfway through? Instant watery disaster. Think about that load of laundry. Before the clothes begin to spin, they lie limply on the bottom of the washer, overcome by the downward force of gravity. But click on the spin cycle, and the clothes are picked up and thrown to the sides. Slow or stop the spin, and the clothes come tumbling down.

Likewise, swing the pail too slowly, and the water will begin to tumble down and out. Stop the pail abruptly, and you're soaked. Gravity wins again.

Then there's Plan C: The Letting Go. Remove the centripetal force, and a moving object's own inertia is revealed.

The bucket is restrained by your grip on the handle or rope. And the water is stopped by the bottom of the pail. So if you let go of your bucket midswing, it will take off on a straight path into the wild blue yonder. Freed from the centripetal force you supplied, the bucket and its contents will continue on their merry way (well, at least for a short freedom-filled distance).

Now think about Earth. If our orbiting planet were to slow down, or suddenly careen to a stop, it would be pulled by gravity into the Sun—just as the water fell from the bucket when it slowed or stopped.

On the other hand, what if an annoyed Sun were to disappear in a huff, taking its gravity with it? The speeding Earth would be freed from the centripetal force that keeps it running around the big star like a faithful puppy. Our planet would slingshot off in a straight line. Zooming off into the wild black yonder of space, Earth would continue on its merry way until it was captured by the gravity of another star, slammed into a fellow planet, or sucked into a black hole.

How does a finger on a straw keep liquid in?

Put a finger over the end of your straw before lifting it from your beverage of choice, and it's like you've invented your own antigravity device. The liquid, amazingly, stays suspended in the straw, rather than pouring out onto the table. But lift your finger, and, well . . . oops.

How does one little finger make water defy the pull of gravity? As it turns out, the power isn't exactly in your finger. It's in something virtually invisible: the air around us.

At close range, in a quiet room, air is both unseen and unfelt. Only when air currents move against us in a breeze, or when we look at the blue sky (the mass of air from a distance is blue) do we feel and "see" the air.

But at sea level, the Earth's atmosphere exerts about 14.7 pounds of pressure on each square inch of us. The air also presses on your beverage, including the liquid inside the straw. But sealing the open end with your finger changes everything.

How? When you cover the top with your finger and lift the filled straw, the liquid begins to fall downward. At first, you'll lose a few drops. But as the liquid sags down into the straw, the air trapped in the space between the liquid and your finger spreads out, becoming less dense. Result: less pressure on the liquid remaining in the straw.

Since the pressure from above has decreased, it's now lower than the pressure from the air at the straw's bottom. With the pressures unbalanced, the liquid experiences a greater "upward" force from the air below. This force is strong enough to offset the force of gravity, and support the liquid's weight.

Why do we fall forward when the bus driver suddenly brakes?

Inertia Rules! ... Unless the FORCE is with you!

Just try to get Darth to stop mowing the lawn!

or attempt to make lazy Princess Leia clean up her room!

But save the elbow grease for Luke Skywalker, battling inertia on the planet Hoth!

He's evil 'n' FAST!

Mañana!

Ride yourself to school!

It can happen on the bus, but also on a train, in a car, or on a bike. You're riding along. Suddenly, there's a dog crossing the road, or someone's pulled the emergency cord, and bang— the brakes are on. And you're thrown forward. If you're unlucky (or un-seatbelted), your tender forehead may hit a windshield, or you may go flying over the handlebars. Which is why subway poles, metal bus straps, and seatbelts are such good ideas.

It might seem like we should stop when the vehicle we're riding on does. But because of inertia, a feature built into the universe we live in, we keep right on moving.

Inertia means that whatever you're doing, you'll tend to continue doing it unless some force intervenes. We've all experienced the inertia of habits, which leads us to mindlessly part our hair on the same side every morning, or (better) brush our teeth before bed every night. Inertia can be very useful. It helps us finish a task, once started: picking up stick after stick in the yard, pedaling mile after mile on a bike, putting a pile of laundry away, sock by sock. But it can also keep us planted firmly on the couch, channel-surfing. Whether you're sitting still, or just continuing to move in the same old direction, it's all inertia.

So much for psychological inertia. What throws you forward on a bus is real, physical inertia, and it's out of your control. As scientist Isaac Newton observed back in the late 1600s, "Every body continues in its state of rest, or of uniform motion in a straight line, unless it is compelled to change that state by forces impressed thereon."

On a smoothly moving train, we may feel like we're sitting perfectly still. Of course, when you're riding, say, on the subway, you and the train are both traveling forward in space. When the brakes are suddenly applied, frictional forces make the wheels stop. But because of inertia, your (brakeless) body goes on blithely traveling forward—at the original speed of the train.

In a suddenly stopped car, a seatbelt applies a counterforce, keeping you from hitting the dashboard. In a train, the seat in front of you may stop your forward motion.

In a swiftly descending elevator that abruptly stops, the elevator floor keeps you from continuing to fall. However, inertia of motion may cause some blood to rush from your head. Likewise, a football player's head may strike the ground, but his brain continues moving forward in his skull, leading to a possible concussion.

And the more massive the object, the more inertia it has. That makes massive objects harder to move when they're stopped—and harder to stop when they're moving. It's hard to budge an enormous boulder, sitting stock-still. But once you get it rolling down a hill, it's also very hard to stop.

Of course, in the real world, objects in motion don't stay in motion forever. Imagine a ball rolling across a smooth, icy pond. Even if the pond stretched on to the horizon, the force of friction between the ball's surface and the ice will gradually slow its progress, and eventually bring it to a stop. In this universe, perpetual motion machines aren't allowed.

How does a yo-yo work?

Meditations on a yo-yo's return...

Yo-yo has fallen in love with hand and can't stay away...

Yo-yo is afraid of floor and must escape...

Yo-yo is never happy and must stay on the move!

Can you Hop the Fence, Milk the Cow, Ride the Horse, and then Walk the Dog—without ever setting foot on a farm? If so, you're probably familiar with yo-yo tricks.

A simple wooden yo-yo, physicists say, illustrates many of the discoveries of science. Case in point: A fundamental law of the universe is that energy can't be created or destroyed. Scientists call it the "conservation of energy." Energy already exists, but its form can change in an instant.

Imagine water behind a dam. When the dam is closed and the water is waiting, it has potential energy. Open the dam, and the water cascades down, pulled by the force of gravity. Suddenly, the water's potential energy has been transformed into kinetic energy—energy of motion.

Rushing against the blades of a turbine, the water's kinetic energy powers the turbine, which is connected to an electrical generation system. So the water's kinetic energy has been changed into electrical energy. And so on, into your home—

where the electrical energy is transformed into heat energy, warming your house.

Something similar happens with a yo-yo. A yo-yo drops, and its potential energy changes to kinetic energy. But unlike water falling over a dam, a yo-yo rotates as it drops, its rate depending on the thickness of the bundle of string wound around its middle.

As the yo-yo falls, its string unspooling, it spins faster. Some of the energy that would go into falling has been transformed into the rotational energy of spinning. So about halfway through the fall, the yo-yo's descent speed actually slows.

At the end of the string, the yo-yo bounces. The string begins to rewrap around the shaft, yo-yo still spinning. If the bounce it felt wasn't hard enough, the yo-yo will "sleep," according to physicist Jearl Walker of Cleveland State University. To wake it up, he says, jerk back on the string. If there is enough friction between the loops of rewrapping string, the yo-yo will keep turning—and therefore rising.

Back at the top, its kinetic energy transformed into gravitational potential energy, the yo-yo plunges again. But because of friction, a yo-yo's kinetic energy gradually changes into increasing heat energy in the string and spool. (Just as friction between a moving tire and pavement heats the tire surface.) If the yo-yo-er fails to tug up on the string each time, the yo-yo will lose more and more momentum, finally coming to a full stop at the bottom.

How big can yo-yos get and still work? In 2010, a yo-yo that weighed 1,600 pounds broke the Guinness world record. But the most recent world record for largest working wooden yo-yo belongs to inventor Beth Johnson of La Rue, Ohio.

Fast Fact

The ancient Greeks had yo-yos by 500 BC; a painting on a vase shows a kid playing with one. While inventors use the science behind yo-yos to come up with more advanced designs (a $400 yo-yo made of magnesium alloy, equipped with ball bearings and counterweights), the simplest wooden yo-yo is amazingly ingenious already.

The striped yo-yo, which was tested in Cincinnati in 2012 as it dangled from a crane, measured 11.75 feet across and weighed more than 4,600 pounds.

Measure FOR Measure
1,600 pounds = 725.7 kg
11.75 feet = 3.58 m
4,600 pounds = 2,086.5 kg

Why does a bouncing ball bounce lower and lower each time?

No matter how bouncy the ball, the first bounce is always the best. Even a small rubber SuperBall will high-bounce only so many times before it peters out. And each bounce is a little less high than the last. It's almost as if the ball were becoming tired from all the effort of springing into the air. Until at last, utterly exhausted, it stops dead-still on the ground.

Left to its own devices, a bouncing ball gradually loses energy to its surroundings. Imagine holding a ball over a wooden floor, say, 5 feet up. The poised-to-fall ball has potential energy— gravitational potential energy.

Let the ball go, and gravity will cause it to accelerate toward Earth.

When the ball begins falling, its potential energy is transforming into kinetic energy, energy of motion. A tiny bit of energy is lost through friction with the air, changing into heat energy. Just before the ball hits the floor, nearly all of its potential energy has turned into kinetic energy—the ball simply has no farther to fall.

When the ball lands, it presses down on the floor— and the floor presses back. A bit of energy is transferred to the floor, which vibrates from the impact. This

vibration spreads into the air, and we hear the ball's thud. The very fact that we hear a thud means that the ball has lost—to the wood and to the room—some of the energy it started with. The ball and floor are also heated a little by the impact, the heat energy radiating into the air.

Squishing from the impact, the ball is actually motionless for a split second. The flattened part of the ball has in effect absorbed most of the energy the ball had. At this instant, the ball has "elastic" potential energy, just as it had gravitational potential energy when suspended overhead.

As the ball un-squishes, its molecules returning to their former positions, that energy is released—as kinetic energy. And our round friend springs into the air.

However, the ball doesn't make it all the way up to the 5-foot height from which it was dropped. An average ball will rebound 60 percent—3 feet, in this case—on the first bounce. A basketball may rebound 80 percent. An extremely bouncy SuperBall may rebound to 90 percent of its original height.

The amount a ball rebounds, according to University of Virginia physicist Louis Bloomfield, is equal to the amount of energy the ball has held onto. So a ball that rebounds to 60 percent of its former height has retained 60 percent of its original energy—and has lost 40 percent to its surroundings.

Each time the ball falls back to the floor, it loses more energy. So each bounce is a little lower than the last. Until finally, its energy spent, the ball rolls to a rest. To keep a ball bouncing, you need to expend some energy yourself—which is why dribbling a basketball can get tiring.

Measure FOR Measure
5 feet = 1.5 m
3 feet = a little less than 1 m

Why does metal feel colder than clothing at room temperature?

Have you ever climbed into a cast-iron tub before it's filled and touched your bare back to the metal? Even in a warm room, the tub will make you flinch. Or stepped barefoot on ceramic tiles after walking across a carpet? Common sense tells you that the carpet and the tiles are probably at the same temperature. But your bare feet, acting as a handy thermometer, tell a different story: The marble feels much cooler.

While your skin may not be the most accurate thermometer, it is sensing a real difference between materials. It all comes down to the movement of heat between one object and another.

While heat and temperature are related, they're actually two different things. Temperature measures the average amount molecules are moving in a substance, or their average kinetic energy. Heat is the energy a substance has because of the energy of all of its molecules. So while a mug and a bathtub full of water may be at the same temperature—say, 100°F—the big tub of water has much more stored heat.

Put two objects of different temperatures together, and heat energy will be transferred from hotter object to cooler. Pour boiling water into a room-temperature mug, and the mug warms up, even as the water loses heat energy. Eventually, both will reach the same temperature.

What does all this have to do with objects around the house that feel oddly cool (or strangely warm) to the touch? Your body, a substantial reservoir of heat energy, maintains a temperature of about 98.6°F. So your own temperature is, on average, more than 20°F higher than that of the room's air and the objects in it. Making you a walking, talking oven.

Your Skin Thermometer tells you...

Hot!

Cold!

The temperature of what you are touching...

Which way the heat is moving...

And when it's not moving at all!

So when you touch an object at 72°F—say, your wooden desk—you are transferring heat energy from your warm fingertips to the cooler wood. As they gain energy, molecules in the wood begin moving more energetically. And as heat energy is transferred from your hand at the point of contact, the temperature in your fingertips drops. And your skin senses coolness. (However, since your

body's metabolic furnace works hard to maintain your high temperature, you and your desk will never reach temperature equilibrium.)

But why does metal feel extra-cool? Metal is an especially good conductor of heat, losing and gaining heat quickly. So when you touch a metal cake pan at room temperature, heat flows swiftly from your hand into the pan. With the quicker, steeper drop in your fingertip

temperature, you sense that the pan is cooler than your wooden desk. Besides wood, other slow heat conductors, like carpeting and clothing, also feel warmer to the touch than metal.

Measure FOR Measure
100°F = 38°C
98.6°F = 37°C
15°F = −9°C
more than 20°F higher =
  more than 11°C higher
72°F = 22°C

How does dry ice make fog?

You're on Thin Ice...

I can't see!

BLAM!!

I'll sublimate you next!

If you're skating on dry ice... If it's in your Thermos... Or if you decide to have a snowball fight with it.

Leave an ice cube on the kitchen counter, and you'll return to find nothing but a puddle of water. But a left-behind chunk of dry ice, made of carbon dioxide instead of H_2O, will turn to fog and disappear—with no wet trace. Scientists call the sudden change from solid to gas, with no liquidy interval, sublimation.

Luckily, our winter coats don't suddenly dissolve into colored clouds when we enter a warm school or office. Still, sublimation doesn't happen just to frozen carbon dioxide. In fact, it's happening all around us—in the room you're sitting in, and in the depths of space.

Sublimation depends on the physical properties of a substance, its temperature, and the pressure it feels from outside. At sea level, Earth's atmosphere exerts a pressure of nearly 15 pounds per square inch. Water in your kitchen responds by remaining liquid at room temperature, freezing into ice at 32°F (0°C) or below, and boiling into a steamy gas at 212°F (100°C).

PARTY TRICK

Put pellets of dry ice into a balloon, tie it shut, and throw it into a swimming pool. The balloon will sink. But as the CO_2 ice warms and turns to gas, the balloon will inflate, swiftly rise to the surface, and explode with a bang.

But carbon dioxide (CO_2) is different. At room temperature in the ordinary atmospheric pressure of Earth, CO_2 is already a gas. It can be contained inside a soda can, but open the lid, and the gas escapes, leaving a flat drink.

As it's chilled to $-109.3°F$ ($-78.5°C$) at ordinary pressures, carbon dioxide goes straight from gas to a snowy solid, skipping the liquid phase on its way. To turn carbon dioxide into a liquid requires a big squeeze—at room temperature, a pressure of 30 atmospheres. Many fire extinguishers contain liquid carbon dioxide, held under just such high pressure.

When CO_2 ice is suddenly exposed to a lower pressure and higher temperature, its molecules gain energy, like H_2O molecules in a heating teakettle. A block of dry ice, placed out in the open in a school lab, immediately expands into a gas, molecules flying off in all directions.

Carbon dioxide gas itself is invisible. So why the spooky fog effect? When frigid CO_2 gas hits the air, it causes water vapor to condense into tiny droplets—creating instant (real) fog.

Sublimation can happen slowly, too. Stray atoms escape from the surface of ice cubes in your freezer, causing gradual shrinkage. Atoms even flee into the air from the surface of your desk (and everything else in the room), although the process is so slow as to be undetectable.

Fast Fact

Dry ice must be handled with tongs and insulating gloves, since skin will freeze to it on contact. Vapors can be a breathing hazard, so always use in a well-ventilated space.

Sometimes, however, sublimation is spectacularly visible—in the night sky. Comets, speeding through the solar system on arcs around the Sun, are made mostly of ice. As a comet nears the Sun, sunlight warms the frozen water. Energized H_2O molecules immediately expand into gas in the near vacuum of space. Since a comet's gravity is too low to hold onto an atmosphere, the released gas streams behind it. A comet with its glowing tail, seemingly hanging in the night, is a sublime effect of sublimation.

Does hot water really freeze faster than cold water?

It sounds like one of those questions that must have been answered hundreds of years ago by a scientist whose name is in our textbooks. The commonsense answer: no, of course not. Water freezes because it loses heat. Cold water has already lost more heat than hot water. So since it's already closer to the freezing point, cold water should freeze faster.

But the real answer to the question is: It depends.

Experiments show that hot water *will* sometimes freeze faster than cooler water, depending on the starting temperatures, the containers holding the water, and the freezing conditions. (For example, hot water will not freeze first if the cooler water's temperature is already almost at the freezing point.)

Imagine two identical buckets, open at the top. Put hot water in one and an equal amount of lukewarm water in the other. Set them outside when the temperature is well below freezing, or in a big freezer. According to one argument—the evaporation theory—the hotter water will evaporate faster. With less water to cool, the water in the "hot" pail may cool to freezing first. Also, evaporation itself makes water lose heat quickly—like sweat evaporating from your skin cools you.

But in the pail of cooler water, a thin layer of ice will quickly form on the surface, insulating the water from further evaporation— and slowing the rate of ice formation below the surface.

There may also be a supercooling effect, in which water remains liquid below its normal freezing point of 32°F (0°C), then freezes faster. How? Normally, ice crystals form at places in water where there is suspended dust or gas bubbles. Hot water that's been boiled has fewer dissolved bubbles. With fewer impurities, water can evaporate and cool without forming a layer of insulating ice on top. As it chills to below freezing, ice crystals form spontaneously, spread into an icy slush, and the water quickly freezes solid.

(There's also a simpler reason why hot water may freeze faster. Put a tray of hot water in your freezer, and its heat may trigger the refrigerator's thermostat, causing the compressor to start. With the refrigerator pumping heat out of the freezer, your hot tray may enjoy a quicker trip to icehood than a cooler tray would.)

Aristotle noticed the hot water phenomenon back in 300 BC, but scientific discussion of the mystery had all but ceased by the 20th century. Until a boy in Africa, Erasto Mpemba, noticed something funny when he was making ice cream: If he started with hot milk, his ice cream froze *faster*.

Later, in high school in Tanzania, Mpemba pestered his teachers for an explanation. A professor of physics visiting the school was intrigued, and a series of experiments in his lab confirmed the boy's results. In 1969, the professor and Mpemba published their findings. Today, the phenomenon of hot water freezing faster than cooler is often called the Mpemba effect.

Scientists watch hot and cold water freeze...

Why does your tongue stick to freezing-cold metal?

In the 1983 movie *A Christmas Story*, it's a triple-dog-dare that prompts Ralphie's friend Flick to taste a freezing-cold flagpole on a winter's day in Indiana. When he can't get his tongue unstuck, Ralphie's

friend is rescued by the local fire department, while his classmates watch from the school windows.

Wet fingers can stick to metal, too, but tongues are especially vulnerable. The tongue is naturally moist, its surface riddled with tiny fissures where water can collects. Touch your tongue to metal whose temperature is below the freezing point of water (32°F [0°C]), and the water on its surface freezes solid, forming an icy bond between you and the metal.

Chemist Francis DiSalvo of Cornell University says that ice forms so quickly because metals are so good at

conducting heat. Touch your tongue to a frozen rubber pencil eraser, and you can't make it stick. That's because the thermal conductivity of rubber is about 100 times lower than that of metal. Cold rubber just can't remove enough heat from the water on your tongue to freeze it.

But metals have high thermal conductivity, quickly siphoning off heat from water and lowering its temperature to freezing. In an instant, you're (painfully) attached to a frigid flagpole. The remedy for un-sticking: a glass of warm water, poured over your tongue to melt the ice.

Why do ice cubes swell as they freeze?

If Freezing Ice Didn't Expand...

Icebergs would sit safely on the ocean floor.

Iced drinks wouldn't be much fun.

You can say that again.

Ice skaters would have to wear wet suits.

Water is peculiar. When most substances change from liquid to solid form, they shrink, becoming denser, their molecules packing more closely together. But when water changes from a sloshy liquid to solid ice, it expands, becoming less dense. Which is why ice bobs to the top of your Coke, rather than sinking to the bottom.

At normal atmospheric pressure, molecules usually behave in predictable ways as their temperature changes. Molecules fly apart into a gas when heated, condense into a flowing liquid when cooled, and shrink into a frozen solid when chilled still further. The changes in state parallel changes in energy: from high energy to medium energy to barely jiggling.

Boiling water expands into a gas (steam) and wafts off into the kitchen. But we also see water expand when

WHAT IF . . .

If frozen water weren't less dense than liquid, there would be no floating icebergs to sight off the bow of a ship. There would be no skating on ice-covered ponds, while fish and other life shelter in insulated water below. If water froze from the bottom up, much of Earth's water would solidify in winter, and life might be impossible.

chilled in the freezer. An ice cube tray filled to the rim the night before overflows with big cubes of ice in the morning.

How does it work? Water starts out behaving normally. As its temperature drops, water obediently shrinks together—until it reaches

Measure FOR Measure

39°F = 4°C
32°F = 0°C
10 cups = 2.37 l
11 cups = 2.6 l

39°F. Then, amazingly, water reverses course, its volume slowly increasing as it chills. When water finally freezes, at 32°F, it expands dramatically.

Scientists say water's quirky behavior is caused by the shape of its molecule and by how the molecules bond to one another. Each water molecule is two hydrogen atoms bonded to one oxygen (H_2O). Because of how the atoms share electrons, a water molecule has a slight positive charge at the end with the hydrogen atoms and a slight negative charge at the end with the oxygen atom.

Result? The molecule's charged ends attract the oppositely charged ends of other water molecules (aka hydrogen bonding).

In liquid water, as molecules slip-slide past one another, bonds form, break, and re-form. But by the time water has cooled to 39°F, the molecules' energy has dropped enough that they

Fast Fact

When water freezes and expands, water pipes can freeze and then burst in unheated houses. Water in roadway cracks turns to ice in winter, expanding crevices into gaping potholes.

are very near one another. So each H_2O molecule forms more stable hydrogen bonds with up to four fellow molecules.

By 32°F, the H_2O molecules are snappily lined up in a frozen crystal lattice, an open hexagonal (six-sided) shape. Unlike in liquid, molecules in ice are held rigidly apart. That means more empty space between molecules—so frozen water occupies more room.

Presto: Put 10 cups of water in the freezer, take out nearly 11 cups of ice!

How can ice cubes grow sharp spikes?

ICE SPIKES AROUND THE HOUSE...

subzero olive holders...

chilly hat and glove hooks...

a frosty back-scratcher

Are your ice cubes mysteriously sporting Mohawks? If so, you've probably been making ice the old-fashioned way, in an ice cube tray. Cubes that tumble out of an ice maker tend to be uniformly shaped. But water left to freeze in open trays can undergo a startlingly spiky transformation.

One clue as to why spikes form: Have you ever noticed that after you fill an ice cube tray, the frozen cubes bulge above the rim? Water is peculiar. When other substances transform from liquids to solids, molecules packing together, they contract. But when liquid H_2O changes into solid ice, it actually expands—by about 9 percent.

Why? At 32°F (0°C), water molecules lock into a rigid, open lattice. The result is open spaces inside each cube, causing ice to swell out of the tray.

Scientists say that under the right conditions, thin ice sheets form on the surface first, near the edges of each tray compartment. Meanwhile, ice also forms on the bottom of each compartment. As the freezing, glacierlike sheets advance in from the sides and up from the bottom, liquid water may find itself trapped between the jagged sheets.

As the freezing water expands, the still-liquid water may be squeezed through gaps in the icy sheets. Once at the cube's surface, the water may erupt in a tiny geyser, freezing in place. Presto: a hollow, pointy ice spike. A spike's angle varies, depending on the shape of the funnel the water squeezed through. The more tilted the funnel, the more slanted the spike.

For spikes to form, freezing must be rapid, but not too rapid. At too-low temperatures, water that wells up through a surface hole will simply freeze over into an unsightly ice wart. According to studies, the ideal temperature for growing spikes is around 19°F (7°C). It can take up to 10 minutes for a fledgling spike to grow to its full height. The tallest spikes may reach 2 inches (5 cm), making convenient handles for pulling cubes from trays.

Want to make your own spiky cubes? According to researchers at Caltech, plastic trays work best, providing just the right amount of

Fast Fact

On a frigid day in winter, look for larger ice spikes wherever water collects in a contained space, from driveway puddles to plastic birdbaths.

insulation on sides and bottom. To grow the most spikes, fill the tray with distilled water. Dissolved minerals in tap water slow down freezing. Distilled water can "supercool," staying liquid as the temperature drops below 32°F (0°C), and then freezing rapidly. Leave the ice cube tray undisturbed for a few hours, and you may return to find icy thorns.

What exactly is fire, anyway?

It's easy to figure out water. Sipped from a glass? Liquid. Floating in cubes? Solid. Jetting out of the spout of a furiously boiling teakettle? Gas.

But fire doesn't look, or feel, like any of these familiar states of matter. And ever since human beings started wondering about the world around them, they've tried to crack the mystery of fire.

The ancient Greeks thought fire was one of four basic elements: earth, water, air, and fire. Philosopher Heraclitus thought that fire was, in fact, the primary element. The world, he said, "was ever, is now, and ever shall be an ever-living fire." The philosopher Anaximander believed Earth was surrounded by huge, misty spheres, but beyond lay an enormous fire. The stars and the Sun were just glimpses of the fire, like the glow seen through cutouts in a lampshade.

Many believed that the great fire was the source

of both creation and destruction. Which makes sense, since even a small fire is constantly in motion, like energy dancing in place—and capable of devouring everything around it.

Fire was so dazzling, terrifying, and mysterious (and yet useful) throughout human history that trying to solve its riddle helped develop a whole branch of science: chemistry.

In trying to figure out fire, human beings discovered something even more fundamental: oxygen. In the early 1500s, inventor and artist Leonardo da Vinci was among the first to make note that a flame goes out without air, like a living creature suffocates. Others discovered that when metals were heated in a flame, the powder left behind weighed more than the original metal. It was as if an invisible substance had been added.

By the 1700s, French chemist Antoine-Laurent

In trying to figure out fire, human beings discovered oxygen.

Lavoisier and others realized that air is made up of gases. And that it was one of these gases—oxygen—that was sucked into all burning materials, adding its own weight to burned metals.

Scientists soon figured out how it works. Over time, oxygen atoms combine with carbon and hydrogen atoms in so-called hydrocarbons like wood. From the gradual yellowing of aging paper to the controlled "burning" of food in the body to an actual wood fire, oxidation goes on every second, all around us.

Fire is just oxidation, sped up by intense heat. If a fuel like wood is heated—say,

by a struck match—oxygen in the air swiftly bonds to the wood's hydrogen and carbon atoms. If the process accelerates to the ignition point, you'll feel heat, and see a red glow. The first flames will appear. And your match will have created a campfire.

Fuel burned in a fire can be solid (a chunk of wood or lump of coal); liquid (gasoline or kerosene); or gas (natural gas or propane). According to scientists, an object can even be on fire without producing a flame (like a red-hot coal).

But what about the dancing fire itself? Flames are a collection of very hot, glowing gases such as carbon dioxide, along with steam, rising from a burning material. (How hot? A candle flame's temperature is about 1,800°F [982°C].) Sitting by a campfire, you may also notice solid bits of soot, glowing embers carried up toward the night sky.

Why do flames point up?

WHY DOES A FLAME POINT UP?

Because it's impolite to point at people...

Because it doesn't want to appear sad...

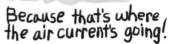

Because that's where the air current's going!

If you've ever picked up a burning candle—say, from your birthday cake—and tilted it to one side, you may have noticed that while the candle leans sideways, the flame continues to point straight up toward the ceiling. Even if a candle is flipped all the way upside down, the flame will turn skyward, making a mess of hot, dripping wax as it envelops the candle.

> Even if a candle is flipped upside down, its flame will turn skyward.

Most everyone keeps at least a few candles around the house, whether for special dinners or lights-out emergencies. Of all the everyday objects around us, a candle—a pillar of wax with an embedded string—seems among the simplest and most "homemade."

But Michael Faraday, the brilliant 19th-century English scientist, thought candles were far from simple. Faraday did a lecture series in London aimed at young people, and six of the talks were about candles. "There is no more open door by which you can enter into the study of [science] than by considering the physical phenomena of a candle," he said, going on to discuss what makes a candle flame bright, how it burns, why flames come in different colors, and why a burning candle produces water vapor.

As a flame burns, it heats the surrounding air, creating currents. The heated air near the flame spreads out and rises, since it's lighter than the air around it. Cooler air rushes in to replace it, heats up, and likewise rises. So there is always an upward-flowing current of air (convection current) around a candle flame. It is this upward current that keeps a flame pointing up. Soot particles sputtering off the end of the burning wick are also carried upward by the current and incinerated, making the flame yellow.

So a flame points upward—no matter how we tilt the candle—in the same way that a hot-air balloon pulls straight up into the sky, even if its passenger basket is tilted sideways by the ground crew.

LOW-GRAVITY FLAMES

On your Earthbound dining room table, rising hot gases shape a candle flame into an arrowhead or feather shape. But a flame would act and look strikingly different in a place where gravitational forces are effectively very tiny—such as in the free-fall environment of a space station. To keep astronauts safe, scientists have studied how fires ignite in conditions of microgravity. In the process, they've discovered some odd things about how flames behave. Experiments show that in microgravity, a flame loses its familiar feather shape and also changes color.

How come? In microgravity, the concepts of "lighter" and "heavier" and "up" and "down" are almost meaningless. The air near a flame still heats up, but there are no briskly "rising" air currents. With few air currents to quickly replenish oxygen, a flame burns slower, but hotter. The result? A blue flame, reduced from an up-rushing arrowhead to a compact dome.

Why do Cheerios clump together in the bowl?

Together wherever we go-oh! Because...

We're lost...
Where did the box go?

we like each other...
You smell good!
This is fun!

We're afraid!
oh my gosh!
White stuff!
eeeek!

Whatever your favorite floaty cereal, you may have noticed the phenomenon: Clumpy bunches of Os, or Lucky Charms, or Cocoa Puffs huddled together in the milk. Along with a ring of cereal bits, clinging to the walls of the bowl.

Scientists call it the "Cheerios effect," but small, O-shaped rings of oats aren't the only objects that do this. When a man shaves in the morning, the shorn hairs that fall into the sink water will tend to clump together, too. Yuck-O.

What's the attraction? Do small bits feel the need to huddle in the deep middle of a scary pool of liquid? Do the rest cling to the sides, like non-swimmers along the wall of a pool?

Believe it or not, it wasn't until 2005 that science completely explained the Cheerios mystery (even though its namesake cereal had been around since 1941). Scientists say the Cheerios effect is due to surface tension, gravity, buoyancy, and something called the meniscus effect,

SNAP, CRACKLE, POP

Why do Rice Krispies make noise when doused with milk? Cereal makers oven-toast the rice, which has been conditioned with water. As the water turns to steam, the rice kernels puff out like popcorn.

But unlike the compact, hard walls of an uncooked rice kernel, the walls of puffed rice are stretched thin, making each kernel fragile. The shock of cold milk makes the walls crack like a thin glass crystal. As the milk is (unevenly) absorbed by the puffed rice, the snapping and crackling sounds come from the fracturing of the walls and the escape of air trapped inside the kernels.

which involves the attraction between liquids and solids.

Cheerios and other cereals that float are able to resist the force of gravity because of the buoyant effect. If an object (like a single Cheerio) is less dense than milk and weighs less than an equal (Cheerio-size) volume of milk, it will float.

And then there's surface tension. Molecules at the surface of a liquid are strongly attracted to each other and also attracted to the molecules beneath. But they're much less attracted to air molecules moving above the surface. The result: The surface has a skinlike tension. Thanks to surface tension, some insects can stride across a pond, feet indenting the water as if it were a rubbery sheet.

When a Cheerio floats on milk, it creates a dent in the surface. Each bobbing Cheerio makes its own dimple in the ordinarily smooth surface "skin" of the milk. As the Cheerios drift near one another, they seem to attract like magnets. Actually, researchers say, they consolidate their troughs, creating a bigger and bigger dimple as more Cheerios drift in. Escaping from the bunch is hard, since it requires a Cheerio to travel up a hill, against the force of gravity. So the Os tend to stay clumped.

So why do Cheerios often cling to the sides of the bowl? Water (or milk) near the side of a glass behaves differently than water (or milk) in the middle. The crescent shape of a liquid where it meets a solid surface is called a meniscus. The liquid can bulge into a convex shape when it's repelled by the solid, or dip down in a concave shape when it's attracted.

Since water molecules are attracted to glass, and milk is mostly water, milk will dip down near the wall of a glass bowl. So Cheerios at the boundaries of the milk will float upward where the dip meets the wall, forming a ring of cereal.

Why do Wint-O-Green Life Savers emit sparks when chewed in the dark?

Life Savers sparks are actually a mysterious glow called triboluminescence, produced when sugar and other crystals are crushed or rubbed together.

When you scrape two dry sticks together, the friction can generate enough heat to spark a small flame. Likewise, friction produced in the right materials, like sugar, can create not a flame, but a burst of static electricity, like the sparks that crackle through a dry, clingy blanket on a winter night.

Here's how it works: When you crush Wint-O-Green Life Savers (or any hard candy made of real sugar), the naturally asymmetrical sugar crystals tend to break in a lopsided way that separates electric charges in the molecules. So negative electrons are split off from positive protons. Sparks fly when the charges reconnect, like a lightning bolt that reunites positive and negative charges from cloud to ground.

Like regular lightning, mini-lightning occurs when the electric current excites nitrogen molecules in the air. The nitrogen molecule emits photons of light, mostly in the invisible-to-us ultraviolet range. So by themselves, the sugar sparks are hard to see. (Many UV-sensitive insects, birds, and reptiles, however, might find the sweet lightning very entertaining.) That's where the flavoring in Wint-O-Green Life Savers comes in handy.

Wintergreen oil (methyl salicylate) is key to the electric Life Savers effect. Wintergreen is a fluorescent

SPARKY EXPERIMENT

To perform your own electric candy experiment, take some Wint-O-Green Life Savers into a very dark bathroom or other room with a mirror. Let your eyes get accustomed to the dark for about 10 minutes. Then chomp down on the candy while you look in the mirror and watch the (blue) sparks fly. Even better, use a pair of pliers to crush your Wint-O-Green Life Savers in the dark—since it's wet in your mouth, using a tool to smash the candy should make brighter sparks. (It will also preserve your teeth.)

You can also try smashing a sugar cube, or even ripping a piece of adhesive tape off its roll, to see a more muted display of tiny lightning.

nitrogen molecules in the air of your mouth, emitting a flood of visible bluish light. Voilà: mouth sparks.

Interestingly, much of the mystery behind Life Savers lightning was solved by a scientist named Sweeting. The late Linda Sweeting's experiments showed that impurities in a crystal structure could produce triboluminescence, even in symmetrical compounds.

compound; it absorbs high-energy, short-wavelength light and re-emits lower-energy, longer-wavelength light. So wintergreen absorbs the UV light made by the

4th of July- Candy Style
oh say... can you see... my sparkling candy?

Why are Brazil nuts always at the top of the mixed nuts can?

It's like a Brazil nut conspiracy. The big, heavy nuts sit like bullying boulders at the top of the can, shoving all the tasty almonds, pecans, cashews, and peanuts to the bottom. Doesn't gravity make heavier things sink?

But there's no antigravity device inside that Planter's can. Nor is there one in your bag of granola, where the biggest clumps seem to make their way to the top. In fact, it's the Earthward tug of gravity that prompts small bits to slip down through the spaces between big chunks.

Since at least the 1930s, scientists have been trying to solve the mystery: If a container of particles is shaken up and down, why would a big particle buried inside rise? The so-called Brazil nut effect is surprisingly hard to explain.

What role does friction play? What about air pressure in the spaces between particles? The container's shape? Or the frequency of its vibration?

Why does it matter? Besides a desire to explain how the world works, the Brazil nut effect is important in everything from rock-filled landslides to the smooth mixing of medicines to how dunes formed on Saturn's biggest moon, Titan.

Experiments show that part of the effect is due to particle percolation. In a vibrating container, particles shift around. Small gaps that open up under big particles can only be filled by small particles. As small particles sift into empty spots, big ones are lifted toward the top.

Other experiments found that shaking triggers convection currents in the container. Upward currents running through the center ferry bigger particles to the surface. Downward currents streaming along the sides are too narrow for big particles to join. So post-shaking, Brazil nuts are stuck near the top.

Why does the shower curtain blow in and cling to my legs?

Ever find yourself standing in the shower, eyes squeezed shut and covered with soap, when a sticky (or worse, slimy) shower curtain suddenly billows in and wraps cozily around your legs? Your shower curtain hasn't gone psycho; it's simply reacting to a dramatic change of pressure in the shower.

Until several years ago, no one had solved the mystery behind the dreaded shower curtain blowback (or blow-in), although there were plenty of ideas. Some suggested that rising shower air, heated by warm water, is replaced by cold room air

seeping in from the bottom, causing the curtain to blow in. The problem: A very cold shower also causes blow-in.

Other explanations involved Bernoulli's principle. Mathematician Daniel Bernoulli, born in the Netherlands in 1700, is most famous for discovering a fundamental fact of fluids: The pressure of a fluid varies inversely with its speed. So as a fluid speeds up, its pressure

---

Shower air whirls, like a dust devil tipped on its side.

---

drops, and vice versa.

(As water flows through a pipe, it flows faster through narrower sections, its pressure dropping as it does. It seems like the fluid's pressure should rise. Instead, it falls, thanks to the conservation of energy. Speeding up means more of the water's total energy has been converted to kinetic energy—energy of motion. So its potential energy and pressure must drop accordingly.)

Bernoulli's principle applies to everything from the fluid air streaming over a jet's wings to the blood pulsing through our veins.

While Bernoulli was silent

on the subject of shower curtains, many thought that his principle could explain the Cling Wrap phenomenon. The air inside a shower, driven by the water, flows faster along the curtain. The resulting low pressure causes the curtain to sink inward.

Well, not exactly. A holiday trip was one scientist's catalyst for finally solving the mystery. University of Massachusetts engineering professor David Schmidt took a shower at his mother-in-law's house and was plagued by an especially clingy curtain. Back home, he modeled a typical shower on his computer, dividing the splashing shower into 50,000 tiny cells. The model accounted for the spray of droplets, including the way drops change shape and break up as they fall. The simulation ran for weeks, doing more than a trillion calculations as it created a 30-second snapshot of shower time.

Schmidt found the Bernoulli effect operating near the showerhead, with air moving faster and pressure dropping on the inside of the shower curtain. However, the spray of water droplets created an even stronger effect. As they accelerate toward the shower floor due to gravity, drops are slowed by friction with the air. (This "aerodynamic drag" affects everything from falling baseballs to returning space vehicles.)

The shower air reacts by beginning to move in a circle, like mini-tornado. However, unlike a real tornado, the shower twister is tipped on its side, its low-pressure vortex aimed right at the innocent shower curtain.

A heavy shower curtain, or one with magnets, can resist the pull. Low-flow showers create a weaker vortex than big-bruiser showerheads. Curving shower rods, popular in hotels, hold the threatening curtain farther away from the splashing water (and you). Or do away with fickle fabric entirely, and install a shower door.

THE GREAT BEYOND

It's hard to imagine the size of the universe, born in the "Big Bang" some 13.8 billion years ago. Our own solar system seems big enough: The Sun is 93 million miles from Earth, while dwarf planet Pluto orbits the Sun at nearly 3.7 billion miles out. Other dwarf planets, comets, and trillions of other small, icy objects swarm at still greater distances, extending more than a trillion miles from the Sun.

But the Sun is only one of hundreds of billions of stars that make up our home galaxy, the Milky Way. On a clear night, we see the Milky Way as a powdery band of stars across the sky. But we are actually looking at the galactic center from our solar system's position in the outskirts, on one of its spiral arms of stars. (It's a lot like looking at the lights of the skyscrapered center of your city from the suburbs.)

Within our galaxy, distances are vast: Many trillions of miles separate each star, or

multistar system, from the next. And scientists estimate that our galaxy may harbor at least 1.6 planets per star. (If the Milky Way contains 200 billion stars, that's at least 320 billion planets.) So when we look up at the night sky, we're seeing not lonely stars, but other solar systems, harboring planets of all sizes, colors, and compositions.

In the sea of space, galaxies are like islands, made of stars. The Milky Way is one of hundreds of billions of galaxies, strewn across the fabric of space. To measure such unfathomable expanses, miles or kilometers are much too small. Instead, distances are measured in "light-years." Each light-year is how far light travels through space in one Earth-year. (At 186,000 miles a second, light covers about 6 trillion miles in a year.) The nearest solar system to ours, the Alpha Centauri system, is about 4.3 light-years away, or more than 25 trillion miles.

Our Milky Way is about 120,000 light-years across. The next-nearest spiral galaxy, Andromeda, is 2.54 million light-years away. And it takes light from the most distant galaxies more than 13 billion years to cross the lonely dark expanses to us.

Since the universe is so unimaginably vast, looking out into space is also looking back into time. Our own Sun is 8 light-minutes away, so we see the Sun as it appeared 8 minutes ago. But when we look at the Milky Way, we are seeing the center of our galaxy as it was 27,000 years ago—around the time humans first ventured into what's now North America. And when the Hubble Space Telescope detects the light of stars more than 13 billion light-years away, we are looking back to near the beginning of the known universe.

Measure FOR Measure
93 million miles = 149 million km
3.7 billion miles = 6 billion km
The speed of light = 299,792,458 m/s (exactly)
6 trillion miles = 9.7 trillion km
4.3 light-years = more than 40 trillion km

Why do the Moon and Sun change colors?

It just wouldn't be fall without a huge Halloween moon glowing orange at the horizon, rising above a spooky landscape of black tree limbs and piled-up leaves.

The Moon is actually a rocky gray-and-brown ball, lit up by brilliant sunlight. But the color we on Earth see depends on where the Moon is located in the sky. No matter what the time of year, as the Moon first peeks over the horizon, it may appear yellow, orange, or nearly red. Gradually, as the Earth turns eastward and the Moon rises higher in the sky, the color pales to white.

Similar tricks of light happen with the Sun. In the middle of the day, the Sun normally looks yellowish-white. But at sunrise and sunset, it may turn red or orange or a rosy pink. How come?

Our Moon and Sun are not really changing colors hour by hour, way out there in space. The clue is that the colors appear to change only when you look at either body through the Earth's atmosphere. Looking at the Moon or the Sun through air is like looking through a veil. Light, which has to pass through the air before it reaches our eyes, is changed by its trip.

Nitrogen, oxygen, and other gases that make up our air, plus the tiny particles of dust, smoke, and pollutants that are always floating through, redden the light that reaches our eyes.

How? White light is made of a hidden rainbow of colors—red, orange, yellow, green, blue, indigo, and violet. So sunlight is invisibly full of color as it zips through space at 186,000 miles per second (299,793,458 m/s exactly). (And moonlight, of course, is simply reflected sunlight.) The color changes occur because of how the Earth's atmosphere plays with the streaming-in sunlight and moonlight.

When it enters the Earth's atmosphere, some of the light slices cleanly through, reaching the ground without encountering a single air molecule—staying white.

Since the Earth's air is made of gas molecules, some of the light will run into these molecules on its way down. When it does, light is scattered.

It is mostly bluer light that is scattered out of the beam of white light, turning the sky blue. By the time sunlight reaches our eyes, the colors left in the beam are warmer. This makes the Sun look a bit yellower to us than it actually is.

The Sun looks closest to its true color when it is directly overhead. Then, its light must pass through only the air above us—air that becomes thinner and thinner higher up. And much of the sunlight reaches our eyes unscathed.

But when the Sun is near the horizon, its color changes dramatically. Then, its light must travel through the heavy blanket of air near the ground that extends from us to the horizon. Even more of the blue end of the spectrum is scattered out of the light beam. This leaves mostly yellow, orange, and red light in the beam by the time it reaches our eyes. And so we see the Sun as a fiery orange ball at sunrise and sunset.

Likewise, a rising Moon may look red-orange. But as the Moon rises higher, we see it through thinner air. Since we are able to see more of the entire spectrum of moonlight, with more blues left in the beam, we see a whiter Moon.

Where is the rest of the Moon when only half or a sliver of it is in the sky?

On a clear, cold fall night you go outdoors. The Moon has just risen; it is huge and orange, a Halloween moon.

But a few nights later, the Moon is less round. And as the days pass, it seems to shrink into a cartoon moon: It looks like a crescent, or an animal's horns. Finally, the Moon seems to disappear entirely.

What's going on? Unlike the Sun, which shows us its full, fiery face all day long, the Moon has phases. Each month, the Moon goes through its phases, seeming to blow up and then deflate like a balloon. The truth is, the Moon is really an unchanging solid, rocky ball. What changes as the month passes is our view of light and shadows on its surface, day and night on the Moon.

"Moonlight" is actually sunlight, reflected off the Moon's rocky gray surface. As the Moon travels with the Earth around the Sun, it is spotlit by the Sun. As a month passes, we see more and then less of the sunlit half of the Moon because the

Fast Fact

Planets have phases, too. Scientists looking at Mercury and Venus through telescopes have seen them as crescents. And spacecraft sent to study other planets have sent back pictures of the Earth as a silvery crescent, backlit by the Sun.

Earth and the Moon are always changing positions in relation to the Sun.

What we call "phases" are simply the glimpses we get of the sunlit half of the Moon. There's the full moon when we see one entire side of the Moon lit. Then, as we see less of the lighted part a few days later, the phase is called a "gibbous" moon. ("Gibbous" comes from the Latin word for "hump"—and a three-quarters-full moon does look like a hump.)

Next comes the half moon, and then the beautiful crescent moon. Finally, when the side of the Moon we are facing lies in total darkness, we call this phase the "new moon"—a moon waiting to be born. And indeed, as the Earth and Moon move on, we see a sliver of the daylight side, and then more and more, as the whole cycle repeats.

Take a good look when the Moon is just a crescent, and you will see the rest of the Moon—the shadowed part—outlined dimly against the sky.

How does the Moon cause tides in the oceans?

The Earth is awash in water. More than 70 percent of our planet's surface is covered by oceans. If something falls to Earth from space, odds are it will splash down in seawater.

Thanks to the gravitational pull of our circling Moon, Earth's oceans rhythmically rise and fall. When the tide is high, the ocean climbs far up the beach, advancing on lifeguards and hot dog stands. When the tide is low, the ocean retreats, exposing wet sand, broken shells, slimy seaweed.

Gravity increases with mass, and the Sun is 27 million times more massive than our Moon. But gravity weakens quickly over distance. With each doubling of the distance between one body and another, the gravitational tug decreases to just one-quarter of its former strength. The Sun is 93 million miles from Earth; the Moon is only 240,000 miles away. Yet the enormous Sun still exerts more than 174 times the gravitational pull on our planet.

Even so, it's the Moon that has the biggest influence on our planet's sloshing waters. How does it work? When we stand on the surface of the Earth, the mass of our planet is tugging on us, keeping our feet planted on the ground. But if you could measure the force of gravity at different points on your body, you'd discover that the force was ever so slightly weaker at your head than at your feet, simply because your head is farther away from the mass of the planet.

Something similar happens with the Earth and the Moon. The Earth is about 8,000 miles wide. That means that the side of the planet that happens to be facing the

Measure FOR Measure
93 million miles = 149.7 million km
240,000 miles = 386,243 km
8,000 miles = 12,875 km

When the Sun, the Moon, and Earth are aligned, as they are when the Moon is new or full, the ocean's tides are extra high and extra low.

Moon is 8,000 miles closer than the other side of the planet—and thus feels a stronger pull from the Moon's gravity.

This varying force of gravity across an object is called the "tidal force" or the "tidal effect." The Sun is so far away from the Earth that there is only a difference of 0.0017 percent in its gravitational pull over the width of our planet. But while the nearby Moon's gravity is much weaker, its force varies by a full 6.8 percent across the Earth. Result? The Sun's tidal effect on Earth and its oceans is less than half that of the Moon's.

So as the Moon orbits the Earth, and the Earth spins, our planet and its oceans

Oh, the Ebb and Flow of it?

LOW TIDE   HIGH TIDE   RIPTIDE

experience changing tidal forces. The pull of lunar gravity deforms the Earth's crust by several feet, and makes ocean waters under the Moon bulge up several feet more. As the Earth turns and the bulge sloshes against land, it is thrust up still higher. Presto: high tide. Away from the tidal bulge, lower-than-average waters mean low tide on other coasts.

Strangely, high tide on one side of the planet also means high tide on the opposite side. The orbiting Moon tugs the Earth and its movable ocean toward it, resulting in a tidal bulge on the near side. On the far side of the planet, think of the Earth as pulling away from the ocean—leading to a matching tidal bulge, like the two ends of an egg.

When the Sun, the Earth, and the Moon are aligned, as they are when the Moon is full or dark, the high tides are especially high, and the low tides especially low. These are the "spring" tides, when the range between high and low tide is at its maximum. (Think of a natural spring, with water shooting out of the ground.)

Why do the Moon and Mars seem to have a man's face on them?

While we can't see the small "face on Mars" just by looking at the Red Planet in the night sky, we're all familiar with the enormous face on Earth's Moon. When the Moon is full and bright, there are those hollowed-out eyes, nose, and hint of a mouth. When the Moon is a quarter crescent, we see the Man in the Moon in profile, grinning as he looks out into space. (From Earth's Southern Hemisphere, the Moon is viewed "upside-down," and people say they see a different face, or none at all.)

But while the "Man" has been immortalized in songs, poems, and movie titles, he's really an illusion, the convergence of flowing lava, light and shadow, and human imagination. In fact, over many thousands of years, we humans have described other images in the Moon, too, from a basket-carrying woman to

> The Man in the Moon is the creation of flowing lava, tricks of light, and human imagination.

a man with a dog to a very large rabbit.

So where do the men, women, and bunnies come from? Billions of years ago, the Moon wasn't the rather quiet gray world it is today. Like all rocky worlds, the Moon has a long history of exploding volcanoes, with hot, glowing lava flowing across its surface. In some areas, the molten rock cooled into solid, flat plains called maria (from the Latin word for "seas"). Scientists say that most of the plains formed between 3 billion and 4.2 billion years ago.

There are 14 maria, all of them on the side of the Moon

facing Earth. The hardened lava makes each plain appear as a dark-gray patch on the Moon. Each one is huge and can easily be seen on a clear night. Looking at the Moon—especially through a telescope or binoculars—we can see that it's these scattered dark plains that form "eyes," "nose," and "mouth."

But why a face? Human beings (and other animals) have brains that can assemble unrelated features into patterns or pictures. Is that a pile of black clothing in that dark corner, or your black cat? A threatening leopard hidden in the bushes, or dappled sunlight on leaves?

Besides helping us survive, our pattern-making penchant serves us well in art and science. It's why we see animals in billowy cumulus clouds, and people (Orion the hunter) or objects (a Big Dipper) in the random arrangement of stars. So it's no wonder we see faces, figures, and animals in the light-and-shadows surface of the Moon.

Scientists say it's the same with the "face" on Mars. First noticed in a photograph taken by the unmanned *Viking 1* orbiter in 1976, some thought the mile-wide surface feature resembled a stone sculpture, like the Great Pyramid of Giza. Was it a very old artifact, evidence that a culture like that of ancient Egypt once thrived on Mars?

More than 20 years later, the Mars Global Surveyor sent back images much sharper and more detailed than the low-res *Viking* pictures. Alas, the "face" turns out to be an ordinary Martian hill, likely built by a long-ago lava flow rather than industrious Martians.

Why do we sometimes see a halo around the Moon?

Circles Round the Moon

Are they rings around the collar?... **Certainly Not!**

Telltale perspiration?... **How embarrassing**

Ice looking for a party about to happen? **Sounds like Fun!**

Pale, shimmery haloes materialize when moonlight sifts through high, icy clouds. The haloes may glow in white or in faint rainbow colors. Besides being beautiful, haloes have traditionally been used to predict the weather: "Ring around the moon, rain or snow is coming soon."

While moon rings depend on ice in the atmosphere, haloes aren't just a winter phenomenon. Even in the heat of summer—or in the balmy tropics—the highest clouds are made of glittering ice rather than liquid droplets of water. When moonlight (or sunlight) passes just so through the ice crystals of these frigid clouds, we see a ring around the Moon or Sun.

The droplets of water that make up warm clouds are round spheres. But high, cold cirrus-type clouds are made of six-sided ice crystals frozen into many different shapes, from columns to flat plates. Many of these crystals resemble the six-sided glass prisms that hang from a chandelier, or the hexagonal barrel of your No. 2 pencil.

Ice crystals hang in the air and fall within their clouds, tending to line up with the air current they fall through. These glittering crystals are responsible for the glowing ring around the Moon, even when all we see of clouds is a bit of haze in the night sky.

Most moon rings are created when moonlight enters and exits through the sides of crystal columns at least 15,000 feet up in the air. As moonlight pierces

Moon and Sun haloes appear when light is bent by tiny ice crystals, high in the sky.

one side of a tiny ice prism, it bends (refracts). Shooting through the center of the prism and out the other side, the moonbeam bends more as it emerges into open air. The two bends mean that moonlight veers off at a 22-degree angle from its original path. If enough randomly oriented crystals are scattered across the sky, the angled moonlight streams from all directions, forming a cone of light. And we see a halo.

Occasionally, even bigger rings spring up in the night sky. Huge (but faint) 46-degree haloes can appear when moonlight passes first through the side and then through the base of ice crystals.

Shimmering rainbow-colored haloes can also appear around the Sun, as brilliant sunlight is refracted by the same high ice crystals. Since moonlight is much weaker than direct sunlight, moon ring colors are more muted. But look closely, and you may see a pale rainbow spectrum, with red on the inside of the ring and violet on the outmost edge.

As for the ring's accuracy in predicting the weather, meteorologists say that high cirrus clouds often gather a day or two before rain clouds appear.

Why do we sometimes see the Moon in the daytime?

The Moon in the daytime, bleached white against the blue sky, is beautiful but seems strangely out of place. In fact, you're nearly as likely to see the Moon in the daytime as you are at night—if you're paying close attention.

Moons and planets shine by reflected light. In our solar system, light from the Sun bounces off all eight planets (nine, counting Pluto) and their dozens of moons. During the daytime, the skies of Earth are full of stars and planets, just as they are at night. However, the Sun's glare, reflecting off the gas molecules in Earth's atmosphere, drowns the whole panorama in light.

But if you took off in a rocket ship from your

backyard one sunny afternoon, and kept rising and rising, above the clouds and through the thinning air, you'd soon see stars. Surrounding the blanket of Earth's atmosphere is the nearly limitless dark emptiness of space. It's always there, just beyond the glare.

How can we see the Moon in the daytime? The Moon is made of grayish rock, and reflects only about 7 percent of the light striking its surface—sunlight reflecting off the Moon is a lot like light reflecting off an asphalt parking lot at the mall. The Moon looks so brilliantly bright at night only in comparison to the pitch-blackness of the sky around it.

But the Moon is so close to us (about 240,000 miles/386,243 km) that the light it mirrors back to us is still much brighter than that of the nearest bright stars. For example, the Moon is 33,000 times as bright as Sirius, the star that shines brightest in the night sky.

For part of each month, the Moon rises in the morning or afternoon. So we sometimes see a crescent or half moon in the daytime sky. As the month wears on, the Moon rises later and later, until it is rising while or after the Sun sets. (In all locations except near the North and South Poles, the full moon sets as the Sun rises—which is why we see full moons only at night.)

So the Moon is as much a daytime object as it is a nighttime sentinel. Even if, in the afternoon, it looks like a pale, ghostly version of its vibrant after-dark self.

 During the daytime, the skies of Earth are full of stars and planets, just as they are at night.

And although they don't shine as brightly as the Moon, you can often see the brightest planets and stars around sunset and sunrise, when the sky is still light. You may even see the planet Venus in broad daylight—resembling a dazzlingly bright star—if you happen to be looking in just the right spot.

Why does the Moon look gigantic on the horizon, but small overhead?

Have you ever been riding in a car in the evening and noticed something huge and yellow behind the trees and buildings in the east—and then realized it was the Moon? Especially in the fall, the pumpkin-colored harvest Moon, looming up over the horizon, looks enormous and even spooky. It's not hard to imagine a broomstick-riding witch flying across.

But picture this Halloween scene when the Moon is high in the sky, small and white, and it's just not the same.

Scientists say that to most of us the horizon Moon appears to be twice as big as the overhead Moon. People have been arguing over why for more than 1,000 years. Astronomers, psychologists, and nonscientists all have their theories. In 1989, researchers even published a book of such explanations, titled *The Moon Illusion*.

You can prove to yourself that the Moon is actually the same size no matter where it is in the sky, using a ruler or an object like a car key. Note (or mark) the Moon's width at the horizon. Later, compare it to the Moon's width overhead. You should find that the Moon's face is no wider at the horizon than it is at the top of the night sky.

You may even make the size illusion vanish. Some people suggest bending over and looking at the horizon Moon upside down, in a kind of lunar yoga. Others recommend looking at the Moon through a cardboard tube that blocks out landscape features.

What causes the illusion? Most agree that the illusion is a matter of perception—a trick of the brain. Some argue that the horizon Moon looks bigger because it is framed by smaller objects like trees, houses, and hills, making it huge by comparison.

However, that doesn't explain why the Moon also looks so big rising over the flat expanse of the ocean.

Several complicated theories involving the brain's visual system also try to explain the Moon paradox.

Here's a simplified version of one popular explanation: The brain perceives the sky (and Moon) above us as closer than the sky (and Moon) at the horizon. When an object is perceived to be nearer, the brain may compensate by making it look smaller to us. Likewise, an object thought to be farther away will be seen as larger.

For now, the Moon illusion remains one of nature's loveliest unsolved mysteries.

How come we see only one side of the Moon?

Standing on Earth and observing the Moon night after night, it would be easy to decide that our Moon doesn't rotate at all. Whether it's full-on bright or coyly lit in slices, the Moon always shows us the same man in the Moon, with the Mona Lisa smile. The other side is mysteriously and forever turned away.

However, the Moon didn't always just stare at us. Billions of years ago, an Earthbound observer (had there been one) could have seen all sides of our newborn satellite. Why does the opposite side no longer spin into view? The Moon's slow-poke rotation means Moon days are now about 656 hours, or 27.3 Earth days, long. Which exactly matches how long the rocky satellite takes to journey around our planet.

To see why synchronous rotation means the Moon never turns its back on us, put a chair in the middle of the room and have a friend sit in it. The chair is the Earth; you are the Moon. Walk slowly around the chair, facing it at all times. Your friend will see only your smiling face. But you'll find, when you've gone once around, that

---

 Synchronous rotation means the Moon never turns its back on us.

---

you've faced all sides of the room.

Congratulations: You've rotated on your axis, even though the chair observer has never seen your backside.

But it's no coincidence that the Moon behaves this way. In fact, it's a typically Moon-y thing to do. Just as the Moon's gravity creates tides in the oceans of Earth, so has Earth's greater gravity raised tides in the first-molten, now-stony body of the Moon. In the distant past, the Moon was spinning faster and orbiting closer. But the Earth's pull, offset by the tendency of a moving body to fly off in a straight line, deformed the Moon, making it slightly egg-shaped. And the Moon's rotation gradually

slowed as it lost energy to the internal upheaval.

As its spinning braked, the Moon bulged more on one side than the other, the man-in-the-Moon side jutting out some 2 miles (3.2 km) more and feeling more of the Earth's gravitational force. This is the side that ended up facing us when the Moon reached a comfortable equilibrium, becoming tidally locked by the Earth.

Scientists say that many moons became tidally locked after they formed and now show only one face to their home planets. Among the dozens in synchronous rotation in our solar system are Mars's Phobos and Deimos; Jupiter's Io, Europa, Ganymede, and Callisto; at least 17 of Saturn's moons, including Enceladus and Titan; Uranus's Miranda and

Fast Fact

Since the Moon's orbit is also pulled this way and that by the Sun and other planets, we actually get glimpses of about 9 percent of the Moon's back side.

Ariel; Neptune's Triton; and dwarf planet Pluto's companion, Charon.

The Man in the Moon on Synchronous Rotation...

656-hour days can be really BORING!

Would you rather stare into a black void 24/7?

...Or gravitate toward the action on the Earth?

What are shooting stars?

Once in a while, if we're lucky, we see it: A star appears to tear itself away from the others and plunge through the skies of Earth.

But what we're really seeing is not a star, but a meteor. Although from a distance meteors and stars look alike, they actually are very different. Stars are huge, glowing balls of gas, which only look small because they are very far away. (Our Sun is just an average-size star, but it is big enough to hold more than a million Earths.)

The meteors that flare so brightly across our skies are really broken-off fragments of icy comets or rocky asteroids. Asteroids are part of the debris left over from the formation of the planets.

When asteroids collide, as they have for billions of years, they send rock fragments—meteoroids— flying in all directions. These fragments keep moving, because there's no friction in the emptiness of space to slow them down.

Meteoroids, some up to boulder size, whiz silently by Earth all the time, darkly

PIECES OF OTHER WORLDS FOUND ON EARTH!

Judging from the kind of rock found in some fallen-to-Earth meteorites, not all are fragments of asteroids or comets. Some are pieces of other worlds. More than 130 Moon rocks have turned up, found in deserts in Antarctica, northern Africa, and Oman. Scientists figured out where they came from by comparing their composition to the rocks brought back from the Apollo Moon missions. (From 1969 to 1972, Apollo astronauts collected more than 840 pounds of rocks, sand, and dust on the Moon.)

But how did more than 100 pounds of Moon rocks get here on their own? Scientists think meteorites slamming into the Moon shattered rocks and sent them flying out into space. Because the Moon's gravity is so weak, the rocks kept going. Some were captured by Earth's gravity and ended up tumbling down to the ground. Scientists say that most of the lunar rocks fell from the sky in the last 100,000 years.

Even more startling: Another 130 meteorites have turned out to be bits and pieces of the planet Mars. Scientists confirmed that the rocks are from the Red Planet by comparing their composition to that of rocks analyzed by NASA's Mars landers, including trapped gases that match those in the Martian atmosphere.

In 2014, scientists announced that most of the rocks were probably blasted off Mars less than 5 million years ago, when an enormous meteorite smashed into the planet, carving a crater 36 miles wide.

And somewhere on Mars, or perhaps Venus, there may be little pieces of Earth—chipped off in the distant past by some huge meteorite that careened into our own planet.

invisible. But if they pass too near our planet, the fragments are sometimes caught by the Earth's gravity. And some hit our atmosphere, traveling at about 20,000 to 135,000 miles per hour (about 32,000 to 217,000 km/h).

Most meteoroids range from the size of a grain of sand to the size of a pea. As a typical stony meteoroid is pulled in by the Earth's gravity and tears down through the air, it quickly heats up. The heat is caused by friction between air molecules and the rocky surface.

As the rock falls through the atmosphere, a shell of gas around it (a corona) heats to well over 2,000°F. This heat causes meteors to glow as they plunge toward Earth, before they go out like snuffed candles. How can something so small burn so brightly? The combination of glowing rock and corona makes the meteor appear much bigger than it actually is.

A tiny meteor may have time for one brief flash before it burns up. A larger meteor may be lit up for more than a minute as it streaks down across the sky. Go out to the country—or better yet, the desert—on a clear, dark night, far from city lights. Let your eyes wander across the sky, and be patient. Chances are, you'll see a meteor flash by. Such solitary meteors are called "sporadic." On a clear night, you might see 10 in an hour. But in a meteor shower, the number can increase dramatically.

The meteors that streak across the sky in a meteor shower come from the debris field of a passing comet. Meteor showers reoccur each year as the Earth orbits the Sun and circles back near the path of certain comets, each on its own unique orbit around the Sun. There are about 18 major meteor showers each year, from the early-January Quadrantids to the mid-August Perseids to the mid-November Leonids. A shower gets its name from the constellation that happens to be its backdrop in space.

A meteor shower can range from a bit of a dud to a blazing storm. In an ordinary meteor shower, a sharp-eyed observer might see 15 to 1,000 meteors an hour. But when shower turns to storm, the number may increase to 6,000 or more an hour. The denser the stream of comet grit the Earth is passing through, the more meteors per hour streak by.

Then, as country singer Hank Williams wrote, you may be looking when "the silence of a falling star lights up a purple sky."

Fast Fact

Most meteor craters have disappeared, covered by oceans and lava, or erased by rain and blowing sand. One survivor, Meteor Crater in Arizona, is about three-quarters of a mile wide and nearly 600 feet deep. The hole was blasted out about 50,000 years ago, when a rock the size of a 15-story building and weighing some 600 million pounds dropped out of the sky.

Measure FOR Measure

840 pounds = 381 kg
100 pounds = 45 kg
36 miles = about 58 km
2,000°F = 1,093°C
600 feet = 183 m
600 million pounds =
   about 272 million kg

How does the Sun hold the planets in orbit?

If you've ever let go of a helium-filled balloon, you know what happens: It rises through the air.

The Sun is made of gases, and mostly of two that are lighter than air. About 72 percent of the Sun's mass is hydrogen; 26 percent is helium, the gas used in party balloons. (The other 2 percent is composed of heavier elements, from oxygen to neon to sulfur.)

But while the Sun is made mainly of the universe's two lightest elements, its wispiness is deceiving. In the core, where our star's gravity is at its most crushing, compressed gases are 20 times denser than iron, and a 1-inch-square cube of sun-stuff would weigh about 6 pounds.

Our star's enormous gravity is due to its enormous size. Our rocky planet Earth has a mass of about 6.6 sextillion tons. The total mass of the gaseous Sun? An astonishing 2.2 octillion tons, about 300,000 times that of Earth's.

And when it comes to gravity, mass rules.

Like a pony tethered to a pole, carrying kids around and around, an orbiting object is tied to the Sun by the invisible threads of gravity. If it weren't for gravity, planets would go flying away from their home suns like so many billiard balls.

In fact, gravity is what pulls planets and stars into balls to begin with. And just as gravity holds the Earth together, it tugs raindrops down from clouds, and makes baseballs trace arcs across the sky rather than go flying into space.

Still, even as the Earth's gravity pins our feet to the ground, other bodies tug at us from the sky. Even if we don't notice the gravitational pull of the Moon, the oceans do. In fact, each bit of matter in the universe tugs on every other bit.

The more matter clumped together in one place, the more powerful the force of gravity. The Sun and the

Measure FOR Measure

1 square inch = 6.5 cm²
6 pounds = 2.7 kg
186,000,000 miles = 299,337,984 km

Earth are each attracted to the other. But because the Sun is 300,000 times more massive, it pulls harder. And while the force drops off quickly over distance, the Sun's gravity is strong enough to hold onto eight full-fledged planets, with more than 146 moons; hundreds of dwarf planets (some with their own moons); millions of asteroids; and perhaps a trillion comets.

Left all on their own, these bodies would tend to whiz off in straight lines. They orbit instead because their attraction to the Sun (and, in the case of moons, to their home planets) continuously pulls their paths into curves, like horses on a merry-go-round.

Scientists think that gravity actually shapes space itself. Imagine holding a sheet with someone, pulled taut, and placing a heavy ball in the center. The sheet will curve around the ball, and other balls dropped on the sheet will tend to roll toward the depression. Likewise, a star's enormous mass distorts the fabric of space, forcing already-in-motion objects like planets to travel in roughly circular paths, rather than flying off at tangents into space.

Where do comets come from?

If you've been lucky enough to see a comet, you've seen an artifact from the earliest days of our solar system. Scientists think these "dirty snowballs" may even predate Earth and its sibling planets.

Why "dirty snowball"? Judging from the most famous comet, Halley's, the icy core of a comet is mostly frozen water (about 80 percent), with 15 percent carbon monoxide ice, along with traces of carbon dioxide and methane ices. Surrounding the frozen core is a dark shell of dust and rock.

Measure FOR Measure

3 to 9 billion miles = 4.8 to 14.5 billion km

180 billion miles = 289.7 billion km

These dark, icy objects bide their time in vast gangs on the outskirts of the solar system.

Before becoming official "comets" by sweeping in toward the Sun, these dark, icy objects bide their time in vast gangs on the outskirts of the solar system. Some comets are "short-period" (although their period may be longer than a human life). These comets' paths take them back through the inner solar system in 200 years or less. The most well-known short-timer, Halley's Comet, returns about every 76 years. A little girl first dazzled by Halley's from a perch on her father's shoulders may see the comet return when she is a great-grandmother.

A comet that puts in very rare appearances—every 200 years to 30 million years—is a long-period visitor. Scientists think that whether a comet has a long or a short period depends in part on where it started its journey.

Oort Cloud or Kuiper Belt? Those seem to be the two choices, the bus stations of the comet world, where comets hang out and wait for a boost toward the Sun.

The Kuiper Belt is closest at some 3 to 9 billion miles from the Sun, a stone's throw on the cosmic bus routes. In 1951, scientist Gerard Kuiper predicted this band of debris existed and was a source of short-period comets. In the 1990s, Earth telescopes and the Hubble Space Telescope finally imaged some dark objects in the right place. Scientists estimate that some 200 million icy chunks orbit in the dark space beyond Neptune.

The existence of a more enormous—and enormously distant—field of long-period comets was suggested by astronomer Jan Oort in 1950. The Oort Cloud has never been seen, but may surround our solar system like a dark halo. Starting more than 180 billion miles out, the Oort Cloud is a vast comet prairie that may stretch almost one-fourth of the way to the next nearest star. The "cloud" may contain up to 2 trillion tailless comets, separated by hundreds or millions of miles of empty space—a little like a herd of lonely cows that goes on and on in every direction. Too distant from the Sun to be lit by its light, the comets are nearly as dark as the space around them.

Comets "fall in" from the Kuiper Belt or Oort Cloud because they are tugged by gravity. With Kuiper comets, the gravity of one of the giant planets may start the ball rolling. Oort objects may be sent flying by the gravity of stars our solar system passes on its journey around the Milky Way.

Comets go from dark to glowing as they approach the inner solar system. Sunlight and the solar wind (charged particles streaming from the Sun) cause comets to grow streaming tails of shining dust and glowing gases.

A comet's slingshot trajectory may send it around the Sun and into a long, egg-shaped orbit. But many comets never return, disintegrating from the heat and gravitational forces they encounter on their first trip in.

Fast Fact

A comet loses about one-tenth of 1 percent of its ice each time it passes the Sun and its ice vaporizes, forming a beautiful streaming tail. After about 1,000 trips around the Sun, all traces of a comet's ice will have disappeared, leaving only a collection of rocks and dust.

Is our next-door neighbor Venus similar to Earth?

Seen from Earth, Venus is impossibly beautiful, a planet masquerading as one of the brightest stars in the sky. In fact, Venus is also known as the Evening Star, because it's often found in the western sky, shining diamondlike in the twilight. Venus's brilliance comes from its thick layer of clouds, which reflect back 75 percent of the sunlight that strikes them.

Before we knew what Venus was really like, we thought of her as Earth's sister planet. After all, Earth and Venus are both rocky worlds, nearly the same size. Of all our solar system's planets, Venus is nearest to Earth, and only 30 percent closer to the Sun.

And since Venus is completely covered by heavy layers of clouds, for most of history, Earth-bound humans could only guess at what was underneath them. As usually happens, whenever we try to imagine what another planet must be like, we picture it as familiar—somehow like Earth.

Back in 1686, French writer Bernard le Bovier de Fontenelle wrote that he was sure that the "inhabitants of Venus" were people with skin "burned by the sun," who were "full of wit and fire, always in love, writing verse, fond of music, arranging festivals, dances, and tournaments every day." Later, science-fiction stories also imagined a balmy tropical climate on Venus, with steamy swamps and thundering dinosaurs. In the 1958 movie *Queen of Outer Space*, Venus is peopled by glamorous women in high

Fast Fact

Venus, the second planet from the Sun, is even hotter than Mercury, the closest.

heels, including actress Zsa Zsa Gabor.

But truth is stranger than fiction. On Venus, there are no rollicking music festivals, no rampaging dinosaurs. Instead, imagine a vast rocky landscape simmering in heat like the inside of a pizza oven, with temperatures around 870°F. And with a carbon-dioxide atmosphere so thick and heavy that it presses down with the force of about 1,300 pounds per square inch at the surface. At around 90 times the pressure of Earth's air, the Venusian atmosphere would crush any sunburned dinosaurs, bad poets, or Hungarian film stars.

What about those heavy clouds roiling overhead, that look so pretty from space?

MAPPING VENUS

In the later 1960s and early 1970s, the former Soviet Union sent a number of space probes, the Venera series, to Venus. (*Venera* is the Russian name for Venus.) They showed the planet to be a desolate, rocky place—no watery swamps in sight, and none possible, since water would boil away on the scorching-hot surface. (Since the pressure of Venus's atmosphere is 90 times that of Earth's, water would begin to boil at well over 300°F, rather than 212°F at sea level here.) In 1990, the U.S. *Magellan* orbiter beamed radio signals down to Venus, and mapped the cloud-hidden surface by tracking what signals were absorbed and which bounced back. *Magellan* found that Venus is dotted with thousands of volcanoes, ancient lava channels, and seven flat-topped hills made of hardened lava, more than 8,000 feet high.

Unfortunately, they're not made of water, like clouds on Earth. Instead, Venus's clouds are made of droplets of corrosive sulfuric acid. Up to 25 lightning bolts a second rip through the poisonous clouds.

And if you could—with the right equipment—survive a full day on the inferno that is Venus, it would be a very long day indeed: about 5,832 hours long, the equivalent of eight months on Earth.

Planet Mercury, a full 20 million miles closer to the Sun, actually enjoys somewhat cooler weather: Daytime temperatures may reach 800°F, but at night the surface may cool to a frigid −279°F. Meanwhile, Venus remains blast-furnace hot whether the Sun is shining or not.

Why? It all comes down to atmosphere. Mercury has little; Venus has a lot. And

Measure FOR Measure

870°F = 466°C
20 million miles = 32,186,800 km
800°F = 427°C
−279°F = −173°C
300°F = 149°C
212°F = 100°C
8,000 feet = 2,438 m

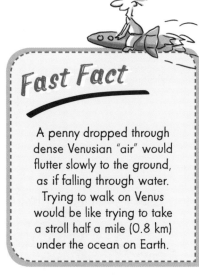

Venus's atmosphere is 97 percent carbon dioxide—the "greenhouse gas" implicated in planetwide warming here on Earth. How does it work? A rocky planet's surface absorbs sunlight, then reradiates heat into space. But while sunlight penetrates Venus's thick atmosphere, heat is trapped underneath it.

With its runaway greenhouse effect, Venus is so hot that a lead cannonball—not to mention a strolling, sunburned troubadour—would simply melt into a puddle.

Fast Fact

A penny dropped through dense Venusian "air" would flutter slowly to the ground, as if falling through water. Trying to walk on Venus would be like trying to take a stroll half a mile (0.8 km) under the ocean on Earth.

Why is Mars red?

Start a rust collection... VACATIONING ON MARS give up bathing... Mars Hilton Sorry No H₂O ...try to find Mount Olympus in a dust storm

Scan the night sky some night, and you may see one "star" that appears to glow steadily—and with a reddish light. But that's no star. That's our next-door-neighbor planet, Mars, basking in the light of the Sun.

To the naked eye, other planets in our solar system look white. (Think of brilliant Venus, just after sunset or before sunrise.) Mars alone is red—which is why ancient people named the planet after the Roman god of war.

But there's nothing angry about Mars, any more than an old iron frying pan or a bike left out too long in the rain are angry. Mars is red because it's a rusty little planet.

Pictures sent back from space probes that have landed on Mars show that the planet looks a lot like parts of Arizona in the United States. The ground is rocky, with boulders strewn among sifting sand dunes. Even on summer mornings, a light coating of water frost decorates the red rocks as the sun rises.

On Mars, as on the Earth

and the Moon, there is iron mixed into the minerals that make up rocks. Add some water and warm-enough temperatures, and you have a recipe for rust. The rust on Martian rocks tells us that long ago, Mars was wetter and warmer than it is now, with a thicker atmosphere. (Scientists think, in fact, that rivers of water once ran on Mars.) When iron combines with oxygen (found in water and in atmospheric gases on Mars, like carbon dioxide), rust can form.

Unlike Earth, Mars has no protective ozone layer, and UV light from the Sun can easily break up water (H_2O) molecules into hydrogen and oxygen. Lightweight hydrogen escapes into space, but freed-up oxygen reacts with other elements to form rust.

On Earth, according to NASA scientists, oxidized iron-rich minerals are often carried away by rain and rivers and deposited in lakes and oceans. But no rain falls on Mars, and there are no longer any flowing waters.

When the *Viking* space probes landed on Mars in 1976 and tested the planet's soil, they found that 19 percent of it was ferric oxide—rust.

LIFE ON MARS

The Red Planet is just over half the size of Earth. Because Mars has less mass, its gravity is weaker—a little more than a third as strong as our planet's gravity. (A person who weighs 100 pounds [45.4 kg] would weigh only 38 pounds [17 kg] on Mars.) Martian air is very thin—only 1 percent as dense as our atmosphere. Our air is mostly nitrogen and oxygen; Mars's atmosphere is 96 percent carbon dioxide gas, the kind in soda pop.

Fast Fact

Olympus Mons (Mount Olympus), a volcanic mountain on Mars, is nearly 16 miles (25 km) high.

About 75 percent of the Martian surface is covered in sand tinted orange-red by these rusty particles. Which is why pictures of Mars show vast expanses of red desert. If you want to see the color of Mars up close, just look at a rusty old frying pan.

Wind spreads the soil particles across the Martian landscape, covering dark-gray volcanic rocks with a layer of rust. Dust devils—spinning tornadoes—whip more soil into the air. And huge dust storms sometimes rage out of control, blanketing much of the planet in a blinding red-tinged haze.

What are the rings of Saturn made of, and how did they form?

Saturn's rings are one of the most spectacular sights in our solar system. As far as we know, the first person to see them was Galileo, in 1610. Looking through his telescope at Saturn, he saw what he said looked like "two ears" on the planet.

In 1655, Dutch astronomer Christian Huygens realized that the two "earlike" projections Galileo had noticed around Saturn in 1610 were something extraordinary. His newer, more powerful telescope allowed him to see that the mystery Galileo had puzzled over appeared to be one enormous, shining ring.

By the 1800s, astronomers had figured out the ring, far from being solid, was made of countless smaller particles. Eventually, with better telescopes and data sent back from robot explorers in the 1970s and '80s, astronomers found out that there wasn't one ring, but many.

Scientists also confirmed the existence of several (dark) rings around Uranus and Jupiter, too. Rings around outer planet Neptune were discovered in the 1980s. Which meant that the four largest planets in our solar system—the so-called "gas giants"—had decorations that rocky planets like Earth lacked.

Saturn's ring system, at around 175,000 miles wide, is the biggest and the brightest, the circles-within-circles structure of its 12 rings resembling a cosmic compact disc.

Why are the rings so luminous? Saturn's rings are made mainly of millions of pieces of water ice. The icy bits range in size from tiny grains to crushed soft-drink ice to snowballs, snow boulders, and even icebergs. Tumbling together around Saturn at nearly 50,000 miles per hour, glittering in the light from the faraway Sun, the icy collection appeared to Huygens as a single, shining ring.

Scientists still don't know exactly how the rings formed, or when. Their particles could be the leftovers of a moon, slammed by an asteroid or comet during the tumultuous times of the early solar system, more than 4 billion years ago. Since Saturn has so many moons (current count: 62), some ring material may also spiral in when meteorites strike the moons, sending fragments into space.

Saturn's enormous gravity may also have ripped apart a massive object whizzing by it, leaving only bits and pieces. Likewise, comets venturing too near could have been torn into icy fragments, left to circle their captor. A new theory by French researchers is that in the high-drama, demolition-derby days of our solar system, most of its planets, including Earth, had rings of circling debris. Some 4 billion years ago, Saturn's ring system may have been 5,000 times more massive.

Saturn's largest moons probably formed along with the planet from the rotating cloud of gas and dust that formed the Sun and other planets. But other, smaller moons, researchers say, may have coalesced later, from icy bits in the rings.

Measure FOR Measure

175,000 miles = about 282,600 km
50,000 miles = about 80,500 km

Why do stars seem to form pictures?

TEENAGE SKY

Think of the night sky as a giant connect-the-dots drawing, with each star a dot. Except that there's no right or wrong way to connect them. The pictures the dots form can be yours alone—just like those shapes you see in puffy clouds on sunny days.

Of course, there's a difference between stars and clouds. Clouds are collections of water vapor, constantly shifting and re-forming. That pug you see one minute is a Beluga whale the next. Stars, on the other hand, are faraway suns. Their enormous

distance makes their positions appear fixed in the sky. So as the Earth turns, star patterns remain the same, for as long as they're visible during the night.

While you can dream up your own constellations, chances are you'll be

> A million years ago, the Big Dipper looked like a long spear.

renaming groups of stars people have been describing for thousands of years. We know, for example, that the Sumerians drew constellations at least 4,000 years ago.

Throughout history, when people saw pictures in the night sky, they saw what interested them. European sailors saw stars patterned in the shape of a compass. (In fact, astronomers say that one of the most important uses for star pictures was to help people navigate the featureless sea—for example, by looking for the northerly Big Dipper.)

And the pictures could be wildly creative. In a big group of stars surrounding the Dipper, ancient Egyptians saw a bull, a reclining man, and a hippopotamus walking on two legs—carrying a crocodile on his back.

Modern astronomy divides the sky into 88 separate areas, each represented by a named constellation. These include Orion's starry belt, Leo the lion, a giraffe, a chameleon, a dolphin, a telescope, a painter's easel, and a winged horse.

Each half of the Earth sees a different night sky. The Big Dipper is the most familiar "star picture" in the Northern Hemisphere, easy to recognize and visible in the northern sky all night in most of the United States. (The Big Dipper is actually an "asterism," a group of stars within a constellation. The Big Dipper's parent constellation is Ursa Major, the Great Bear.) In the Southern Hemisphere, the best known is the kite-shaped Southern Cross.

But you don't have to cross the equator to see the other hemisphere's most familiar star patterns. In the Florida Keys and Hawaii, look for the Southern Cross just above the southern horizon. In northernmost spots in the Southern Hemisphere, you'll find the Big Dipper resting on the northern horizon—upside down.

Stars are always being born or dying, and constantly moving through space. So over millennia, constellations change. A million years ago, the Big Dipper looked more like a long spear.

From some far-off solar system, our Sun may be a star in another culture's constellation—perhaps a point in the outline of an exotic animal found on their home planet.

Why is the space between planets dark?

It's something of a mystery: Light leaves the blazing surface of the Sun, lighting the side of every planet turned toward it. Giving us sunny afternoons on Earth (and dimmer afternoons on more-distant Mars, which has a much thinner atmosphere). But between Earth and Mars, even as sunlight zips through, space is black—like a corridor with the lights turned out.

So what happens to all that sunlight on its journey? Why isn't the space between the Earth and Mars, or Venus and Earth, lit up like Vegas?

First, a little about where all that light comes from. Sunlight is made deep inside our yellow-white star when hydrogen atoms fuse together under great pressure, making helium atoms. In the process, each reaction also releases particles of light, or photons.

Since the Sun is so enormous—more than a million planet Earths could fit neatly inside—a colossal amount of light is produced every ticking second. Scientists say that if the Sun were a lamp, it would be glowing with the light of 4 trillion trillion 100-watt lightbulbs. (Which is why its noontime face is so blinding.)

But it's not an easy or quick journey out of the Sun for all those photons. Photons produced in the Sun's interior collide with electrons, other photons, and the nuclei of atoms, again and again, in a kind of superhot pinball game. After many trillions of collisions, a photon of light may, by accident, have made its way through layer after layer of gases to the surface of the Sun. There, like a fish breaking water, the photon will zip away from the Sun's gases, zooming straight ahead into empty space at about 186,000 miles per second.

A photon of light takes only eight minutes to travel the 93-million-mile distance from the Sun's surface to the Earth. But its frustrating, zigzag journey through the enormous Sun itself can last a million years. So the light shining on your face today may have been born in the Sun when primitive humans using stone tools roamed the Earth.

Why is the Night Sky Black?

So we know when to go to sleep ...

...Because it's the only way to watch fireworks...

... And drive-in Movies!

But the emptiness that allows light to zip unhindered through the space between planets is also responsible for the darkness. If you were an astronaut in a ship traveling from Earth to Mars, you would find your ship lit brilliantly by the sunlight. But outside the window, space would remain black.

Why? The skies of Earth and Mars are lit up by the noonday Sun because each planet has its own atmosphere made of zillions of gas molecules. When photons of sunlight encounter molecules of gas, they are absorbed and re-emitted, scattering light across the sky.

In addition, all planets and moons, whether they have atmospheres or not, reflect light back to our eyes; that's why the full moon is so brilliant. But in the near-vacuum of space itself, with little gas or dust to reflect light, space stays dark . . . even as it is crisscrossed by countless photons of light.

Measure FOR Measure

186,000 miles per second = 299,792,458 m/s (exactly)
93 million miles = about 149,700 km

Why do stars twinkle?

To understand why stars twinkle, think about an asphalt road on a summer day. You can almost see the heat rising, as the air above the hot asphalt waves and shimmers, making the road, trees, and cars ahead appear to shimmer, too.

Now think about planet Earth, and the heated, swirling air around it. It's this turbulent atmosphere that makes the light of distant stars—steadily shining, like our own Sun—shimmer and twinkle.

How it works: All day long, the surface of our planet heats in the sun. And all night long, the ground radiates stored heat into space. As air just above the ground warms and rises, it mixes with cooler air, creating roiling motion, like water boiling in a pot. Starlight, on its way to the ground, passes through this turbulent air, and is bent this way and that by its run-ins with gas molecules. The shifting pockets of air, in effect, act like lenses.

The result? As you look at a star, its light seems to shimmer, making the star appear larger and less focused. The star also seems to dim and brighten, jump and sparkle. That's because its light rays alternately bunch up (causing brightening) and then spread out (causing dimming) as they pass through the unstable air. Scientists call the effect scintillation.

Stars sparkle most when near the horizon, as we look through extra-dense air. A bright star, low in the sky, may also change color rapidly. As white starlight travels through the atmosphere, different wavelengths of light (colors) are bent more or less. Just as with a prism, we see rainbow colors, a star flashing red, orange, yellow, green, indigo blue, and violet.

Scientists say that sunlight reflected off Earth's sibling planets is also bent this way and that by our atmosphere. But since these planets are near enough to appear as discs rather than pinpoints, our eyes receive light from many points on a planet's face. Light rays bent one way are canceled out by light rays bent the opposite way. And so we see a steadily shining (round) planet.

However, under the right conditions, even planets can twinkle. When the atmosphere is especially unstable (like after a storm), or when the planet is near the horizon, its light passing through thick layers of churning air, we may catch it twinkling, like its background of stars.

Fast Fact

On a world without an atmosphere, like the Moon, stars shine steadily in the dark sky (and don't look pointy). Twinkling may be beautiful, but it's a real headache for Earthbound astronomers, as bright images dance this way and that. Computer programs can adjust a telescope lens as stars twinkle. But the Hubble Space Telescope, orbiting above the atmosphere, sees stars as they really are.

Can you really figure out where you're going by using the Pole Star?

Imagine setting up a camera near the North Pole in winter, pointing it at the sky, and then taking pictures over one (long, dark) day. Here's what you'd see in the time-lapse video: Polaris, almost directly overhead, like a beacon. And, over 24 hours, the rest of the stars, appearing to slowly circle it.

But Polaris's exalted status is just a coincidence. The stars' circling is really an illusion; it's the Earth that's spinning under the stars, taking 24 hours to turn once around. While the Earth turns, Polaris appears to stand still only because of its position in the sky: lined up almost perfectly with our planet's axis.

How does it work? Earth's North (celestial) pole traces a small circle over 24 hours as the planet turns. Since the pole happens to be pointed at Polaris, the medium-bright star is always directly overhead there. That makes Polaris the Earth's North Star. (There is no corresponding South Star, simply because the South celestial pole isn't pointing at any easily visible star.)

Since Polaris stands above the North Pole like a glowing directional beacon, it's the star to steer by in the Northern Hemisphere. Polaris has also been called the Lodestar, since, like a compass or lodestone, it helps us locate north. The ancient Romans also called the star *Navigatoria*. Sailors, hikers, and even birds have used it to find their way, for as long as they've been navigating the darkness.

While Polaris is directly overhead at the top of our

👑 Vega will wear the Pole Star crown in about 11,700 years.

planet, it sits on the horizon at the Earth's equator. Just south of the equator, Polaris disappears from view.

Between the North Pole and the equator, Polaris is at an in-between position in the sky, corresponding to your latitude north of the equator. So the Pole Star can help you figure out where you are, even in the middle of the featureless sea.

Polaris is not the brightest star in the night sky. But you can easily find it on a clear night in the Northern Hemisphere. Follow an imaginary line from the outermost stars in the Big Dipper's bowl, to the tip of the Little Dipper's handle. That's Polaris.

But the role of the Pole Star is played by different celestial actors over the millennia. Everything in space is in constant motion relative to everything else. As the Earth rotates, it wobbles on its axis, rather like a spinning toy top. So the North Pole points toward different stars over thousands of years.

It takes nearly 26,000 years for the Earth to execute a full wobble. While Polaris wears the Pole Star crown for now, a star called Thuban held the honor 5,000 years ago. By the year 13,727, the fifth-brightest star in the night sky, Vega, will reign as our new Pole Star—at least until the Earth tilts away again. Then Thuban returns to true north, followed again by Polaris.

But as Earth changes position relative to the stars, there are centuries in which there is no Pole Star to guide us. And there will be again, as the North Pole gradually points away from Polaris in coming centuries.

What is the last number in the universe?

A song says that "one is the loneliest number," but it would be even lonelier to be the last number. Hanging out there at the end of the line—right at the edge of the abyss—it would be cold comfort to have an incredibly long list of numerals in your name.

But while there may be a zillion good reasons for not having finished a homework assignment, even a gazillion doesn't come close to being the last number, since a bazillion (or more) is always just over the horizon.

From the beginning, human beings have been preoccupied with counting things and making up names for big numbers. For example, the largest named number in ancient Greece was 10,000; they called it a *myriad*. (Today, the word just means "many.") But the ancient Greek scientist Archimedes recognized that the world contains numbers of objects far greater than a myriad. In his work *Sand Reckoning*, Archimedes estimated that it would take about 10^{64} grains of sand (the number 1 followed by 64 zeroes) to fill the universe.

While scientists like to write numbers using powers of ten (10^3 is $10 \times 10 \times 10$, or 1,000), they have also named many large numbers. The number 1,000,000,000 is a billion in American English and is sometimes called a milliard in British English. And while a zillion isn't a real number, an octillion is: It's the number 1 followed by 27 zeroes. An octovigintillion is 1,000 followed by 28 groups of three zeroes.

One very big number was named by nine-year-old Milton Sirotta in 1938.

Milton's mathematician uncle, Edward Kasner, asked his nephew what he would call the number one followed by a hundred zeroes. Milton decided it was a "googol."

Beyond the googol, there's the googolplex, the number 1 followed by a googol zeroes. A googolplex is so enormous, astronomer Carl Sagan noted, that if it could be written out on a strip of paper, the paper couldn't be stuffed into the known universe.

And the universe is vast: 76 sextillion miles (122.3 sextillion km) separate us from the most distant quasar. (Quasars are bright objects at the center of massive galaxies.) To appreciate such numbers, Kasner, like Archimedes, suggested thinking about grains of sand. A thimble, he said, can hold many more atoms than there are grains of sand on New York's Coney Island beach—about an octillion, in fact.

A googolplex is the highest number that English has a name for, but it isn't the end of the line for numbers. To any imaginable number, we can always add 1 (or 1 million). Even if we tire of naming numbers, there's no end to the counting, even when the universe has run out of objects to be counted. There is no last number; numbers can mount up forever.

Scientists have proposed different rules for naming large numbers, resulting in tongue twisters like septenquadragintillion (1,000

Fast Fact

In our 13.8-billion-year-old universe, there may be more than 300 billion galaxies, each a collection of hundreds of billions of stars and perhaps up to a trillion planets.

followed by 47 groups of three zeroes). But the biggest numbers you can think of are up for grabs, so feel free to make up your own name for your favorite gigantic number.

Suggested Big Number Names...

Huge-a-gabillion — The number of hot dogs I can eat.

Mega-Quin-tuple-zillion — The number of times I like to watch a movie.

Grande-Sex-octo-bazillion — The number of minutes I talk on the phone each month.

HOME PLANET

Seen from space, Earth, the third planet from the Sun, is a blue-and-white world with one large, silvery companion moon. Compared with the giant gaseous planets of the outer solar system, Earth is rather small. And unlike any of its planetary siblings, Earth has oceans of liquid water, where scientists think life got its start.

Earth has changed a lot over its 4.5-billion-year lifetime. Scientists say that the Earth formed from a cloud of gas and dust in space, and grew bigger from a steady hail of debris raining in from the early solar system. Our planet evolved into a ball of molten rock, and then, after slowly cooling, emerged awash in water. Continents grew, moved, slammed together, broke up.

Today, it's a blue-and-white planet, blue from the waters on its surface, white from water vapor afloat in the skies above. As Earth spins like a carousel at 1,000 miles per hour at the equator, volcanoes belch rivers of hot, liquid rock from its insides. Icebergs the size of houses break off its ice sheets and drift into its oceans. Bowls carved out by glaciers fill with rain. Islands thrust themselves up from the bottom of the sea. Above it all, shape-changing clouds send bolts of lightning thundering to the ground.

Life appeared, evolved, and took many strange and astonishing forms—most now extinct. For millions of years, dinosaurs large and small roamed the planet. Then, they too vanished.

Now we humans, toolmakers living in every nook and cranny of the planet, have ushered in a new stage in the history of the Earth. Our technology has altered the planet in ways we are only beginning to discover. We are just starting to understand the responsibility we share for the caretaking of this, our only home.

How was the Earth formed?

Seen from space, Earth looks familiar, like home: bright blue oceans; gray, snowcapped mountains; sandy deserts; patches of green. But once upon a time, there was a very young Earth, as different from the grown-up planet as Earth today is from Mars.

About 4.6 billion years ago—when the universe was already about 9.3 billion years old—our Sun was born. The Sun is one of hundreds of billions of stars in the Milky Way galaxy, born out of a rotating cloud of gas and dust between other stars. Newborn stars are surrounded by orbiting debris, circling in a flattened disk. Particles collide and make bigger particles, like snowflakes clumping as they fall. Over millions of years, planets form.

Our Earth started as a rock, slowly growing bigger as a rain of debris, from sand- to mountain-size, fell onto its surface. In the beginning, more than 60 million tons of material may have fallen on to the Earth each day. (Now, the daily dose is about 5 to 300 tons of stuff—most of it dust particles too small to notice.)

The unceasing impacts heated the rocky surface to a liquid. Earth was covered in a sea of molten lava, topped with a thin layer of dark, cooler rock, like the scum on a pond. Cracks revealed the fiery glow beneath; dust hurled into the sky by the bombardment made days as black as nights.

Falling material vaporized on contact, adding gases to Earth's atmosphere. Over millions of years, the impacts grew fewer. Why? There were fewer objects tumbling through the solar system that hadn't been swept up into planets. So Earth's surface began to cool, and a true crust formed.

Volcanoes belched carbon dioxide and steam into the air. The cooled, cratered surface was soon covered with water, as steam condensed and rained down in drops. Icy comets from the outer solar system added more water as they crashed in. By about 4 billion years ago, Earth was entirely covered by a warm-water ocean, topped by clouds, and pelted continuously by rain.

The newly formed Moon was nearer than it is today, so tides surged wildly. Asteroids striking the ocean created monstrous tidal waves, the force of which created craters and rocks on the seabed.

Much of the air's load of carbon dioxide gradually dissolved into the ocean. As the air thinned, days brightened. The global ocean began to evaporate, exposing more and more rocky, fractured land.

By about 3.4 billion years ago, broad landmasses broke up the once endless expanse of ocean. By about 2.9 billion years ago, tiny organisms known as *cyanobacteria* (also called blue-green algae) had evolved. Like today's plants, the cyanobacteria used sunlight to split up carbon dioxide, creating carbohydrates for themselves and leaving oxygen as a waste product. The algae's leftover oxygen had begun to accumulate in Earth's air by about 2.4 billion years ago.

By making the atmosphere breathable—over a billion long years—bacteria and plants created the conditions for the evolution and spread of animal life, which began about 600 million years ago. Thanks to them, you are reading this today. And the rest, as they say, is history.

A STAR is Born... and then some planets

Somewhere in the Milky Way...

Clouds of dust and gas attract and compress...

and the next thing you know...

It's a sun!

Millions of years later, after much clumping, colliding, compression, and attraction...

grandchildren!

How come the Earth is tilted?

If you could watch the Earth circling the Sun, you might decide our planet has very poor posture.

The Earth—tipped over about 23.5 degrees from straight up-and-down—rides around the Sun leaning to one side. It got that way, scientists say, in the demolition derby that formed our solar system more than 4.5 billion years ago.

The Sun, the Earth, and its sibling planets formed from a rotating cloud of gas and dust in space. Scientists say the Earth grew into a planet-size body as particles collided with other particles. Over millions of years, the colliding chunks got bigger, worldlets crashed into other worldlets, and planets grew. (The Moon may have formed when a particularly big body slammed into the still red-hot Earth.) According to astronomer Clark Chapman, there must have been one final enormous collision that knocked the poor battered Earth over into its current position.

The tilt makes life on our planet more interesting. It makes leaves turn red in October in Maine. It bakes Ohio in August, sending kids splashing into pools. And it

TOPSY-TURVY WORLD

The Earth is not the only planet leaning to one side. Mars is tipped over by about 25 degrees, and it, too, has seasons.

But the planet with the biggest tilt is distant Uranus. Some terrible impact, probably more than 4 billion years ago, when Uranus was very young, knocked Uranus completely over. Today, the whole planet, rings and all, rides around the Sun lying on its side.

Uranus is odd in another way, too: It spins backward, turning from east to west. Scientists call its rotation "retrograde."

At 1.79 billion miles (2.88 billion km) from the Sun, Uranus is a frigid world; the average temperature of the atmosphere is about −350°F (−212°C). As Uranus makes its long orbit of the Sun—one Uranian year is 84 Earth-years long—first one of its poles, and then the other basks in the Sun. When it is summer at its north pole, the Sun shines continuously, day in and day out. Meanwhile, it is winter at the south pole, and pitch-black. Each "season" lasts about 21 Earth-years.

When the U.S. space probe *Voyager 2* flew past Uranus in 1986, it found some surprises. For example, the temperature of the atmosphere at the shadowed pole was 4°F to 6°F (2.2°C to 3.4°C) warmer than the temperature at the sunlit pole.

This may be due, scientists say, to a "seasonal lag" in temperature. Cold objects lose heat more slowly than hot objects. Since Uranus is already so frigid, it takes a long time to cool further. So a pole that has spent 21 years in light—but is currently in darkness—will take a long time to lose the heat it collected during its years in the sun.

sometimes delivers January snows that shut down New York City. In short, the tilt makes seasons—four of them.

How? Because of the tilt, the North Pole leans toward the Sun for half the year and away from the Sun for the rest. The Northern Hemisphere gets more sunlight and warmer weather when the North Pole is tipped toward the Sun, longer nights and colder weather when it's tipped away.

In the Southern Hemisphere, it's just the opposite: Winter in Boston is summer in São Paulo. Near the equator, there is only a kind of endless summer.

If the Earth were to be pushed straight up on its axis, Chapman says, the seasons would nearly disappear. Since the Earth's orbit around the Sun is not a perfect circle, temperatures would drop a bit as the Earth made its farthest swing from the Sun. Then things would warm up as our planet came closer to the Sun again. But these slight variations would be a far cry from real seasons—fall, winter, spring, and summer. Without the Earth's tilt, these words wouldn't even be in the language.

Why isn't the first day of summer, the longest day, also the hottest?

As spring slips into summer, the days get longer and longer, the nights shorter and shorter. Days lengthen from about 9.3 hours in late December to more than 12 hours in late March to about 15 hours in early June in the northern United States.

How come days and nights aren't always 12 hours each? Blame it on (or thank) the Earth's tilt. Imagine a spinning top, whirling around an imaginary vertical axis. Now imagine the top still spinning, but tilted a bit to one side. Like the top, our spinning blue planet is tipped at a 23.5-degree angle from the straight-up-and-down. So we travel around the Sun at a slant.

One trip around our star equals one year. As the year unfolds, Earth's fixed tilt means that the top half of the planet is leaning toward the Sun for half the year, away the other half. When the Northern Hemisphere is tipped toward our fiery star, it's summer vacation time. Meanwhile, in the Southern Hemisphere, the tip-away means winter cold and long nights.

As a hemisphere leans toward the Sun, days lengthen as sunlight hours increase. And the Sun's rays hit the hemisphere more directly than in winter, as the Sun climbs higher and higher in the sky.

All of this means a gradual heating of the atmosphere, soil, and oceans.

The summer solstice is not actually a day, but a single moment in time. In the Northern Hemisphere, it marks the point at which the Sun is highest and farthest to the north in the sky for the year.

According to the U.S. Naval Observatory, the official summer solstice for 2015 is June 21 at 16:38 Universal Time (4:38 p.m.). Universal Time is five hours ahead of U.S. Eastern Standard Time, four hours ahead of Eastern Daylight Time. So on the U.S. East

Coast, for example, the 2015 summer solstice is at 12:38 p.m. on Friday, June 21.

After the solstice—which means "sun stands still"—things begin to go backward. Earth's orbit begins to shift the Northern Hemisphere away from the Sun. The Sun appears a bit lower in the sky each day and more southerly. And days gradually get shorter, losing minutes each week.

But summer temperatures don't reach their peak until a month after the longest days. Why? The ground heats more slowly than the air, the oceans more slowly still. So the atmosphere loses some of its late spring/early summer heat to the cooler oceans and land. While the air receives less heat from the Sun in the post-solstice weeks, it keeps more as soil and oceans warm up. (Meanwhile, the slower-to-heat ocean holds on to its heat longest of all.) So heat is still accumulating after the solstice, and temperatures hit their average maximum in July and August.

Fast Fact

Summer solstice day is the longest of the year, but only by seconds. The two days before and after the solstice are almost equally long: nearly 15 hours, 6 minutes, in New York City.

Diary: Planet Earth

Vernal Equinox — Must change tilt for a total tan.

Summer Solstice — Out all day and night—things are heating up.

Autumnal Equinox — Whew! Time to cool down.

Why does the Earth keep rotating on its axis once every 24 hours?

Although the Earth is spinning at about 1,000 miles per hour (1,609.3 km/h) at the equator, no one needed to give Earth a shove to start it whirling like a top. Earth and its planetary siblings were born from a cloud of spinning gas and dust in space, with the Sun forming at the center. Our star and its planets began their lives whirling in space. And without the friction that a spinning object encounters here on Earth, they continue to spin.

The young planets' speed and direction of rotation depended on what collisions they suffered in the early years of the solar

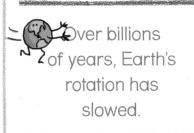

Over billions of years, Earth's rotation has slowed.

system. Each planet in our solar system emerged with a different mass, circumference, rotational speed, and day length. (A day on Jupiter is less than 10 hours long, but days on Mercury last an interminable 1,407 hours, or nearly 2 Earth months.)

Even though Earth was born spinning, our planet didn't come equipped with

rotational cruise control. According to some models, after a collision with a Mars-size body some 4.5 billion years ago, the hot, molten Earth may have begun whirling around on its axis in six hours—making days a brief six hours long from one sunrise to the next.

But over billions of years, Earth's rotation has slowed. A main cause of the deceleration is the rising and falling of Earth's immense oceans. Sloshing ocean tides affect a planet like the brakes on a speeding car. The tides are created mainly by the gravitational pull of the Earth's big Moon. By the time dinosaurs first roamed the planet, they probably enjoyed days that were only about an hour shorter than ours.

About a century ago, a day on Earth was 1.7 milliseconds longer than it is today. (A millisecond is a thousandth of a second.) In another 200 million to 300 million years, according to some estimates, the Earth's deceleration will have added a full hour to each day. (And if gas stations and stores are still around, some will undoubtedly be open 25/7.)

Besides Moon-whipped tides, events like earthquakes and hurricanes, shifting ocean currents, and "wobbles" between the Earth's molten core and mantle can temporarily change the speed of spinning by a few microseconds (millionths of a second) either way.

 Some scientists think that global warming will be a small countervailing force to the gradual slowing. As ice melts and sea levels rise, water shifts toward the North and South Poles. Just as a figure skater pulling in her arms spins faster, this small redistribution of the Earth's mass may cause our planet to spin a bit faster, too.

If the Earth is spinning, why can't we feel it? Why don't we fly off?

The next time you get on an elevator in the lobby of a tall building, close your eyes. As the box you're riding in smoothly ascends, you may feel like you're not moving at all—at least, until it slows to a stop at your floor. Think about it, and you'll realize you've had the same experience in a train or a car. Or even on a jet plane, traveling through the clouds at more than 500 miles per hour.

We're traveling on our planet, too, circling the Sun, journeying through space with the rest of the solar system, all while Earth spins on its axis like a top.

In fact, our planet's rotational speed at the equator is higher than a commercial jet's cruising speed. The Earth measures about 24,900 miles around at its widest. Divide that by the 24 hours it takes to turn once, and we

get the Earth's speed at the equator: a dizzying 1,040 miles per hour.

But since the distance around the planet shrinks as we travel toward the poles, the relative speed changes, too. So at the latitude of New York City, the Earth's rotational speed is about 783 miles per hour. Which means that each second ("one hippopotamus, two hippopotamus") you've traveled 1,148 feet forward on your planetary merry-go-round. And as in a plane at constant speed, you're just not feelin' it.

Physicists discovered this principle centuries ago:

In a closed box, no windows to peek from, there's no way to tell whether we're stopped still, or moving at an unvarying speed. But if the "box" (or elevator, or plane) speeds up or slows down, the feeling of movement suddenly appears, too. We experience motion when it's changing.

Since Earth's rotational speed is so constant, we (thankfully) can't feel how fast we're really spinning. The same goes for our 365-day trip around the Sun, which our speedy planet whizzes through at 67,000 miles per hour.

Although you're being spun to the east at, say, nearly 800 miles per hour, the matter in your body is strongly attracted to the much greater mass of matter of the planet. The centrifugal, outward "force" created by rotation is a tiny fraction of the strength of our planet's downward-directed gravitational force.

But if the Earth's rotational speed changed suddenly, we'd realize we're moving at breakneck speed. If the Earth suddenly slowed, scientists say, we'd tumble forward; if it sped up, we'd fall over backward.

And if Earth's rotational speed at the equator increased

If the Earth's rotational speed suddenly changed, we'd realize we're moving at breakneck speed.

to more than 18,000 miles per hour, with a day lasting just 80 minutes, gravity could no longer keep us safely planted to the ground. And we would, indeed, go flying off into the dark.

Measure FOR Measure
500 miles per hour = 805 km/h
24,900 miles = 40,073 km
1,040 miles per hour = 1,674 km/h
783 miles per hour = 1,260 km/h
1,148 feet = 350 m
67,000 miles per hour = 108,000 km/h
800 miles per hour = 1,288 km/h
18,000 miles per hour = 29,000 km/h

What would happen if the Earth stopped spinning?

The Earth condensed from a spinning cloud of gas and dust in space. Born turning, its rotational speed has slowed over the last 4.5 billion years, due to its gravitational interaction with the Moon. But scientists say our planetary carousel is in no danger of stopping.

But what if? If the Earth suddenly stopped spinning, it would be an instant catastrophe, according to astronomer Sten Odenwald. As the Earth screeched to a halt, the atmosphere would continue spinning at more than 1,000 miles per hour (1,609 km/h) at the equator. Buildings, trees, dirt, plants, animals, and people would be swept up into the sky,

rather like Dorothy, Toto, and the cow in *The Wizard of Oz*.

But assume instead the Earth slowed to a stop gradually, over billions of years. One side of the Earth would be lit up by the Sun. The other side would be cloaked in endless night.

The daylight side would get very hot. The nighttime side would grow frigidly cold. Neither side would be a very pleasant place.

But any remaining Earthlings would soon learn that they only had to put up with the daylight (or its absence) for about six months. As the Earth traveled around the Sun, day would turn to night, and vice versa. (See for yourself: Mark a small ball with an X, then move it around a lightbulb, holding it with the X pointing forward. See how the X is first in light, then in darkness?)

During the half-year of daylight, the Sun would vary in its position in the sky, moving closer to the horizon as summer turned to fall. Then the Sun would sink below the Earth's rim,

ushering in 6 months of darkness. And during the very long night, the constellations wouldn't vary over the course of hours, as they do now.

Because the Earth is tilted, there would still be seasons. But with no spin to cause rotating hurricanes and ocean currents, the weather would be very different from today's. According to Odenwald, the steep temperature difference between the night and day sides of a stalled Earth would create winds that blew from the equator to the poles, rather than around the planet.

Earth's gravity, which is based on its mass, wouldn't change. However, a spinning planet produces a centrifugal effect, which makes everything on board want to fly off on a tangent, like passengers in a car rounding a curve. So the Earth's spin has

If the Earth stopped spinning, one side would be lit up by the Sun, the other cloaked in frigid darkness.

a tiny counterbalancing effect on its gravitational force. If the Earth were to stop spinning, a 150-pound (68-kg) person would weigh in several ounces higher on a scale.

What makes the wind blow?

Wind whips flags, ruffles your hair, and pushes you down the sidewalk, like a strong hand at your back. Yet despite all the commotion, wind is invisible, seeming to come out of everywhere and nowhere at the same time.

Of course, it's actually the air around us, moving this way and that, that may become a wind, whirling dry leaves like a tiny tornado. Surprisingly, it's our home star, the Sun, that is the force behind the winds of Earth. Sunlight warms the ground, which—like an electric heater—warms the air above it. Warm air rises; cooler air rushes in to take its place. This flow of air—the movements of great bunches of gas molecules, swept along together—is what we call wind.

How does it work? Warming air expands and thins. As its gas molecules spread farther apart, a parcel of air weighs less, creating less pressure on objects beneath it. But cold air shrinks together, so a parcel of colder air presses down with more force.

Like water flowing out the nozzle of a hose, air tends to flow from an area of high pressure to an area of low. In their attempt to equalize the pressure, air molecules rush in to spaces where air is thinner, creating a breeze.

But winds don't just blow by your front door; they also blow around the whole planet. Rising air from Earth's hot equator regions meets cold, sinking air from the north and south poles, causing global winds to blow. But our planet's winds don't simply blow from high- to low-pressure regions. Since Earth and its atmosphere are always rotating, global winds are forced to follow a curving path.

Smaller, local winds aren't much affected by the Earth's turning. Winds along coastlines, for example, blow in from the sea during the day, but stream from the land out to sea at night. Why? Imagine a hot, sunny day, beach sand warming fast. Air over the beach heats and rises, and cooler ocean air rushes in to replace it—creating a welcome sea breeze.

But at night, coastal land radiates heat into space more rapidly than does ocean water, which tends to hold onto heat. So as air cools above the beach, it flows out to fill in the thinner, warmer air above the water. Out on a boat at night, you may feel a breeze blowing from shore.

Fast Fact

Air seems insubstantial, weightless. But above our heads, stretching into space, the whole atmosphere of gas molecules weighs more than 5 quadrillion tons. Even as you read this, the air around you is pressing on each square inch of your body with nearly 15 pounds of force.

The greater the pressure difference between two regions of air, the faster air flows between them. Encountering a pocket of especially low pressure, air may suddenly gust in, taking the hat right off your head.

How can you calculate the distance around the Earth?

Nowadays you can find out the circumference of the Earth using surveying instruments and satellites. But you don't need fancy equipment to measure a planet. You could do what Eratosthenes did more than 2,000 years ago: He correctly figured out the size of the Earth without leaving the grounds of the library where he worked.

Eratosthenes was an ancient Greek mathematician and geographer who lived in Alexandria, a city in Egypt, between about 276 and 196 BC. He worked at the Alexandrian Museum, which was part museum, part

An ancient Greek mathematician and geographer, Eratosthenes, figured out the Earth's circumference more than 2,000 years ago.

research center. It had botanic gardens, zoos, an astronomic observatory, and laboratories. Scholars gave talks in the museum's lecture hall; others relaxed, ate meals, and talked in the museum's dining room.

Eratosthenes was head of the museum's library, the most important in the ancient world. The Library of Alexandria may have contained a half million books and documents, all written on scrolls of papyrus (a kind of paper made from the papyrus reed). Eratosthenes was interested in everything: He had studied philosophy, history, geography, math, music theory, and the sciences. Some of his fellow scholars thought he was a dilettante—someone who dabbled in many things, but wasn't really first-rate at any of them.

Eratosthenes had heard from travelers about

something peculiar they had seen in Syene, a town far south of Alexandria. At noon on the first day of summer—the longest day of the year—shadows disappeared in Syene. The Sun stood directly overhead; its rays beamed straight down. Looking into a deep well, you could see a reflection of the Sun's disc in the water at the bottom.

However, back in Alexandria, Eratosthenes had seen museum walls casting shadows at noon on that very same day. From this simple observation, he was able to calculate the size of a whole planet.

Here's how. Eratosthenes knew that because of the enormous distance of the Sun from Earth, its rays reached both Alexandria and Syene in side-by-side, parallel beams.

If the Earth were flat, then shadows would disappear everywhere on June 21. But since, he reasoned, the Earth is curved, the walls and columns of Alexandria—about 500 miles north of Syene—were poking out from the Earth's surface at a different angle.

So at noon on the first day of summer, Eratosthenes measured the shadow cast by

Eratosthenes Pop Quiz

Q. I have a little shadow that goes in and out with me and what can be the use of it is more than I can see.

A. 1. A cool place to relax
2. To tell time
3. Help measure the circumference of the Earth.

an obelisk outside the museum. Since he knew the height of the obelisk, he could imagine a line from the top of the obelisk to the tip of the shadow, making a measurable triangle.

After "drawing" the triangle, Eratosthenes used a simple rule of geometry to find that the top of the obelisk pointed away from the Sun by a little more than 7 degrees.

Since there were no shadows at noon in Syene on that first summer day, the angle in Syene must be 0 degrees—in other words, no angle at all. This means that Alexandria was a bit more than 7 degrees away from Syene along the circumference of the Earth.

All circles have 360 degrees, and the Earth's circumference is no exception. The 7-degree angle between the two cities was about 1/50th of a circle. So Eratosthenes multiplied the distance between Syene and Alexandria—about 500 miles—by 50, getting 25,000 miles for the distance around the Earth. Modern astronomers put Earth's actual circumference at about 24,894 miles. Eratosthenes had proved himself a first-rate scholar indeed.

Today, there is a whole science, called "geodesy,"

Fast Fact

Earth is about 24,894 miles around. (That's about 40,063 km.)

devoted to sizing up our planet. Geodesists use special surveying instruments to measure angles of the Earth. They measure gravity to determine the exact shape of the planet, and they make use of the position of satellites in the sky to measure triangles, with a satellite at the apex and two ground stations marking the other two points of the triangle.

Measure FOR Measure

500 miles = 805 km
25,000 miles = 40,234 km
24,894 miles = 40,063 km

Why is the ocean salty?

Salt Water Taste Test

Crisp and lightly salted, tastes like... the Adriatic?

Full-bodied and firmly salty, from... the Dead sea?

Fruity yet delightfully salty, could it be... my bathwater?

Ever get splashed by a wave and taste a mouthful of ocean? Seawater is about as salty as a glass of tap water, with a teaspoon of salt stirred in.

"Water, water everywhere, nor any drop to drink," wrote Samuel Taylor Coleridge, in his *Rime of the Ancient Mariner*. At sea, the ocean stretches to the horizon. But the water is undrinkable, thanks to its heavy load of salt.

Leaving pollution aside, water from rivers and freshwater lakes *is* drinkable. So it's surprising to find out that our planet's salty seas get their salt courtesy of those same rivers.

And the oceans contain a staggering amount: If you were to weigh seawater, 100 pounds of water would contain about 3.5 pounds of dissolved salt. By contrast, the average river would contain a

scant 8/100ths of an ounce of salt, less than half a teaspoon, in 100 pounds of water.

In fact, about 85 percent of the 50 quadrillion tons of solids in the Earth's seas are the minerals sodium and chloride (aka table salt).

Since fresh water from rivers continuously pours into the oceans all around the world, we might assume the oceans' salt becomes more diluted over time. It

THE (LESS) SALTY SEA

The sea's surface water varies in saltiness from place to place. But scientists have discovered that the average saltiness of ocean water can be an indicator of climate change. As the average temperature rises and polar ice melts faster, salt is diluted in the surrounding sea.

Scientists note that ocean water near the poles has become dramatically fresher in the last 45 years, even as tropical waters have become saltier. If the North Atlantic loses too much salt, its surface waters will sink less, altering ocean circulation and weather patterns.

seems to make sense that in the distant future, we might find ourselves swimming in freshwater oceans—with many "drops to drink."

But rivers dump billions of tons of solids into the oceans each year. Pouring rain and flowing rivers leach salt out of rocks and soil on land, eventually carrying it into the sea. Erupting volcanoes belch salts into the air, and much of it lands in the ocean. And more salts seep into seawater from volcanic vents, hidden on the ocean floor.

The result: Over billions of years, the salt deposited in the oceans has built up to its current enormous level (enough, if removed and dried, to bury our entire planet's land mass under 500 feet of white crystals).

But thanks mainly to the Sun, the salt tends to stay put. Day in and day out, the Sun's heat evaporates water from the ocean's surface. Our star acts like a water distiller; water molecules fly off into the atmosphere, but nearly all the salt is left behind. And then there's sea ice. When ice forms from seawater, the water freezes, but the salt is expelled into the ocean.

So when ocean water evaporates or freezes, the surface water is left with an extra load of salt. This denser water sinks toward the seafloor, playing an important part in the circulation of ocean waters worldwide.

Scientists say a sodium atom washed into the ocean from a river will, on average, remain for 237 million years. But some minerals seem to vanish. Rivers dump much more calcium than chloride into the sea, but the oceans have about 46 times more chloride than calcium.

How come? Shellfish extract calcium to build their shells or carapaces. And excess calcium is deposited on the seafloor as calcium carbonate—the main building material of coral reefs.

Measure FOR Measure

100 pounds = 45.4 kg
3.5 pounds = 1.59 kg
8/100ths of an ounce = 2.3 g
500 feet = 152.4 m

If rivers drain into oceans, why don't the oceans overflow?

Human beings have always been confounded by the puzzle of rivers. As the Bible says, "All rivers run into the sea; yet the sea is not full."

From space, rivers look like running faucets, flowing into Earth's oceans. The 4,000-mile-long Amazon River pours continuously into the Atlantic; the 1,200-mile Columbia River empties day and night into the Pacific. Meanwhile, the 1,700-mile Zambezi River gushes nonstop into the Indian Ocean. Yet unlike a bathtub with its faucets left on, overflowing onto the bathroom floor, the oceans never seem to fill.

Water from rain and melting snow flows down the towering mountains and gentle hills of Earth in streams; streams collect together into rivers. Rivers widen as they are joined by streams along the way. Smaller rivers feed big, deep rivers, like the mighty Mississippi. And all of that water flows down, down, down, toward the sea.

The biggest rivers dump stadiums full of water into the oceans. Runoff is greatest in places with the most yearly precipitation, like the torrentially rainy tropics. Some tropical rivers can pour out 700,000 cubic feet in a second, the time it takes to say "one Mississippi." The Amazon alone drains one-fifth of the Earth's total runoff into the Atlantic Ocean.

So why don't seas simply overflow? Think of an ocean as a fountain in a public square. In the fountain, water continuously sprays into a wide basin. But the basin doesn't overflow, because water is pulled up to spurt out of the fountain's top again. The water in the fountain

Measure FOR Measure

4,000 miles = 6,437 km
1,200 miles = 1,931 km
1,700 miles = 2,736 km
700,000 cubic feet = 19,822 m³
400 feet = 122 m

continuously recycles.

A similar kind of recycling happens in the oceans. Water rains down on the land and flows into the sea. But on the surface of the oceans, water continuously escapes into the sky, evaporating like the liquid in a glass left on the kitchen counter. Molecule by molecule, water breaks free from the oceans, saturating the air above, and forming clouds. As a cloud's water droplets or ice crystals grow larger, gravity tugs them to Earth, in the form of rain and snow. And water makes its way back to the oceans, in pouring rivers.

But the water level in ocean basins isn't unchanging. Earth's periodic ice ages have a big effect on sea level. When glaciers covered nearly one-third of the land, the average sea level was much lower than it is today. Water continued to evaporate from the oceans, forming clouds. But rain and snow falling on the continents quickly froze onto the massive sheets of ice, rather than flowing back into the sea.

However, as centuries passed and the ice slowly melted, sea level rose again, increasing at least 400 feet since the depths of the last Ice Age (about 20,000 years ago). Scientists say that global warming is now making sea level rise even faster.

The Water Cycle... Great for oceans, lousy for picnics!

Why don't oceans freeze?

Even as freshwater ponds and lakes obligingly freeze over in winter, the ocean stays stubbornly liquid, waves rolling into shore in January just like in July.

How come? First, a big parcel of water acts as a heat reservoir. Since oceans are so much bigger than lakes, they hold onto much more heat, and for much longer. Second, oceans never stand still; tides and rolling waves make it difficult for ice to form.

Finally, there's the freezing point of water. Which—surprisingly—isn't a constant. Under everyday conditions, fresh water (like tap water) begins to freeze at 32°F. At

32°F, some water molecules are locking into crystal lattices (freezing), even as others are breaking away (melting). But as the temperature drops, freezing outpaces melting. Presto: ice cubes!

But when salt is dissolved in water, freezing is short-circuited. A dissolved salt molecule separates into its atoms, sodium and chlorine.

These charged atoms (ions), electrically attracted to water's H_2O molecules, cluster around them. Result: Some water molecules are kept from attaching to the forming ice crystals. And freezing slows down, while melting continues as usual.

So salt dissolved in water lowers its freezing point, and sea water must reach a temperature of about 28.4°F before it starts to freeze. Combine a lowered freezing point with the ocean's retained heat and constant movement, and salty seas stay sloshy.

But in the frigid waters of the Arctic and Antarctica, a cap of frozen saltwater forms in winter, extending 3 to 15 feet under the surface.

Measure FOR Measure
32°F = 0°C
28.4°F = −2°C
−58°F = −50°C
3 to 15 feet = 0.9 to 4.6 m

Is it true that water swirls down a drain in opposite directions north and south of the equator?

Perhaps you heard it from a friend, or even learned it in school: Draining bathtub water swirls clockwise in the Southern Hemisphere, counterclockwise in the Northern Hemisphere. What might make this happen? The Coriolis effect.

No, the Coriolis effect is not this summer's blockbuster movie. It's simply the effect that a turning planet— ours, in this case—has on moving bodies on or above the planet's surface. The Coriolis effect helps curve storm systems into spinning cyclones, spawning hurricanes on Earth (and the Great Red Spot on Jupiter).

Thanks to the Coriolis effect, hurricanes turn counterclockwise in the Northern Hemisphere, while in the Southern Hemisphere, tropical cyclones spin clockwise. And that's how the story about draining bathtubs (and flushing toilets) got started. People believed that if the Coriolis effect influences the spinning of storms, then small vortexes of water, like mini-hurricanes, must swirl in opposite directions in New York City and Melbourne, Australia.

So if, in your Northern Hemisphere bathroom, you fill the tub and pull the plug, will the water depart in a counterclockwise swirl? Maybe. Or maybe not. Whether your bathwater is

The Coriolis Effect and The Goldfish That Went to Heaven...

Hey, he's going the wrong way!

north or south of the equator turns out to be the least important factor in how it circles the drain.

For cyclonic storms like hurricanes, however, it's location, location, location. How come? Imagine a ball lying on a patch of ground at the North Pole, and another sitting on the ground at the equator. Meanwhile, the Earth is speedily spinning, though

 The spinning of the Earth makes hurricanes in the Northern Hemisphere turn counterclockwise.

we don't sense its carousel movement.

At its bulging waistline, our spherical planet measures nearly 25,000 miles around. In the 24 hours it takes Earth to turn once, the ball at the North Pole, at the top of Earth's axis, has effectively stood still. But the ball at the equator has been carried almost 25,000 miles, at a speed of more than 1,000 miles per hour. (At the in-between latitude of New York City, the Earth rotates at about 783 miles per hour.)

Now imagine that the North Pole ball is picked up and thrown by a pitcher with superhuman strength—all the way to Florida. Because the Earth is turning faster nearer the equator, the ball's path would gradually appear to curve, the ball landing to the right of its target. Starting from the South Pole, a ball's path would be deflected to the left.

A liquid or gas flowing across the spinning Earth feels an accelerating force, at a 90-degree angle to its forward motion, thanks to the Coriolis effect. North of the equator, as rushing air drops into a low-pressure area, it's deflected in a counterclockwise direction. Result: counterclockwise hurricanes. South of the equator, low-pressure storms are nudged into a clockwise rotation.

But the Earth's rotation has virtually no effect on water in a bathtub. Scientists say that the rotation rate of a tiny parcel of water around a drain (one rotation in a few seconds) is tens of thousands of times higher than the rotation rate of the Earth (one rotation in 24 hours). The Coriolis effect, at just 3 ten-millionths of the strength of gravity, is too weak to make swiftly spinning bathwater behave.

Instead, the directional die is cast as water swirls and sloshes against the sides of the tub, developing a slight rotating motion that increases when you open the drain.

To show the Coriolis effect working as it really does in nature, on the scale of a hurricane, bathtubs would have to measure hundreds of miles across—fit for a race of giants.

Measure for Measure

25,000 miles = 40,233 km
1,000 miles per hour = 1,609 km/h
783 miles per hour = 1,260 km/h

Why is it so easy to float in salt water?

Archimedes At the Beach ...

Can we have our ball back now?

HA! try that in the Dead Sea!

If you've ever compared floating in a backyard swimming pool to floating in the ocean, you know there's a difference. It's just easier to float lazily around in a calm, salty sea, with no pesky sinking knees. In the even saltier Great Salt Lake in Utah, you'd bob like a buoy.

Objects sink through water for the same reason they fall through the air: gravity. Gravity is the attraction matter feels for other matter. The more matter packed densely together in one place, the greater its gravitational pull. An enormous chunk of matter like Earth has enough gravitational pull to make a

baseball fall down through the air and a stone sink in a pond of liquid water.

So an object that floats rather than sinks is floating because the liquid is pushing it up, exerting a force opposite to the force of gravity. A scientist from ancient Greece named Archimedes summed up what happens: An object in

It takes
about 9 pounds
of force to press
a beach ball
underwater.

a fluid is buoyed up by a force equal to the weight of the fluid it displaces.

But whether an object floats or sinks depends on whether it displaces enough water to hold its own weight. So when it comes to floating, what counts most is density—how much mass is packed into a given volume. If a solid object is denser than the water it displaced, it will sink. An iron frying pan is denser and weightier than a frying pan–sized volume of water. So tossed into a lake, it will sink straight to the bottom, tugged down by gravity.

But if an object is less dense than water, like an inflated beach ball, it will float. A beach ball is a thin elastic sheet surrounding a big bunch of thin air. But a beach ball–size parcel of water is much more densely packed and heavier than an actual beach ball. A beach ball not only floats, it actually takes about 9 pounds of force to press a gallon-size beach ball underwater.

But even objects whose average density is greater than water (and end up sinking) also experience its buoyant force. A rock sinks, but some of its weight is buoyed up, making the rock lighter underwater than on land.

The denser the liquid, the more weight it will hold up. A solid chunk of steel, for example, would bob around nicely in even-denser liquid mercury.

Which brings us to salt. When you take a certain volume of water and add salt, you are making a denser liquid. One cubic foot of freshwater weighs about 62.4 pounds, but an equal volume of salty ocean water weighs about 64 pounds. So an object that sinks in freshwater may float in saltwater. (Utah's Great Salt Lake is 12 to 25 times as salty as the sea, and most people float effortlessly on its surface. The tricky part is staying submerged.)

See for yourself how salt water makes objects more buoyant: Fill a glass about halfway with tap water. Gently slide an egg into the glass—and watch it sink, since it's denser than water. Now stir in some salt. Keep adding salt, about a tablespoon at a time, until your egg rises off the bottom and begins to float.

Measure FOR Measure
9 pounds = 4.1 kg
62.4 pounds = 28.3 kg
64 pounds = 29 kg

What makes dew appear on grass?

It appears seemingly from nowhere, glistening on every blade of grass, leaf, and flower. Dew, people once believed, was nectar from heaven. Rolling in dew was a favorite part of some ancient ceremonies, as was washing in it, or drinking a bit for instant invigoration and good health.

But dew isn't confined to early-morning grass. A kind of dew appears on cold pipes in hot weather (we say "the pipes are sweating"), and on the outside of ice-filled glasses in summer. Dew happens when water-filled air comes into contact with cooler surfaces—a blade of grass, a cold-water pipe, an ice-filled glass.

Air has what scientists call a dew-point temperature.

> Dew forms most often on nights with clear skies.

That means that at a particular temperature and pressure, a parcel of air is holding all the water vapor it possibly can. The air is saturated, like a washcloth full of water just before it begins to drip on your bathroom floor.

Whether dew is present in the morning depends on what happened the night before. After the sun goes down, the Earth's surface begins to lose the heat it stored up all day long. The moist air just above the ground loses heat, too. As long as the sky is clear, the heat simply radiates into space.

Cool air, which is more tightly packed, can't hold as much water vapor as warm air. So it quickly reaches its dew point, when it is as full of water as it can be without "spilling." If conditions remain calm—if no breeze springs up to mix in warm air from higher up—dew forms.

How does it work? The air, overfull of water vapor, touches a cool blade of grass. As the water vapor cools when it touches the grass, it condenses into liquid and drips onto the grass (rather like your dripping washcloth).

Plumber's Dew

Nectar from heaven — or a leak from the third floor?

Those droplets combine with water naturally evaporating from the plants. Soon, the whole lawn is covered with drops, which will glisten and shine when the Sun rises in the morning.

Dew forms most often at night when the sky is clear, since a clear sky means no clouds to keep heat from radiating into space. So an old farmers' adage says that morning dew means no rain

that day, whereas no dew means a storm is on the way.

Dew can have strange and wonderful effects on light. It can make a halo appear on the head of your shadow. If you happen to be on an evenly clipped lawn in early morning, just after the Sun has come up, you may see it. With your back to the Sun, look at the top of your long shadow on the wet grass. You may see a

luminous halo surrounding your head.

You don't need to be a saint to wear the dew halo. Such halos form in a similar way to ordinary rainbows. Sunlight from behind the viewer strikes dewdrops in front of him or her, creating a little halo on the grass— much the same way a rainbow is created when you hold a spraying hose at just the right angle to the summer sunlight.

How come it's still light for an hour after the Sun sets?

Twilight time: a time of purple clouds, deepening shadows, and a fading glow in the sky. Still light enough to play outside, but getting harder and harder to read without a lamp. As a song made popular by the Platters in 1958 goes, "Heavenly shades of night are falling; it's twilight time."

Twilight is usually thought of as the time just after the Sun sets in the evening. But the word also refers to the time just before the Sun rises in the morning. During twilight, although the Sun is below the horizon, the sky is still aglow with light, gradually dimming (after sunset) or intensifying (before sunrise).

How come? The light for our evening (or early-morning) activities comes courtesy of the upper

Twilight is the time just after the Sun sets in the evening, but it's also the time just before the Sun rises in the morning.

atmosphere. Light rays from the hidden Sun are bent (refracted) as they pass from the near vacuum of space into the gas molecules of the atmosphere. This means that the sky is lit by sunlight even though the Sun is hidden below the horizon. Since sunlight is also scattered every which way by gas molecules in the air, some of the light even reaches the ground. So it's the still-illuminated sky that creates twilight in the evening—the afterglow before night sets in.

In fact, there are actually four categories of twilight. During the evening, the first twilight period starts with

STAGES OF TWILIGHT TENNIS

CIVIL TWILIGHT
YOU CAN SEE THE NET, the PERSON YOU'RE Playing with but NOT the...

NAUTICAL TWILIGHT
YOU CAN SEE THE HORIZON, NAVIGATE TO the SNACK BAR BUT NOT DETECT THE...

ASTRONOMICAL TWILIGHT
YOU CAN SEE THE STARS BUT NOT YOUR TENNIS PARTNER AND HIS LAST...

sunset. Sunset twilight ends when the Sun has dipped a little less than 1 degree below the horizon.

Next comes civil twilight. During civil twilight, it is still light enough to carry on most outdoor activities, like playing tag on the lawn or watering a garden. Big shapes are still visible during this early twilight, even without streetlamps or porch lights lit. You may see a few bright stars or planets in the sky. In the continental United States, civil twilight lasts for about 30 to 40 minutes, depending on the time of the year and the location. It ends when the Sun is 6 degrees below the horizon.

Then there's nautical twilight. During nautical twilight, the sky is dark enough that the brighter stars are visible. The horizon is still visible, too, so a sailor at sea could navigate by measuring the altitude of certain beacon stars. By the end of nautical twilight, the Sun has slid 12 degrees below the horizon, and the horizon line is fading into darkness.

Finally, there's astronomical twilight. More and more stars can be seen, but the sky is still too light for an astronomer to do any serious work. When the Sun has sunk to 18 degrees below the horizon, twilight is officially over. Astronomical darkness—real night—has begun.

Can we see stars in daytime from the depths of a well?

In Charles Dickens's popular novel *The Pickwick Papers*, first published as a serial in 1836 and 1837, we hear about law clerks working in a very unpleasant office:

In the ground-floor front of a dingy house, at the very farthest end of Freeman's Court, Cornhill, sat the four clerks of Messrs. Dodson & Fogg . . . catching as favourable glimpses of heaven's light and heaven's sun, in the course of their daily labours, as a man might hope to do, were he placed at the bottom of a reasonably deep well; and without the opportunity of perceiving the stars in the day-time, which the latter secluded situation affords.

In other words, if these poor clerks must work in a "dark, mouldy" room behind a high partition during the sunlit hours, they should at least be able to see stars during the daytime—as someone at the bottom of a real well might. Dickens's sentiment should resonate

---

During the day, the Sun drowns out light from distant stars.

---

with any office worker trapped in a dingy cubicle (or student in a dim classroom) on a sunny afternoon.

More than 2,000 years before, the ancient Greek philosopher Aristotle had also mentioned the idea of seeing daytime stars from a deep well. But according to modern astronomers, looking at the sunlit sky from the bottom of a deep hole—like a mineshaft—won't help us see stars. (Unless, of course, we've fallen headfirst into the hole.) In the daytime, the Earth's atmosphere, lit up by our own nearby star, the Sun, drowns out the faint light from distant stars.

According to astronomers, standing at the bottom of a shaft measuring 50 feet deep and 6 feet wide (15.24 m × 1.83 m) is like looking at the sky through a paper towel tube. Neither will help us see stars in the daytime; the sky is just too bright.

(Although looking at the sky through a tube doesn't

increase the contrast between the stars and the sky, there's a good reason why the "well" idea may have taken hold: The darkest, bluest part of the sky is directly overhead. Forced to look straight up, someone in a deep shaft might be a bit more likely to see a star than if he were looking at another part of the sky.)

While a well won't actually do the trick, if you look at the sky just after sunrise, you may be able to see the brightest star, Sirius. And we can also sometimes see planets in the daytime. The brightest planet in our solar system, Venus, can sometimes be seen in the afternoon sky. Even the much dimmer Red Planet, Mars, will be visible in the daytime on its next closest approach to Earth, in 2018.

What causes the Northern Lights?

An aurora is a multicolored glow in the night sky. A typical aurora is a shimmering curtain of blue-green light with patches of pink and red. These ribbons of color may be more than 100 miles wide, and can stretch for 1,000 miles. Dancing like flames in the dark sky, an aurora is a planet's own light show.

Auroras appear on Earth, but are triggered by events on the faraway Sun. Here's how it works.

The Sun is a glowing ball of gas made mostly of hydrogen and helium atoms.

Measure FOR Measure

100 miles = 161 km
1,000 miles = 1,609 km
600 miles per second = 966 km/s

You can see an aurora almost every night at the North Pole.

All atoms have particles called protons at their centers. These are orbited by other particles called electrons. Protons have a positive electrical charge, while electrons are negatively charged.

The halo of superhot gas surrounding the Sun—called the corona—is constantly expanding into space, sending bits and pieces of atoms off in every direction. This is what we call the "solar wind,"

made mostly of protons and electrons zipping along at up to 600 miles per second. Meanwhile, solar flares shoot violently out of the Sun now and then, releasing a gust of new particles into the "wind."

When the solar particles near Earth, they start to feel the effects of our planet's strong magnetic field. The Earth is like a giant magnet, with lines of magnetic force curving out into space and converging near the North and South Poles.

(Our planet's magnetism is believed to be caused by electric currents created by the rotation of its iron core. To see how magnetic fields work, hide a bar magnet under a piece of paper. Now sprinkle iron filings

Aurora Borealis (Suggested Improvements)

① Add Music
(All good light shows are orchestrated.)

② Refreshments
(what's a show without something to eat?)

③ Timing
(Regularly scheduled solar flares, preferably on weekends.)

or tiny iron nails onto the paper. They should line up in curving lines around the magnet, showing the shape of the magnet's force field.)

The Earth's magnetic force lines attract passing charged particles from the Sun, pulling them in. Pulled-in particles travel in "beams" along the lines, which bend back to Earth at the magnetic poles (which are near but not at the North and South Poles).

As the particles travel along the invisible lines, they are unceremoniously dumped into Earth's atmosphere in the far north and south. Now the fun begins.

Our atmosphere is made mostly of nitrogen and oxygen. When electrons and protons stream in from the Sun, they collide with nitrogen and oxygen atoms high up in the air. Some of these atoms lose some of their own electrons, and others get "excited," gaining energy.

When these atoms return to normal after their run-in with the solar protons and electrons, they give off photons of light. Nitrogen that has lost electrons emits

violet and blue light. And excited nitrogen glows a deep red. Excited oxygen gives off green and red light. So the charged particles from the Sun cause the air to shimmer in many colors.

This is the aurora. The glow near the North Pole is called the aurora borealis (it's also known as the Northern Lights). The glow near the South Pole is named the aurora australis (and also called—you guessed it—the Southern Lights).

An aurora appears almost nightly at the North Pole, and 20 to 200 times a year in northern Scandinavia and North America. There are even 5 to 10 aurorae borealis each year near latitudes as far

Fast Fact

Earth is not the only planet with glowing skies. Jupiter has enormous auroras arcing out from its own North Pole, and Saturn has long-lasting auroras that pulse over both poles.

south as those of London, Paris, and Seattle—and the ghostly Northern Lights have even been seen in Mexico.

HOW'S THE WEATHER?

When we ask "What's the weather going to be like tomorrow?," we might as well ask "What's the atmosphere up to now?" Every planet or moon that's surrounded by a layer of gases heavy enough to be held by gravity has weather. (Our own Moon has no atmosphere and, sadly, no weather.)

The Sun heats Earth's atmosphere during the day; at night, the earth and air cool, radiating heat back into space. Heat makes gas molecules fly apart; cooling brings them closer together. Bunches of high-pressure, cooler air stream into emptier pockets of warmer air.

The result is weather: an ocean breeze here, a spinning tornado there, a sunny day in Miami, a steady drizzle in Paris.

Meanwhile, our tilted planet is traveling around the Sun, slowly changing the seasons above and below the equator. How do falling snowflakes or pelting hail first form in clouds? Why do lightning bolts flash between a cloud and the ground? Why are storm clouds dark? What causes that "scent of rain" in the air—and why does rain fall in drops when it finally arrives? Read on and find out.

Why does rain fall in drops? Are they really shaped like tears?

Look at fog swirling in your car headlights or flashlight beam, and you'll see that the floaty mist is made of tiny droplets. And so are actual clouds, high above the ground. Clouds form from the invisible water vapor in the air surrounding Earth. When a cloud forms, the water emerges from hiding. The vapor condenses into liquid droplets or freezes into ice crystals, tumbling and falling in the air.

So rain isn't something "inside" a cloud. Rain is really a cloud falling apart, losing some of itself. This happens when the cloud's droplets or ice crystals grow heavy, and tugged by gravity, fall toward the Earth.

But since the droplets aren't hanging from, say, the lip of a faucet before they fall, they don't start out as elongated teardrops. Instead, the falling droplets are tiny spheres, just as they were in their cloud.

Why spheres? Thank surface tension for molding cloud droplets into tiny, round balls. Molecules in a parcel of liquid water are mutually attracted, but can also slide past each other. (That's how liquid water, unlike solid ice, can assume the shape of the drinking glass it's poured into.)

But water molecules at the surface of a water parcel aren't so attracted to gas molecules whizzing in the air around them. Their main pull is downward, sideways, inward—toward their fellow water molecules. The result is a tense surface, like a thin, rubbery, drumlike skin. This "skin" is strong enough that some insects can saunter across ponds, making visible indentations in the surface with each step.

Surface tension determines the shape water takes in a cloud or fog, pulling each parcel into a nearly perfect ball as it condenses from the air. All molecules on the surface of each watery blob are tugged together with equal tension by their fellow molecules. And so the water shrinks into a tiny, compact sphere—the most efficient shape in nature, with the smallest possible surface area for a given volume. Presto: zillions of miniature round droplets.

But when those droplets, tugged by gravity, tumble from the cloud, shapes can change. The tiniest drops remain almost perfectly round, like plummeting peas. But falling droplets can also latch onto and meld with other droplets, forming much bigger drops. (And as they plunge, drops can reach a maximum speed of 5 to 20 miles per hour, before hitting the ground with tiny splats.)

Bigger drops have more surface area, and so they encounter more air molecules on the long way down. The resistance they meet from the air causes raindrops to flatten out on the bottom, rather as if they were gently landing on a solid surface. So instead of slender, cartoon-y teardrops, big raindrops falling through the air actually look like tiny transparent hamburger buns.

Measure FOR Measure
5 to 20 miles per hour = about 8 to 32 km/h

What causes hail?

While we expect ice in winter, the big, round lumps of ice called hail fall during thunderstorms. So most hail falls in the sweltering months of summer.

Why do violent thunderstorms spew out chunks of ice on hot afternoons? (No, it's not to keep our drinks cold.) Hail-making clouds form when hot meets cold. Heat rising steadily from the ground helps create towering thunderheads. These turbulent, cauliflower-shaped clouds (called cumulonimbus) can extend more than 12 miles up, into regions of the sky where it's always January-cold.

Inside a storm cloud, powerful drafts of warm air soar up, while strong drafts of cold air whoosh down. As large water droplets condense and fall through the roiling clouds, they may be snatched by an updraft rather than falling to earth. The up-rushing wind, which can blow at speeds up to 110 miles per hour, carries the droplets higher and higher into the cloud, where the temperature may be well below 0°F.

As water droplets are lifted up into below-freezing regions, they freeze into ice. (Some hailstones actually start out as ice crystals.) The icy bits may get caught in a windy downdraft, melting a bit as they fall into warmer cloud regions below. Nearer the thundercloud's bottom, the half-frozen drops may be caught in another whooshing updraft, and carried back to the deep freeze higher up. Collecting water vapor and supercooled water droplets that freeze on contact—as well as ice particles and snowflakes—the frozen balls add layer after layer of ice. Their roller-coaster ride through the cloud may last up to 30 minutes.

Measure FOR Measure

12 miles = 19.3 km
110 miles per hour = 177 km/h
0°F = −18°C
24 miles per hour = about 39 km/h
80 miles per hour = about 129 km/h
100 miles per hour = about 161 km/h
8 inches = 20.3 cm
19 inches = 48.3 cm
2 pounds = 0.9 kg

Depending on how it formed, the finished hailstone may look white or clear. Break open a white hailstone, and you may see evidence of its wild ride. Rings, like those on a tree stump, mark off growth layers of ice—a clear

layer, then a milky layer, then another clear layer.

A hailstone that falls out of the cloud after a short ride may be the size of a pea, or a marble. Hailstones that were tossed in the cloud long enough, by very powerful updrafts, can reach the size of a golf ball, a tennis ball, or even (yikes) a grapefruit. Some hailstones are very round; others are studded with icy outcroppings.

It takes a strong updraft to build a big hailstone. According to the U. S. National Weather Service, wind must be blowing at about 24 miles per hour to create a pea-size stone. But tennis-ball hail is made in

HAIL BALL HALL of FAME

STORMY WEATHER

Take one big bunch of cold, dry air from above the Arctic. Send it sweeping down on a collision course with a mass of hot air moseying up from the equator, full of water. Then watch the storms break out.

Like two cars in a head-on collision, the two air masses smack against each other and flatten out. The long, flat area of their impact is called a front.

Remember, warm air rises; colder air tends to fall. A warm front results when a fast-moving warm air mass rides up over the cold air after the collision. Clouds form from the water in the warm air, and it may begin to rain.

In other cases, the cold air moves faster, pushing under the warm air after the collision and giving it a boost up. This is called a cold front, with the cold air forcing the warm air to rise much more quickly than it would on its own. The result? Not just clouds, and rain, but often violent storms, including tornadoes.

updrafts where wind speeds reach around 80 miles per hour. Hailstones fall out of the cloud when the updraft can no longer support their weight, and they are pulled by gravity groundward.

Imagine a baseball made of hard ice, and you can see why heavy hailstones—hurtling down at 80 to 100 miles per hour—can destroy a field of crops, or shatter car windshields. When you hear the pelting sound of hail, and see white gumballs falling from the sky, take shelter.

How do snowflakes form?

In the cold clouds floating around Earth, more than 1,000,000,000,000,000,000,000,000 snow crystals form during a year, a septillion cascading crystals, in a never-ending parade of patterns. Some fall to the ground, where they melt quickly, or pile slowly into a frozen heap. Most vanish on their way down, dissolving to liquid as they pass from their frigid, cloudy nurseries into warmer air below.

Snowflakes can be made from one crystal or many, glommed together. Huge flakes dropping swiftly from a gray winter sky may be clumps of hundreds of crystals. The wetter and stickier the snow, the bigger the falling flakes.

Snow crystals form in cold clouds high above the Earth. At very high altitudes, when the temperature can hover at −40°F, water vapor can suddenly freeze into ice crystals. In lower, warmer clouds, water vapor begins to freeze around blowing

> While we think of snow as being pure ice, it turns out that most snowflakes form around tiny bits of clay, carried into the sky by wind.

particles like soil, dust, salt, and even bacteria when the temperature drops to 32°F or below. Using powerful microscopes, scientists have seen the particles at the secret heart of snow crystals. In one batch of crystals, more than three-fourths had formed around tiny bits of clay from the Earth.

A typical tiny snow crystal contains about 1,000,000,000,000,000,000 (1 quintillion) individual water molecules. When the water molecules freeze together, they arrange themselves into a crystal lattice. The basic form of an ice crystal is a tiny prism with six sides, a hexagon. The prism can be long, like a column. Or it can be nearly

flat, a six-sided plate.

The shape of a snow crystal depends mainly on the temperature and humidity in the region of the cloud where it formed. According to snow research in the lab at Caltech, plates and stars form at about 28°F. Columns and spiky needles appear at around 23°F. When the temperature drops to about 5°F, it's back to plates and stars. And so on, down to temperatures well below 0°F. The higher the humidity, the researchers say, the longer the needles, and the bigger the plates.

When humidity is high, snow crystals often grow into lacy, star-spoked shapes. Icy branches sprout when the hexagon's six jutting-out corners accumulate freezing water molecules faster than the body of the crystal.

Look at a snow crystal through a magnifying glass, and you'll see patterns within

Fast Fact

Once on the ground, the crystals gradually lose their delicate shapes, getting round and nondescript. So if you want to see snowflakes in all their glory, collect them on a dark cloth or mitten as they come down from the sky.

Snowflake Pep Talk

Of course you're special! There's not a snowflake like you in the entire universe. Or so they say...

SNOW DAYS: A RECIPE

For a really good snowfall, enough to build an impressive snowman, conditions must be just right. Beyond the big chill, moist air is a key ingredient in the snowy-day recipe. Snow, after all, is frozen, crystallized water. And warmer air is able to "hold" more water vapor than the same-size parcel of colder air. At 32°F, 1 cubic meter of air contains nearly 0.1 ounce of water. But at 0°F, the same-size parcel holds just 0.02 ounce. And at −40°F—a typical temperature in Antarctica— 1 cubic meter of air contains a mere 0.002 ounce. So as the temperature approaches 0°F, we see less snow, and smaller flakes. Scientists say that we're most likely to see fat, clumpy flakes fall from the sky when the temperature ranges from about 24°F to 32°F.

patterns, stars within stars. In the early 20th century, Vermont farmer Wilson "Snowflake" Bentley set out to photograph snow crystals in their infinite diversity and shimmering design. Bentley set up a big box camera and a microscope and caught falling snowflakes on squares of black fabric. The amazing images were later collected in the 1931 book *Snow Crystals*—more than 2,000 individual photographs. Bentley's book has been updated and is still in print, an indelible record of one of the most beautiful mysteries of winter.

Measure FOR Measure

−40°F = −40°C
32°F = 0°C
28°F = −2°C
23°F = −5°C
5°F = −15°C
0°F = −18°C
0.1 ounce = 2.96 ml
0.02 ounce = 0.59 ml
24°F to 32°F = −4°C to 0°C

Is it true that no two snowflakes are exactly alike?

Rare Crystals

Bahamian Banana Snow, a tropical delight

French Baguette Bread Snow, especially popular if the Brie is falling.

Barking Dachshund Snow, a winter's tale.

Ever hear someone say that two brothers or best friends are as "alike as two peas in a pod"? Green peas may not be perfectly identical, though they're featureless enough to fit the bill. But when it comes to being different or unique, most people usually think not of vegetables, but of snowflakes.

Even the most dissimilar snow crystals have something in common: six sides or points. Snow crystals are hexagonal because the water molecules they are made from link together into a six-sided lattice as they freeze. Photographs of snow crystals reveal miniature frozen landscapes. Hidden in snowflakes are inscribed stars and starbursts, flowers and fern fronds, often layered in dizzying kaleidoscopic patterns.

Scientists have found simple crystal columns

that at first glance look nearly identical. But even human identical twins aren't really identical, and two identical-looking simple crystals would be different on the molecular level.

However, no one has ever found two complex snow crystals that look exactly alike, and scientists say that the odds are low that they ever will. Each growing snow crystal follows its own meandering, bouncing path through a cloud. Crystals experience different temperatures and humidities, and are tossed and twirled different ways. How they drift to earth also determines their final shapes. As snow crystals grow, become heavier, and finally fall through and out of the cloud, their contours change. If they fall in a haphazard, sideways fashion, they end up lopsided. A snow crystal spinning like a top as it falls has the best chance at remaining symmetrical.

CAN A SNOWFLAKE HAVE MORE (OR FEWER) THAN SIX SIDES?

If you like looking for four-leaf clovers in spring, try catching an eight-spoked snowflake on your glove in winter . . . and good luck with that. You'll be in for a long, cold wait. Those crazy-eight flakes may be all over sweaters, scarves, hats, gloves, and holiday decor. But the one place you won't see them is falling from a wintry sky.

While designers may be all about the octagon, nature abhors the stop-sign flake. Except in special cases, snowflakes are hexagons—six-sided stars, plates, and columns. Snow's "sixness" goes all the way down to the molecular level. (Astronomer Johannes Kepler recognized this in 1611, when he wrote his essay "On the Six-Cornered Snowflake.")

Still, there are some snowflakes that at first glance seem to break the mold. One is the so-called triangular snowflake. These snowflakes resemble icy, three-sided triangles. According to a study by scientists at Caltech, such snowflakes may form when particles like dust glom onto one side of the snow crystal. The extra weight makes the snowflake fall at a tilt, with some sides collecting more ice than others.

The end result is a snowflake shaped like a "stubby triangle," with squared-off ends instead of points. But a closer look reveals six sides—three long sides connected by three short sides.

And then there are the rare but spectacular 12-sided flakes. These showy snowflakes are created when ice crystals called capped columns—hexagonal columns with a six-sided plate at each end—form with an inner twist. The result: a pinwheel snowflake, with 12 icy spokes.

How do clouds get electricity to make lightning?

Electricity is something we think is made in power plants, not in puffy masses of water droplets that you can put your hand right through. But there is electricity in clouds, and in this page, and even in you.

Everything is made of atoms, from clouds to trees to human beings. Each atom has a nucleus made up of positively charged protons and neutral neutrons. (Except for the simplest kind of hydrogen atom, which has one proton and no neutrons.) Orbiting the nucleus are negatively charged electrons. Positives and negatives attract, so the electrons circle the nucleus like bees swarming around a sweet roll.

The attraction between protons and electrons is caused by the electromagnetic force. So electricity is already present everywhere we look. It's just hidden inside atoms.

Ordinarily, the positive and negative charges balance each other out in each atom. So objects made of atoms—such as you—don't usually have a positive or negative electric charge. And you don't ordinarily go around zapping other people each time you touch them.

Sometimes, the electric charges in an object can become unbalanced. You've probably experienced this, perhaps on a cold winter day, in your toasty-warm home. Let's say the rooms are very dry. You go scuffing across the carpet. And, unbeknownst to you, some electrons in the rug and in your shoes get sheared away from their atoms.

Now *you* are electrically charged. The number of electrons and protons in you don't balance out. Touch a metal doorknob, and a tiny electric current will flow between you and it. You'll feel the shock. If it's dark, you can even see a spark. (The bright flash occurs because the electrons emit photons of light as they jump.) If it's quiet, you might hear a tiny crackle.

Electricity is always in and around us, and clouds are no exception. They look harmless enough on a bright sunny day. But just like you in your living room, a cloud can build up a charge. If it does, watch out. When a cloud puts its atoms back in balance, there are fireworks.

What happens is this: In dark, towering storm clouds, there are rushing air currents that cause particles in the cloud—including salt from the ocean, dust, soil, and soot—to slam into each other. The colliding particles loosen electrons. The particles then become electrically charged—positively charged if they lose electrons, negatively charged if they gain too many.

For reasons that aren't entirely known, heavier particles tend to get negatively charged, and lighter particles become positive. So the lower layers of the cloud, where the heavier particles fall, become negatively charged.

The negative bottom of the cloud attracts positively charged protons and repels any stray electrons on the Earth below. Soon, a positive charge builds up on the ground beneath the cloud. Then, just as electrons

jumped between you and the doorknob, a tremendous spark—a lightning bolt—connects the cloud and the ground. Electrons zigzag down, meeting protons on their way up from the ground. And instead of a tiny crackle, a clap of thunder erupts.

If we could watch the whole process in slow motion, this is what we would see: A dimly glowing bolt, called a leader, emerges out of the bottom of the cloud. The leader begins to jerkily move down toward the ground. First it jumps 150 feet down to the right, then 150 feet to the left. (That's the zigzag pattern we see in the sky.)

The leader's trip down takes only a fraction of a second. At this point, it carries an electric current of about 200 amperes (normal household current is 15 or 20 amps).

But when the bolt gets to within about 60 feet of the ground, a spark suddenly jumps out of the ground to join it. When the two sparks connect, the current races back up to the cloud, increasing to more than 10,000 amps as it goes.

Another leader snakes out and slams down the channel created by the upward stroke. Then another spark shoots back up to the cloud. Temperatures in the channel can reach 50,000°F. The lightning strokes—firing back and forth many times in less than a second—are what we see as a single bolt.

How much power is in a lightning bolt? Up to 20,000 megawatts, enough to run all the homes and businesses in an entire state—but only for a fraction of a second.

Fast Fact

Only about 25 percent of all lightning is cloud-to-ground. Most lightning flashes from one cloud to another, or within a single cloud.

Measure FOR Measure

150 feet = about 46 m
60 feet = about 18 m
50,000°F = 27,760°C

Does ball lightning really exist?

Close Encounters with Great Balls of Fire...

I saw one crash a party and win the dance contest.

I chased one down the street for a light.

I saw them on tour – they were great!

Stories of ball lightning date back to at least the Middle Ages, and scientists estimate that at least 5 percent of our planet's population have had the privilege (or, sometimes, the misfortune) of seeing the glowing, floating spheres.

According to eyewitnesses, ball lightning appears as a radiant sphere, ranging in size from a baseball to a basketball. It may be white, yellow, red, orange, or blue, and is usually no brighter than a 100-watt lightbulb.

The glowing ball often floats 2 to 6 feet (0.6 to 1.8 m) or more above the ground as it travels, sometimes spinning as it moves back and forth, here and there. After seconds—or minutes—the ball goes out with a hiss, pop, or a loud bang. Like a Fourth of

July sparkler, ball lightning may emit an acrid smell like burning sulfur or ozone, and leave smoke behind. Most ball lightning is seen just before or during a thunderstorm, within seconds of a lightning strike.

Millions have seen ball lightning float through windows and screen doors, cut telephone wires, fall into barrels of water with a sizzle. Passengers and crew on an airliner even watched ball lightning float down the aisle after their plane was struck by lightning.

But ball lightning is still an elusive mystery of science—hard to catch on film, with no agreed-upon explanation for how it works. Most ball lightning theories are extremely complicated, involving, for example, standing radio waves in spheres of plasma. But a newer, simpler theory—based in chemistry—may better explain this otherworldly display. The ingredients for ball lightning, the theory says, are everyday minerals and metals, whipped up by an energizing lightning strike.

John Abrahamson, a chemical engineer who teaches at the University of Canterbury in Christchurch, New Zealand, developed the new theory. He says that when a bolt of lightning hits the ground, it triggers a chemical reaction between silicon compounds and carbon in the soil. The huge blast of energy with its searing heat acts like a factory smelter, creating pure metallic silicon.

The resulting hot vapor of silicon is composed of tiny particles called nanospheres, each as small as a billionth of a meter (0.000000001 m). Trailing out of the hole in the ground carved out by the lightning, rising strings of silicon nanospheres form a spinning ring, rather like a cigarette smoke ring. The

Fast Fact

Ball lightning may be as big as a beachball, and may hiss or buzz menacingly.

ring coalesces into a ball of white-hot metal particles, floating through the air like a spherical fog. The ball's glow is stoked as the silicon particles react with oxygen in the air, keeping the sphere burning brightly for seconds or minutes.

Lit from within, the ball drifts through the air, a ghostly apparition. Eventually, like a fire burning down to ash, the ball runs out of silicon to burn, and disappears in a quiet poof. But if its temperature has risen high enough, ball lightning may also go out violently, with a loud bang.

Why do we see pictures in clouds?

In William Shakespeare's play *Hamlet*, Prince Hamlet and Polonius chat about a passing cloud. "Do you see yonder cloud that's almost in shape of a camel?" Hamlet asks. "By the mass, and 'tis like a camel indeed," replies Polonius.

But as the cloud changes, so does what the two see.

"Methinks it is like a weasel," Hamlet says. "It is backed like a weasel," Polonius notes. "Or like a whale?" Hamlet wonders. Polonius agrees: "Very like a whale."

Our human brains are hard-wired to look for patterns in the world around us. Is that a pile of black clothes on the floor, or

Midnight the cat? Is that a face in the bushes, or just the play of light and shadows? This behavior has survival value, which is why a dog may run toward a rabbit in the yard, only to find a disappointing pile of brown grass.

But while it might seem like a stretch to turn random

NAME THAT CLOUD!

For centuries, scientists and non-scientists proposed various schemes for categorizing clouds. In the 1660s, British scientist Robert Hooke developed a list of sky descriptions, including "checkered," for a summer sky with white fluffy clouds. In 1801, French scientist Jean-Baptiste Lamarck tried to categorize clouds into shapes like massed, dappled, and broomlike.

But in December 1802 in England, a pharmacist and amateur cloud-watcher named Luke Howard cut through the confusion with an elegant proposal. At a meeting in London, Howard presented a paper called "On the Modifications of Clouds." In it, he proposed classifying clouds into a few basic categories, based mainly on shape.

Howard gave the categories names in Latin, the international language of science: *cumulus* ("heap") clouds, the billowing, cauliflower-like clouds that make such good animal shapes. *Stratus* ("layer") clouds, which stretch like a blanket across the sky. And *cirrus* ("curl") clouds, high, icy, and feathery—the clouds that sometimes refract sunlight in rainbow patches. Howard proposed the name *nimbus* ("rain") for systems of clouds from which rain falls. Under the right conditions, sunny-day cumulus clouds can grow into towering cumulonimbus clouds, the thunderstorm-makers.

Howard's categories recognized that there is actually order in the seemingly infinite variety of clouds, that given certain conditions at various sky heights, recognizable cloud shapes would form. The new categories took the weather world by storm. They were soon adopted as the way clouds were categorized everywhere.

stars into Orion the Hunter, the shapes we see in clouds seem obvious to us. We can thank one particular kind of cloud, known as cumulus, for providing a perfect canvas for human imagination.

Fluffy cumulus clouds grow when a parcel of warm, moist air rises—say, from a big, hot parking lot—into higher, colder air. Cooling water vapor condenses around wind-blown bits of dust, clay, or salt. The result? A visible cloud, drifting through the air. Even as new droplets appear at the cloud's bottom, rising moisture evaporates at the top. This shapes cumulus clouds into cauliflower-like blossoms, as if the clouds were boiling.

It's our imagination, and what we've seen or read about, that puts pictures in clouds: cartoon characters, a pointing hand, or camel.

Since clouds change in seconds or minutes, roiling, drifting, disappearing, what we see changes, too. A dog's nose grows into an elephant's trunk; that scary *T. rex* dissolves into a much meeker sheep. To watch the show, just sit on the grass on a summer day. Better yet, bring a friend—and prepare to debate what you see.

Why are rain clouds black?

Dark Clouds Preferred...

By Painters... ...Poets Horror filmmakers

Mountains of the soul...

Mountains in the sky!

Mountains of evil!

A horizon full of dark, menacing storm clouds can be a scary sight. But the reasons rain clouds are black aren't so scary.

First, some basic cloud facts. We sit under an ocean of air that presses on each square inch of our bodies with nearly 15 pounds of force. Clouds form when moisture-laden air rises. As a clump of water-filled air climbs, it spreads out. (Why? Because high up, there is less air surrounding it, and so less air pressure.)

As the parcel of air expands, it cools like fudge spread on wax paper. When the air cools down to a temperature meteorologists call the dew point, its water suddenly condenses from invisible vapor to billions of visible droplets, glommed onto stray bits of dust, dirt, or smoke in the air. A cloud hangs in the sky, where there wasn't one before.

In a storm cloud, rain occurs when these droplets bump into others, and become so heavy that they fall out of the cloud. Or when ice crystals in the cold peaks of the cloud fuse into snowflakes, which melt as they fall to Earth.

Such storm clouds appear gray for several reasons, according to scientists. First, storm clouds are thicker than other clouds (some tower into the sky more than 6 miles), so not as much sunlight can pass through the cloud. Second, water droplets in storm clouds have grown to larger sizes than those in white clouds or fog. Larger drops absorb more light than smaller drops, which tend to scatter sunlight out into the sky. So a cloud with larger drops will appear darker than a cloud with tinier drops.

Finally, not all dark clouds are storm clouds. Some clouds appear dark with glowing white borders, simply because they are lit from behind by the Sun, and light can't easily penetrate their huge, billowing middles.

Older clouds can take on a gray or purple tint, too. Why? As a cloud "ages," most of its small water droplets evaporate into the atmosphere. That leaves fewer drops, and larger ones, which, as we now know, don't scatter sunlight as well. So older clouds are darker than fresh, young clouds, which sparkle in the sun.

Like everything in nature, clouds are always changing— and quickly, too. Clouds spend their hours drifting in the wind, losing droplets and then gaining more as they float into moisture-laden air.

A big cloud's brief life span is determined mainly by the Sun. Clouds stay aloft because of warm air currents rising from Earth's surface.

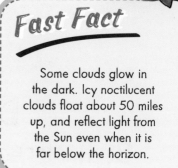

Fast Fact

Some clouds glow in the dark. Icy noctilucent clouds float about 50 miles up, and reflect light from the Sun even when it is far below the horizon.

After the Sun sets for the day, the Earth cools, radiating heat into outer space. As air currents gradually cool, too, there is not as much hot air rising to keep clouds— especially puffy cumulus clouds—afloat. So billowy clouds start to drop.

As a cloud sinks into the warmer air nearer our planet's surface, its droplets begin evaporating. Drop by disappearing drop, the cloud vanishes, never reaching the ground.

Measure FOR Measure

6 miles = 9.7 km
50 miles = 81 km

How can you smell an approaching rainstorm?

It shows up on lists of people's favorite smells, and evokes memories of summer afternoons past, a scent on the air accompanied by the distant rumble of thunder. No one is sure about the complete recipe for the fragrance of approaching rain. But scientists think they've identified the major ingredients.

Surprisingly, the scent recipe doesn't include ozone. Many people think the approaching storm smell comes from ozone produced by lightning, but most scientists say that's unlikely. If you've ever stood on a subway platform in summer as a train pulled in, sparks flying, or watched a fireworks display, you've probably gotten a whiff of ozone. The sharp smell is very different from the fresh scent of approaching rain. Plus, according to scientists, most ozone produced in thunderstorms ends up several miles high in the atmosphere, not down near the ground.

So while traces of ozone waft through the air in and around a thunderstorm, it can't be a main ingredient in the scent of rain. And (pure) water itself has no scent. According to researchers, we have to look elsewhere for the smell—not in the approaching clouds, but in the Earth itself.

When rain is on the way, the air around us becomes saturated with water. High humidity helps our noses function better, and moist air is also good at wafting odors our way, both pleasant and not. Just think of the intoxicating smell of honeysuckle on a summer breeze—or the pungent odor of garbage, baking in a trashcan.

So as a storm approaches, some of the fragrance notes come from volatile molecules released from plants when humidity soars, such as the terpenes in the oily droplets from pine trees. The combined scents create a clean, forest-y smell.

But the most important scent note in the "rain smell," scientists say, is actually created by bacteria. When the air is warm and humid, bacteria called *Streptomyces*, belonging to the group of bacteria known as *actinomycetes*, flourish in soil. But when the soil dries out, the filament-shaped bacteria produce spores. Rain pelting on dry ground sends particles of soil into the air, carrying these tiny spores.

Scientists say that the main scent in the smell of rain comes courtesy of geosmin, an organic compound in the spores and soil. (Geosmin is also the source of the smell

Fast Fact

In the 1960s, Australian scientists I. J. Bear and R. G. Thomas coined the term "petrichor" for the smell of rain hitting hot, dry earth. Petrichor combines *petros*, Greek for "stone," and *ichor*, the fluid flowing through the veins of mythic Greek gods.

we think of as "good soil.") As it turns out, human beings are exquisitely sensitive to geosmin, able to detect its familiar fragrance in as few as five parts per trillion.

Wind carries these scents ahead of an approaching storm, so we "smell rain"—a sweet, earthy scent— even before the first drops arrive.

Why does thunder make different sounds, like a boom or a long rumble?

Ever unfurl a polyester blanket in a dry room? In the dark, tiny sparks will fly. And those snaps, crackles, and pops you hear? Think of them as mini-thunder. Real thunder also snaps, crackles, and pops. But the snaps are cracks, the crackles are rumbles, and the pops are deafening *BOOM*s.

Thunder is the sound trail left by lightning. Lightning announces its arrival in cracks and booms by superheating the air it zigzags through. Just as a spark jumps between your finger and a doorknob in winter, lightning sparks within clouds or between clouds and the ground.

A lightning bolt is an electric current sizzling through the air, connecting positive and negative charges. A typical household current lighting your bedside lamp is 20 amps; the current in a bolt of lightning averages 30,000 amps.

Not surprisingly, this enormous electrical current has a dramatic effect on the air. Within a fraction of a second, the temperature in the air channel carved out by the bolt can reach 50,000°F—much hotter than the 10,000°F surface of the Sun.

The result? The superheated air expands violently, exploding outward in a cylinder-shaped shock wave. Cooling as it goes, the shock wave decays into an ordinary sound wave within a few feet. When the wave reaches our ears, we hear the explosive sound of thunder.

(How come we see lightning before hearing thunder? Light zips along at more than 983 million feet per

Modern Thunder Gods...

Thork... ...Revered by skate boarders his falls shake the heavens...

Big Brat... ...feared by moms, his tantrums convulse the skies...

Miss Munchie BOOM! BOOM! Knocks you out of bed when she falls off her diet.

second; ordinary sound waves travel through air at a pokey 1,100 feet per second. So the flash reaches our eyes before the rumble strikes our ears. To figure out how far away a lightning strike is, count the seconds—"one Mississippi, two Mississippi"—until you hear thunder. Then multiply by 1,100 to get the distance in feet.)

So why doesn't all thunder sound the same? See a lightning bolt flash, hear a dynamite-type explosion seconds later?

Thunder's sound effects depend on lightning's distance, conditions in the atmosphere, and the shape of the Earth in your area, as well as the presence (or absence) of big buildings.

Sound waves arrive at your ears from along the length of a distant lightning channel. The waves must travel different distances, and reach your ears at slightly different times. The closer waves, which reach you first, will be the loudest. Waves that travel longer through the air, dissipating as they go, will sound softer. (Also, longer, low-frequency waves can more easily bend around objects to reach our ears.) The result is that familiar low "rumble."

The longer the channel of lightning (some zigzag 4 miles high), the longer-lasting the sound. Thunder's sound waves also reflect off of mountains, canyons, and big buildings, adding echo effects to the drawn-out rumbling.

But if you're close to a striking bolt, you'll be startled by a sudden *CLAP* or *BANG*. Why? Many high-frequency sound waves from the channel will reach you at the same instant; the closer you are to the expanding shock wave, the louder and more explosive the bang.

THUNDER TALES

Cracks, rumbles, and rolls: As you read this, some 2,000 thunderstorms are in booming progress around Earth, with lightning striking the ground about 100 times each second. It's no wonder so many cultures invented thunder gods to explain the terrible sounds.

In Europe there was red-bearded Thor, who wielded a mean hammer that returned like a boomerang. The Chinese had Lei Gong, a creature with a blue body, claws, and bat wings who beat out thunder with a mallet and drum. In ancient Sumeria it was Ninhar, the roaring bull (married to the much nicer Ninigara, the Lady of Butter and Cream). And some North American native peoples revered the mythical "thunderbird." Lightning flashed from the bird's beak; thunder was the reverberation of its great beating wings.

Measure FOR Measure

50,000°F = 27,760°C
10,000°F = 5,538°C
983 million feet per second = 299.6 million m/s
1,100 feet = 335 m
4 miles = 6.4 km

Why do raindrops seem to fall at a slant when you're riding in a car?

Rain slanting against the windshield as a car drives down a dark country road—can a spooky old house *not* be just around the bend? It's a familiar scene in the movies. But it also rains sideways when you're riding the school bus home—with nary a haunted house in sight.

Wind can blow raindrops sideways, making umbrellas useless as rain pelts your legs. But even when there's no wind, rain will appear to fall slantwise when you see it through the windows of a moving car or other vehicle.

How come? It all depends on your frame of reference. A reference frame could be the inside of your house, the cabin of an airplane, a moving elevator, the back of a merry-go-round horse, the front seat of your car, the surface of a planet—the list is endless.

Depending on your reference point, an object in motion can be seen as moving in different directions. When you drop a penny inside a rising high-speed elevator car, the penny is falling from your reference point. But from the building's reference

Fast Fact

Rather like a car speeding through raindrops, the Earth speeds through starlight on its journey around the Sun. This makes the starlight appear to shift sideways to observers on the ground. Which is why Polaris, the Pole Star, seems to trace a little oval in the sky over the course of a year. Likewise, it's such apparent shifts in the stars that let us deduce that the Earth is, in fact, moving.

point, the penny is rising along with the elevator.

Which brings us to the moving auto. If you were standing on the sidewalk watching a car go by in the rain—on a windless day—the raindrops would appear to fall straight down, the car passing under the perpendicular curtain of water.

But to a passenger inside, it's a different movie. The car is driving forward through the rain at a certain speed. Everything outside the car appears to be moving at an equal speed *backward*. And that includes the raindrops. But the raindrops have a velocity downward, too. So from the passenger point of view, raindrops appear to fall at an angle between the two directions (down and back)— at a slant.

Why is it so quiet after a snowfall?

SOUNDPROOFING WITH FRESHLY FALLEN SNOW...

At the Library...

"It's quiet but freezing!"

In the Recording Studio...

"It's insulated for sound Not temperature"

In your bedroom... the noise of your chattering teeth..."

The snow is falling thick and fast, piling up so quickly that those footprints you recently made have all but disappeared. Also deepening is the sound of silence, as a white blanket is drawn over the landscape.

How come? Some of the quiet is because there are fewer sounds to hear: Birds aren't chirping; drivers are avoiding the roads; people are huddled indoors with cups of warm cocoa and hot tea, noses occasionally pressed against the glass to watch the swiftly falling flakes.

But there is more to snowy silence than the absence of activity. A truck lumbers by, but its grinding brakes and rattling cargo are strangely muted. A dog's bark in the distance sounds muffled.

The hush isn't due to the falling flakes absorbing sounds; the quiet lasts for hours after the snow has stopped. In fact, when we wake up on a winter morning, we may know it has snowed even before we look out the window, simply because of the soft silence.

Scientists say that as new snow piles up on bare ground or old snow, it's the arrangement of the flakes that dampens sounds. Snow crystals come in varied shapes and sizes, from flat plates to pointy stars, and each big flake can be made of dozens of crystals. So as snowflakes land, they don't make a compact, jigsaw-puzzle layer. Instead, they pile up loosely, with plenty of air-filled spaces in between. These spaces or pores in the snow absorb sound, like the pores in acoustic ceiling tiles.

Piled-up flakes have two main effects on sound. Sound waves that would normally hit bare ground or concrete and be partially reflected are instead mostly absorbed into the blanket of snow. More important, sound waves traveling parallel to the snow get muffled, too.

According to researchers, as sound waves travel across a layer of fluffy snow, the pressure of the passing waves briefly pushes air down into the spaces between flakes. So the waves lose more and more energy due to friction and thermal (heat) effects in their sweep across the pore-filled snow layer. By the time snow-skimming sound waves reach your ears, they are weakened. And you hear a softer, more muffled sound.

In fact, experiments show that what would make a loud bang in summer (like a firecracker or a banging trash can lid) makes a quiet *whoomp* in a winter landscape covered with fresh snow. And the sound will not only be softer, but also wavering and drawn out.

But a layer of newly fallen snow, piled up in a delicate stack of oddly shaped flakes, is fragile. Blowing wind flattens it. Sunlight melts it. A freezing rain collapses

When we awake on a winter morning, we may know it's snowed even before we look outside because of the soft silence.

it and adds a coating of solid ice on top. Once the delicate layer caves, its sound-muffling quality (sadly) disappears. The more hard-packed the snow, the more it acts like bare ground or concrete, reflecting and transmitting sound. And noise rises to nearly normal levels.

How do icicles form? Why do they have pointy ends?

The life cycle of an Icicle

A baby is born...

Waaa!

middle age...

Check out my ridges!

The End...

Eeeek!

A snow-covered roof on a sunny but frigid day makes a perfect icicle incubator. Sunlight heats the rooftop snow, which is also warmed from below by heat radiating from the attic. As the snow melts, water trickles down the roof to the icy-cold edges and metal gutters.

Since metal is such a good conductor of thermal energy, the water quickly loses heat to the gutter. And so it refreezes, forming an icy ridge.

As water continues to run down the roof, pulled by gravity, it collects where its fellow molecules have already frozen. (Water molecules are attracted to other water molecules.) Ice adds to ice, drip by drip. And slowly, an icicle grows toward the ground.

But it's not just dripping water that fuels the growth of an icy spike. The temperature of the liquid water dripping off the roof is higher than that of the freezing air. Heat energy flows from warmer objects to cooler objects. So heat diffuses from the thin film of water coating the icicle's surface into the colder air around it.

As it loses some of its heat, the water film freezes, piling on another layer of ice to the growing icicle. The icicle's growth is amplified by a peculiar feature of water: Liquid water actually expands as it freezes (which is why ice cubes bulge out of a tray).

Ever notice an icicle's bumpy ridges? Scientists say the bumps start out as small, random bulges. Since they jut out into the air, these bulges lose heat more quickly than other areas of the icicle. So trickling-down water refreezes on the bumps first, making them thicken into ridges.

The ridges are spaced about 0.4 inch apart, whether the icicle is big or small. And scientists in Japan think they know why: As a ridge gets bigger, the water trickling over it is churned more, like a stream flowing over a rock. The churning water doesn't carry heat away as efficiently, slowing down the ridge's freezing. So a regular pattern of ridges forms, rather than one humongous ice bump.

And what about that sharp point? The secret to an icicle's sharp point is the surrounding air. As water flows down the ice, loses heat to the air, and refreezes, a mini-updraft of warmed air whooshes up the icicle. This warmer air surrounds the top of the icicle like a blanket.

Since the top of the icicle is warmer than the bottom, it grows very slowly. Meanwhile, as long as water continues to drip, the tip grows faster than the base. The result: a long, tapering icicle—with a very pointy end.

Fast Fact

Icicles hanging on a gutter are often as regularly spaced as birds on a wire. Why? Drops of melted water grow as big as they can at the edge of a cold roof before they freeze or fall off. According to some scientists, this results in a certain minimum distance between the drops—and a rather uniform spacing along the roof for a line of icicles.

Spiky, glittering icicles can grow 5 or more feet long before their own weight causes them to crash to the ground, sometimes taking gutters (or tree branches) with them.

Measure FOR Measure
0.4 inch = 1 cm
5 feet = 1.5 m

How does salt melt ice on roads in winter?

Sidewalk Condiments...

The oregano and the dill didn't melt anything, let's try basil.

When salt is sprinkled on an icy sidewalk or road, holes are punched through the snow and ice. It's a mystery: How can a cold bag of salt act like hot gravel?

Here's how it works. In liquid water, molecules slip-slide past one another. The molecules' chemical bonds hold the liquid together. But molecules are always separating and reattaching to other molecules across the way, like dancers at a square dance.

The liquid dance of molecules happens when they are at the right temperature (and pressure). Apply enough heat, and—like dancers escaping an overheated auditorium—the water molecules gain enough thermal energy to fly apart, turning into a gas. At ordinary air pressure, water turns to steam at 212°F and up.

Take too much heat away—chill the water to 32°F and below—and the molecules gradually lose energy. Unable to continue their do-si-do, they will cling stiffly together, turning to ice.

But even when water turns to ice, there is still movement. Individual molecules vibrate slightly in their lattice of crystal. And freezing isn't a smooth process. Some molecules, still in the liquid phase, bump into the forming ice and stick. Others break free from the icy patch and return to being liquid. At 32°F, a parcel of water is balanced between freezing and melting.

All this brings us to salt. Molecules of salt (sodium chloride) are made of linked-up sodium and chlorine atoms. Water molecules are made of two hydrogen atoms and one oxygen atom. Because of how its atoms are arranged, a water molecule generates a tiny electric field.

When salt is dumped onto ice, there is an immediate reaction. Salt molecules come into contact with the electric field of water molecules. This electric field tugs the salt molecules apart. The

Adding salt lowers water's freezing point.

separated atoms are called "ions," because they have an electrical charge. Sodium ions are positive, chloride ions negative. Water molecules, feeling an electrical attraction, cluster around the ions.

The H_2O molecules hanging around the dissolved salt don't glom onto the forming ice. Meanwhile, remember, other water molecules naturally are breaking free from the ice. The result? Since more water is turning from ice to liquid than from liquid to ice, the ice melts. Adding salt short-circuits the freezing process. So salt, in effect, lowers the freezing point of water.

(In fact, dissolving any substance in water—from sugar to alcohol—will do the same thing. Salt is simply cheap and available. And on just 1 mile of pavement, it takes 500 pounds of salt to form a brine of saltwater to keep ice from re-forming.)

However, as the temperature plummets, more water molecules freeze onto ice than escape into liquid, requiring extra salt. Below about 25°F road crews use salt with added calcium chloride, increasing its melting effect. As the temperature drops near 0°F and below, workers spread grit to give tires more traction, since salt mixtures can't keep up with the freezing.

Measure FOR Measure

212°F = 100°C
32°F = 0°C
1 mile = 1.61 km
500 pounds = 226.8 kg
25°F = −4°C
0°F = −18°C

What causes fog?

FOG WEAR
FOR THOSE DAYS when you can't see your hand
IN FRONT OF YOUR FACE

And For real PEA SOUPERS: the Spoon pendant

Lighthouse cap

sensor belt

Warning Bell earrings

Fog is a cloud that hugs the ground. Usually, fogs are made of tiny droplets of water. The droplets sink and then rise again, carried by currents in the air. Sometimes they fall to the ground like rain, but new droplets appear to take their place.

Where do fogs come from? Fogs spring out of the air, where there are always water molecules zipping around. The water molecules jump into the air from oceans, rivers, lakes, and plants, evaporating (turning to water vapor) like water left in the bottom of a glass.

Warm air can hold a lot of water vapor. But as air cools, it reaches its saturation point, like an overfull sponge about to drip. And then, water molecules suddenly condense into visible droplets. Water shapes itself into drops by glomming onto particles of dirt, dust, salt, or pollutants in the air. A liquid droplet forms around a tiny particle, like the grain of sand at the heart of a pearl.

Droplets grow bigger as more and more water molecules collect together.

ICY FOGS

When the temperature plunges well below 0°F (say, to −40°F), fogs made of glittering ice crystals can appear and hang in the air. "Ice fogs" are similar to the icy clouds high in Earth's atmosphere, in which water molecules freeze into ice crystals instead of condensing into liquid droplets.

"Freezing fogs" can appear at slightly higher temperatures. These are made of tiny droplets of supercooled water (with a temperature below 32°F, water's normal freezing point). The fogs waft against tree branches, park benches, car windows. On the cold surfaces, the frigid droplets suddenly freeze into ice crystals—leaving a decorative coating of icy, feathery shards everywhere they touch.

As droplets grow and more droplets form, a light haze can thicken to a dense fog.

The kind of fog that forms at night and hangs around until morning is called a radiation fog. After the sun goes down, the surface of Earth and the air above it cool, radiating away the heat stored during the day. If the air is moist or the cooling very great, a cloud of water droplets may form above the ground. (At night, riding down a dip in a country road, you may suddenly find yourself in a thick fog that your car headlights can't penetrate. That's because cold air tends to sink down the sides of hills and into valleys, carrying heavy fogs with it.)

A radiation fog becomes thickest in the morning, just after sunrise. Why? The first rays of the sun don't heat the air enough to burn off the fog. But the warming air becomes more turbulent. The cool air spreads, making a thicker layer of fog.

As the morning wears on, however, the air heats up. The water evaporates, the droplets splitting into molecules and whizzing off into the air. And the fog disappears.

Another kind of fog forms when warm rain from high clouds falls into a cooler layer of air near the ground. The cool air becomes saturated with water from evaporating raindrops, and fog forms. This fog is similar to the steam that rises from a tub of hot water into the cooler air of the bathroom.

Measure FOR Measure
0°F = −18°C
−40°F = −40°C
32°F = 0°C

How come we see our breath in the cold?

In cold weather, we all become cloud machines. Take the dog for a walk on a wintry morning, and you and Fido puff out a series of tiny white clouds, marking your progress down the road before they disappear behind you.

If the temperature is cool enough, we can see our breath in any season. And just like clouds in the sky and fog near the ground, our visible breath is actually a swirling mist of water vapor.

How does it work, and why don't we see our breath on balmy summer afternoons? It all depends on the air around us.

Earth's atmosphere is a mixed collection of gases. Lurking among the nitrogen, oxygen, and other gases is a

In cold weather, we all become cloud machines.

constantly varying amount of water vapor. Up to about 4 percent of the molecules in a parcel of very warm, humid air may be water vapor; the average is about 2 to 3 percent.

When the air's temperature drops, its molecules have less energy, and pack closer together. Air can only hold a certain amount of water vapor, based on its temperature. When

the "relative humidity" of air reaches 100 percent, the air is holding all the water vapor it can. The air is said to be saturated. When the temperature drops further, some of the vapor condenses out of the air into liquid droplets, as clouds or fog. (Imagine an overfull sponge starting to drip.)

Breath fog forms when the temperature drops, too. On a warm day, the water vapor you exhale (along with carbon dioxide) simply spreads out as H_2O molecules into thin air. And your breath stays invisible.

But when the air outside your body is chilly-to-frigid, it can't hold as much water

vapor as the nicely warmed air inside your lungs. Before you exhale, neither the cold air near your face nor the warm air coming from your lungs is completely saturated with water. But when exhaled water molecules hit the cold air, the small parcel of air in front of your face suddenly becomes "supersaturated" with water.

Result: The water vapor immediately condenses into droplets, forming a tiny cloud. But as the droplets spread out into the wider air, they evaporate, just as a jet's condensation trail fades into the sky.

There is no set temperature at which you will begin to see your own breath. Whether water vapor condenses into droplets depends on both the temperature and the local air pressure. But you will almost certainly see a small cloud with each exhale when the thermometer drops below about 45°F (7°C).

Why do jet airplanes leave trails in the sky that look like clouds?

It's a bird, It's a Plane, It's the Weather Report! 60% chance of rain

A jet climbing the vault of heaven can look like a comet streaking across the sky, trailed by a streaming, glowing tail. Watching the jet trail, you may have noticed its resemblance to those high, streaky clouds known as cirrus. The Latin word *cirrus* means "curl" or "tendril." Icy cirrus clouds look like fluffy locks of hair.

The resemblance of a jet trail to a cirrus cloud is more than skin deep. In fact, a jet trail *is* a cirrus cloud, one produced by the engines of a jet airplane rather than by the sky itself.

Clouds form when water vapor collects in drops around

> 🔍 If the air around a high-flying jet is very moist, you will see the jet growing a longer and longer tail, streaming across the sky.

floating particles of dirt, smoke, plant pollen, or salt in the sky. A jet's cloud is no exception. The water vapor comes from the jet's engines. And the particles come from the jet's exhaust, which spews out incompletely burned particles of sooty smoke.

Because jets fly so high—above 30,000 feet—the air around them is very cold. (When you are flying to visit a far-off relative, the air just outside the window next to your seat, no matter how sunny the day, may be 70°F below zero.) In such cold temperatures, it takes just seconds for the water vapor from the engines to freeze around exhaust particles behind the jet, leaving a long, streaming, icy cloud. (This cloud is also called a contrail, short for "exhaust condensation trail.") A jet is a flying cloud machine.

If the air around the jet is very dry, the contrail cloud will disappear almost as quickly as it forms, as the water dissipates into the cold air. That's why you sometimes see a jet with a short stubby trail, or no trail at all.

But if the air around a high-flying jet is already nicely moist, you will see the jet growing a longer and longer tail, streaming grandly across the sky from one end to the next. You'll notice the end of the trail, the oldest part, ballooning out. That's the cloud swelling as it slowly dissipates into the air. In moist air, a jet cloud can last for hours, drifting through the sky like any other wispy cirrus cloud.

Glowing in the golden light of the setting sun, a jet trail may be one of the most beautiful clouds in the sky. Jet trails can even be used to predict the weather. If a passing jet leaves no trail or one that quickly disappears, then you know the air high up is dry. That usually means that the weather will be clear and dry, too. But jet clouds that last long enough to span the sky mean that the upper atmosphere is full of moisture, a good indication that rain or snow is on the way.

Measure FOR Measure
30,000 feet = 9,144 m
−70°F = −57°C

ANIMAL (AND PLANT) WORLD

Earth was made for life. In cosmic terms, it happened like a shot—the Earth formed some 4.5 billion years ago, and by about 2.9 billion years ago, the planet's first tiny life, the cyanobacteria, had already appeared. How did we get from bacteria to dinosaurs and dragonflies, porcupines and people? Millions of years of evolution took care of that.

Look around even your own small patch of Earth, or sit in a city park, and you'll have a window on the amazing variety of creatures alive today. Trilling songbirds (some 4,000 kinds). Flowering plants (some 400,000 kinds). Bushy-tailed squirrels (more than 270 varieties). Crawling, flying, buzzing insects (more than a million kinds). Giraffes with necks stretching 6 feet; elephants with ears hanging 5 feet. One study estimates that there are more than 8.7 million separate species of plant and animal life on Earth, most of them undiscovered. At the same time, scientists estimate that billions of species of plants and animals have lived on Earth so far—and that more than 99 percent of them have disappeared.

Have you ever wondered *why* an elephant's ears are so outsize? Why so many animals have tails—but we don't? Why dogs bark? How birds know where south is? Why leaves change color in the fall? How a fly can walk up a wall? Take a safari into the heart of Earth's profusion of life—and find out.

Why do plants take in carbon dioxide, while we take in oxygen?

Billions of human beings, and quintillions of other animals (including insects) continuously take in oxygen and release carbon dioxide. Meanwhile, fires burn day and night all over the planet, consuming oxygen as they do. So why doesn't carbon dioxide gas build up in the air? And why doesn't oxygen simply disappear over time?

It took scientists centuries to solve the puzzle. In 1771, British scientist Joseph Priestley noted that a candle flame would go out if covered by a glass jar. But after he put a green plant under the jar, the candle would stay lit. Green plants seemed to give off something that a flame takes away. That "something" turned out to be oxygen. But how do plants do it—and why?

All over the world, as you read this, oxygen is escaping into the air—from trees in the forest, algae in the park pond, the oceans' tiny phytoplankton. On land, the process is invisible: We can't see oxygen gas leaving plants, any more than we can see it in the air we breathe. But underwater, we can actually watch as bubbles of oxygen seep out of waving plants. The result? Earth's air is about one-fifth oxygen gas— perfect for us to breathe.

Here's how it works. Green plants use energy from the Sun to make their own food—sugar. To make it, they also pull water from the soil and carbon dioxide from the air. Oxygen is released as plants make dinner, like the lovely scent wafting from a bakery making bread.

The process is called photosynthesis, from Greek words meaning "putting together with light." And it's the green pigment in plant leaves that starts the process. Green chlorophyll uses energy from sunlight (mainly its red and blue wavelengths) to split H_2O molecules apart, leaving

PHOTOSYNTHESIS FAMILY STYLE...

I don't care if Jr. holds his breath till he turns brown! NO more carbon dioxide today!

oxygen, hydrogen ions, and electrons. (A hydrogen atom is one positively charged proton orbited by a negatively charged electron. With its electron removed, a hydrogen atom has a positive change; charged atoms are called ions.)

Plant cells use these atomic raw materials in a series of complex chemical steps. A compound called ATP is formed, and a molecule in the plant called NADP is altered. In the end, carbon dioxide is used to make a carbohydrate—

glucose (sugar). Presto: plant food! Meanwhile, leftover oxygen escapes into the air. And we breathe easy.

About 70 percent of the oxygen we breathe comes from ocean-dwelling plants, with 28 percent supplied by the rain forests. The photosynthesis of plants and the respiration of animals tend to balance each other out. But since the 1800s, carbon dioxide levels have been increasing. Carbon dioxide traps heat from the Sun, and too much CO_2 creates a "greenhouse effect," raising

Earth's average temperatures. Scientists say the result is melting ice sheets and rising seas, extended heat waves and extreme weather, massive flooding in some places and long droughts in others, crop failures, and, over time, the likely disappearance of many species of plants and animals.

Figuring out how to use less coal, oil, and gas, which produce carbon dioxide when burned, is the first step. Equally important are protecting Earth's oceans and ending the destruction of the rain forests.

Why do the leaves change color in the fall?

Autumn's cool days are trimmed with deep blue skies and golden light, and brilliant leaves of yellow, orange, and red. Leaves changing color in the fall are a tree's way of preparing for long winter, rather like how we put up storm windows and pull warm clothes and blankets out of storage.

In summer, the leaves on trees like pin oaks and sugar maples are green, because they are chock-full of the green pigment chlorophyll.

Trees need sunlight to produce chlorophyll. In turn, chlorophyll uses sunlight's energy to split water (H_2O) into hydrogen and oxygen. Meanwhile, leaves also absorb carbon dioxide gas from the air. The end

> Chilly weather causes chemical reactions that make radish-red pigments in some leaves.

products of leaf chemistry: carbohydrates (homemade plant food for the tree), and oxygen, released into the air (the gas we need to breathe). The whole process is called "photosynthesis."

Along with green chlorophyll, most leaves also contain yellow, orange, and red-orange pigments, the carotenoids. Trees don't need

light to make carotenoids. Botanists call them helper pigments, because carotenoids absorb some sunlight and (nicely) pass the energy along to chlorophyll. We don't see much of these deputy pigments (carotene, lycopene, and xanthophyll) in summer, because they are masked by abundant green chlorophyll.

But the ever-shortening days of fall mean less daylight and colder weather. The average tree is rushing to save all the nutrients it can for its winter hibernation. Nitrogen and phosphorus are pulled from leaves for storage in branches. A layer of corky cells grows between the leaves' stems and their branches, reducing the leaves' supply of nutrients and water.

With diminished sunlight, water, and nutrients, chlorophyll synthesis slows. But old, worn-out chlorophyll breaks down at the usual rate—ironically, sunlight destroys it—so each leaf's stock gradually dwindles. In many trees, as the green fades, yellow and orange pigments emerge from hiding. (These include carotenes, the pigments that color carrots orange.)

But red and purple pigments first form in leaves when the weather turns chilly, tinting leaves of some trees scarlet and burgundy. (The pigments are anthocyanins, which also make radishes red, eggplants purple, and blueberries blue.) Botanists have long wondered why some trees are genetically programmed to manufacture anthocyanins in the fall. New research indicates that anthocyanins may be a tree's own sunscreen.

Anthocyanins are made in a leaf's sugary sap, with the help of lots of sun and cool temperatures. Botanists think that anthocyanins shield the leaves' fading photosynthesis factories from too much sunlight, rather like the pigment melanin protects our skin from the sun. While the red pigments act as a shield, the tree feverishly breaks down and pulls nutrients out of leaves and into its limbs and trunk, before the leaves drop or die.

Anthocyanins may also act like vitamins C or E, scavenging so-called free radicals before they can do oxidizing damage to a fall leaf's fragile structure.

Upper and outer leaves tend to be reddest, since they are most exposed to sunlight and cold. In some trees, like sugar maples, the reds of the anthocyanins combined with the yellows of the carotenoids make especially brilliant orange leaves.

The color that leaves turn is mostly inherited, like our hair color. But whether these colors are dull or bright depends on the weather.

The deepest, most brilliant shades develop after weeks of cool, sunny fall weather. For example, when the temperature drops to between 32°F and 45°F (0°C and 7°C), more anthocyanins form. In the United States, the ideal weather for stunning foliage is found in places like Vermont.

As autumn fades to winter, the colors fade, too, and leaves loosen from their moorings. Leaves are held to branches by their stems. As the weather cools, the cells at the end of each stem fall apart. Eventually, each leaf is held to its branch only by the thin veins through which water and nutrients once flowed. A light wind or rain can break these flimsy threads, sending the leaves drifting to earth in a carpet of color.

The yellow and red pigments may stay in the leaves for days after they have fallen to the ground.

Fast Fact

Trees store up food for winter, just like chipmunks and squirrels do. Only instead of burying nuts in the ground, trees store nutrients in their branches, trunks, and roots.

Gradually, though, the colorful pigments disintegrate. All that's left is the tannins— brown chemicals that also color tea.

The now-brown leaves, cut off from their water supply, dry up. Picked up by the wind, they whirl through the air in leafy cyclones, and crackle underfoot on Halloween.

Why does poison ivy make us itch?

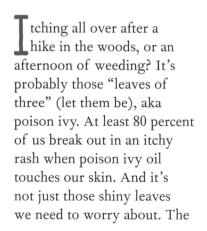

Leaves of three...

Makes a lovely bouquet...

...Charming jewelry...

...Delightful decoration on a gift...

No Way!

Yikes!

Thanks for thinking of me... NOT!

Itching all over after a hike in the woods, or an afternoon of weeding? It's probably those "leaves of three" (let them be), aka poison ivy. At least 80 percent of us break out in an itchy rash when poison ivy oil touches our skin. And it's not just those shiny leaves we need to worry about. The whole poison ivy plant is a menace, from the bottom of its roots to the tip of its stems.

The culprit is urushiol, a yellow oil that sneakily smears on your skin when you brush against any part of the plant. Because a microscopic amount of urushiol (one nanogram, or a billionth of a gram) can cause a reaction, you'll never notice it's there. Until, that is, hours later . . . when a red, itchy, blistering rash sprouts on arms, legs, or face. Just as some react to ragweed pollen by sneezing and sniffling, so do most of us react to urushiol as an attacking foreign body.

So if you think you've come into contact with poison

ivy, rush to the nearest sink and wash skin with cool or lukewarm soapy water. The idea: Remove the poison ivy oil before it bonds to skin proteins. And while touching a poison ivy blister can't spread the rash, urushiol left behind on clothes and shoes can cause a brand-new outbreak.

Hikers beware: It's not your grandmother's poison ivy out there. According to Lewis Ziska, a scientist who studies weeds and other plants for the U.S. Department of Agriculture, the growth rate of poison ivy may have doubled since the 1950s. In the past several years, experiments in the lab and in the forest have proved that poison ivy is thriving on pollution and global warming.

Researchers found that poison ivy plants exposed to higher levels of carbon dioxide, the greenhouse gas, reacted by getting bigger and stronger, outpacing the growth of other plants. And plants exposed to higher CO_2 make a much more toxic brew of urushiol. The result, say some doctors, may be an increase in rarer forms of the poison ivy rash, such as a red rash marked by black spots. Warmer weather and higher CO_2 levels mean that thriving poison ivy will probably continue to overtake other plants, crowding out friendlier vines and bushes.

What does poison ivy look like? Besides the groups of three green leaflets, which turn shades of red and yellow in the fall, poison ivy also sports tiny flowers and green or cream-colored berries. You may see it creeping up a tree, over a rock, up the side of a barn, or in small bunches along a trail. Poison ivy can

Fast Fact

Swallowing poison ivy is especially dangerous, since the result could be a swollen-shut throat, preventing breathing. Never throw poison ivy into a fire; breathing the burning oil can cause a fatal reaction in some people. All of which explains why poison ivy is the plant with its own warning rhyme: "Leaves of three? Let them be."

resemble other harmless plants, like Virginia creeper or wild blackberry. How to tell them apart? Unlike poison ivy, Virginia creeper has groups of five leaves, and blackberry bushes have sharp thorns.

How come flowers have scents?

Ever bury your nose in a rose and take a deep breath? Walk past a fence dripping with honeysuckle just to inhale the heavy perfume? Or breathe in the spicy scent of apple blossoms, bees buzzing all around?

If the scent of flowers attracts you, imagine what it does to insects, which can crawl right into the bloom's perfumed room. Bugs that feel the urge to climb inside a just-bloomed flower and scramble around inside are doing the flower's bidding— whether they know it or not. Their bodies become covered in pollen; when they move on to the next flower, some of the pollen falls off inside. When the pollen works its way into a flower's ovaries,

the plant has been fertilized.

A bumblebee who returns to her nest covered in the perfume of the nectar-filled flowers she found is like a scout who's returned with a scent map. As she buzzes around the nest, the bee also exudes a chemical called a recruitment pheromone. Other bumblebees get the message: "Let's go! There's food out there in flowers that smell like *this*."

Many flowering plants, like snapdragons, release their perfume between about 9 a.m. and 4 p.m., to match the local bees' work shift. Pollinating moths go nectar-hunting at night, so some flowers, like honeysuckle and evening primrose, release their sweet fragrance mostly after dark.

Each flower's fragrance is a unique recipe of a few to hundreds of chemical compounds.

Plants also tailor their perfumes: Some orchids produce scents that, to a male wasp, smell exactly like a female wasp.

But not all scents are pleasant. Interested in attracting a carrion fly or a dung beetle? Some plants are, and that's why their flowers smell like road kill or feces, rotten eggs or rotting fish. Among them are the corpse flower, the skunk cabbage, and the dead-horse arum. Repulsive to us, but quite the lure to many flies, who like nothing better than to lay their eggs in a decaying animal carcass.

Carrion Fly Florist Shop....

Smells like death and decay— my mom will love it!

Other flowering plants can adjust scents as needed, to attract insects that can fly to their rescue in an emergency. One yellow-flowered plant, wild turnip, can become overrun with voracious caterpillars. If so, it dials down its floral scent and releases a fragrance from its leaves that attracts parasitic wasps. The wasps arrive— and kill the caterpillars.

But following the scent trail to waiting flowers is becoming harder for bees and other pollinators. When plants are bred for qualities like new hues, oversized flowers, and disease resistance, their familiar fragrance can disappear. Which is why those rows of roses at the big-box store may be brightly colored, but sadly lacking their unforgettable scent.

Scientists say that in the 1800s, a flower's fragrance could travel nearly 4,000 feet. Today, the scent might be detectable for only 1,000 feet, thanks to masking air pollution. Flower odor molecules also bind with many air pollutants—causing their fragrance to vanish. Pollinators can't find as many flowers, plants don't thrive, and insects like bees, their food supply narrowing, decline even further.

Why is grass green?

Human beings evolved in verdant nature, not in beige cubicles, so we have a natural fondness for green. Green is calming; studies have shown that looking at an expanse of green actually lowers blood pressure.

Green is near the middle of the spectrum of light we call visible. Hidden in ordinary white light is a rainbow of brilliant colors—red, orange, yellow, green, blue, indigo, violet. Pass a beam of sunlight through a prism—or a raindrop—and the colors spread out like a peacock's tail.

Light travels in waves so tiny that they must be measured in billionths of a meter (nanometers). Different colors of light are simply different wavelengths of light. Waves of violet light, the most energetic kind of visible light, measure about 400 nanometers from crest to crest. Less energetic red light has waves about 700 nanometers long. Green is the happy medium: medium energy, with waves about 510 nanometers long.

Green light shimmers all around us outdoors. Grass is green for the same reason most tree leaves are green in

Grass is green for the same reason most tree leaves are green in summer: Each blade is shot through with chlorophyll.

summer: Each blade is shot through with chlorophyll, the ultimate green chemical.

How come? Plants whip up their own sugar diet, and chlorophyll is the key to plant luncheons. Chlorophyll uses energy from sunlight, carbon dioxide from air, and water from the earth and sky to manufacture carbohydrates for plants to consume and store. The process is called photosynthesis, which means "putting together with light."

During photosynthesis, a plant gives off molecules of oxygen, just as we exhale carbon dioxide. Which makes all the chlorophyll around us responsible for the oxygen in our atmosphere. Without oxygen to breathe, we wouldn't be here. No wonder seeing green lowers our blood pressure.

And interestingly, chlorophyll is nearly identical in structure to oxygen-carrying heme in the hemoglobin in our blood. In a chlorophyll molecule, the central atom is magnesium; in heme, the starring atom is iron. One tints plants green, the other colors blood red. (Chlorophyll is also a relative of vitamin B_{12}, which has cobalt in place of magnesium.)

There are actually two forms of chlorophyll, named (not so inventively) chlorophyll A and chlorophyll B. The two differ only in one side chain of atoms. But that slight difference means the chlorophylls complement each

Fast Fact

There is more green chlorophyll on Earth than any other pigment, which is why we see green just about everywhere we look.

other in the wavelengths of light that each absorbs.

The two chlorophylls absorb mainly the blue, violet, and red wavelengths of light. However, both turn up their nose at light with wavelengths around 500 nanometers, the green region of the spectrum. Using the rest of the visible light rainbow while rejecting green means that green is reflected or transmitted rather than absorbed. So green light streams out at us from every chlorophyll-rich object in the world—including blades of grass.

Why is the cashew the only nut you can't buy in its shell?

Cashews—the nut that sounds like a sneeze—are the oddballs of the nut world. Think of nuts on a tree, and you might imagine round walnuts hanging on the branches of a walnut tree, thudding to the ground in late summer or early fall. But cashews come in an elaborate disguise. A cashew wearing its shell looks exactly like a fat worm, wriggling out the bottom of a misshapen apple.

Evergreen cashew trees grow only in a tropical or subtropical climate. They can grow to be more than 40 feet (12.2 m) tall, their green leaves the backdrop for brightly colored cashew

A cashew shell looks like a fat worm, wriggling out the bottom of a misshapen apple.

apples, the tree's "false" fruit. Yellow or red cashew "apples" actually look like pears, or oversize hot peppers. The nuts protruding from the apples' undersides are the tree's real fruit. Hidden inside each nut is a single seed—a delicious cashew.

Why not pluck the nut and sell it with shell intact—like a walnut, pecan, or almond? The problem lies in the cashew's family tree. One of the cashew's close relatives is the pistachio, the tasty green (though often dyed red) nut used for snacks and ice cream. Another is the tropical mango. But other relatives—the black sheep of the Anacardiaceae family—include the not-so-nice poison sumac and poison ivy.

All of these plants contain urushiol, an oily chemical that makes a brush with poison ivy such a painfully itchy experience. The cashew's share of urushiols is concentrated in an oily liquid trapped between the two layers of the shell. (It's no wonder that an old name for the cashew was blister nut.)

Because of the lurking urushiols, cashews must be processed very carefully. The process of removing the shells and extracting the liquid includes roasting, burning, boiling, soaking, cracking, and peeling. Instead of being discarded, the cashew nutshell liquid (CNSL) is often sold for industrial uses. CNSL oils are used in waterproof paints, varnishes, and lacquers, while CNSL particles are used to create more friction in brake linings, so cars and trucks can stop on a dime.

Finally, the cashew seeds are cleaned and roasted. This leaves a batch of pristine (and urushiol-free) cashews, ready to eat.

Despite having poison ivy for a ne'er-do-well first cousin, cashews cause fewer allergic reactions than other nuts. But when cashew processing gets careless, there can be problems. In 1982, more than 50 Pennsylvanians who ate cashews sold by their local Little League ended up with poison-ivy–like rashes.

Fast Fact

The cashews we eat come mainly from India, Vietnam, Brazil, and a number of countries in Africa, including Nigeria and Tanzania.

The culprit: bits of cashew shells mixed in with the cashew pieces.

Fortunately, such glitches are rare. Cashews make an excellent snack, containing heart-healthy oils as well as a good mix of protein and carbohydrates.

Cashews: the Snack that Suffers...

Help!

I'm being roasted to death!

... Then boiled alive...

... Whacked and pulled apart!

I wish I was a peanut.

How can bats catch bugs in the dark?

Bats come out at dusk, swooping across yards and fields like flapping vacuum cleaners. While we can't see what they're doing in the dim light, they are actually snatching up insects as they go.

During the day, bats hang around home—in the rafters of a barn, a hollow tree, or a handy cave. A bat's day is spent dozing and grooming itself, mostly while upside down. (The weight of a bat's hanging body makes her specialized foot tendons go into auto-lock.)

Around sunset, bats fly off in search of food. While some bats eat fruit or frogs and tropical vampire bats feed on the blood of other animals (like cows), most

bats eat lots and lots of bugs. In fact, some can swallow 25 percent of their own weight in teeny insects in just half of a twilight hour. Some bats may catch more than 1,200 insects an hour.

Like many other animals, bats prefer to hunt under the cover of darkness. Bats use regular vision to navigate at dusk. But to locate insects, say, 40 feet away, bats rely on echolocation. Sound sent out and bounced back can detect the exact location of small insects flying across a background of trees, a feat that would be difficult or impossible using sight alone. And in total darkness, a bat can rely on this submarine-style sonar to keep from running into the nearest tree.

(Dolphins, many whales, and some shrews also use echolocation to move through the dark.)

How it works: Bats emit rapid, high-pitched chirps through their mouths or noses, using their big ears to listen for sound reflections. A bat may sweep your yard with sound at 10 or more blips a second, looking for insects. When the sounds echo off a bug, the bat chirps faster, to get a better sense of the insect's size and location.

Bats are mammals, animals that make milk to feed their young. Out of the more than 5,400 mammal species on Earth, more than 1,200 are bats—the only ones that can fly. And scientists think that bats may also be the only mammals with "superfast" muscles, which can contract 100 times faster than ordinary muscles.

Researchers knew that superfast muscles power the twitters and trills of songbirds, as well as a rattlesnake's rattle. Now they've discovered that the muscles also allow bats to take rapid-fire sonar snapshots of their surroundings. As a bat zeroes in on a bug, she may chirp 190 times a second; superfast muscles make it possible.

But many kinds of bats in North America are in danger of extinction, as a disease called white-nose syndrome spreads among cave-dwelling bats. The fungal infection causes hibernating bats to fly out into the frigid cold, using up their fat stores before spring. In some areas of the northeastern United States, bat populations have dropped by 80 percent. Scientists are working hard to understand what's causing the disease—and to keep it from spreading even further.

Bat habitats are also disappearing. Create a bat-friendly yard by avoiding pesticides, and letting part of the backyard go wild.

Bat Air Safety

Control to bat, you are approaching a large towerlike object!

How do fish breathe underwater?

Going for a swim? Be prepared to come up for air every few seconds. You might envy the effortless underwater swimming of fish. Still, their bodies, like our own, run on oxygen.

Of the gases in Earth's air, oxygen makes up about 21 percent, second only to nitrogen's 78 percent. But water is made from oxygen. That's why it's known as H_2O: Each molecule of water is shaped like a triangle, with two hydrogen atoms connected to one oxygen atom.

Multiply an H_2O molecule by uncountable zillions, and you've got a pond. (In fact, just 1 measly cup [0.24 l] of water contains nearly 8 septillion individual H_2O molecules. Written out, that's an 8, followed by a string of 24 zeroes.)

In each of those teeny water molecules, oxygen is tightly bound to hydrogen. So it's not freely available to anyone—human or fish— for "breathing." Thankfully for fish, besides the oxygen trapped in their pond's water molecules, there is oxygen gas dissolved throughout the water. (Think of carbon dioxide, dissolved in an unopened can of soda.) Fish filter out this unfettered oxygen, absorbing it into their bloodstream, where it's ferried to cells throughout the body.

But unlike the 21-percent-oxygen air we breathe, the water a fish swims through contains only about 0.5 percent dissolved oxygen. Water is also 1,000 times heavier than air and at least 50 times as viscous, or syrupy. Our human lungs are designed to operate in gassy air, rather than in dense liquids. So to spend time exploring underwater, we need snorkel tubes to poke above the surface, or scuba tanks full of air.

> The water fish swim through contains only about 0.5 percent dissolved oxygen.

A fish out of water isn't where it oughta be...

They hate going out for walks...

You didn't touch your caviar!

...don't care much for fancy restaurants...

Hey, wake up! These are expensive seats!

...and loathe the theater!

But fish don't need snorkel-like appendages, the fishy equivalent of an elephant's trunk. Instead, they effortlessly extract all the oxygen they need, using organs called gills.

How? Water streams through a fish's mouth, into its muscular throat (pharynx), and through the gills' filaments. Just as our lungs process air, this thready network processes water. Dissolved oxygen enters the fish's bloodstream; carbon dioxide gas leaves it. Water, now carrying the carbon dioxide, flows back through gill slits into the pond. Just as, with each breath, we exhale carbon dioxide into the air.

The gills' surprisingly large surface area—hidden in curtainlike folds—is designed to collect as much (scarce) oxygen as possible. Human lungs extract only about 25 percent of the oxygen in the air we inhale. By contrast, some fish can remove 80 percent of the dissolved oxygen from water passing through their gills, making fish the oxygen-mining champs.

Why do giraffes have such long necks?

The tallest basketball players can thank their long legs and torsos for their towering height. But giraffes win the mammal height contest—by a neck. The tallest male giraffes, from the bottom of their hooves to the top of their heads, measure 20 feet high. And about 6 feet of a giraffe's height is all neck.

A very long neck allows a giraffe to nip at tasty leaves high up in trees, out of the reach of many other plant eaters. The long neck is also startlingly heavy: At up to 600 pounds, a male giraffe's neck and head can weigh as much as three heavyweight boxers. Between meals, a male giraffe wields his weighty neck as a weapon, in fights with other males.

A giraffe's brain is located up to 6 feet away from his beating heart.

How? Swinging their necks in battle, male giraffes—weighing up to 3,500 pounds each—slam heads, with sometimes bone-breaking results. Researchers say that males with the longest, heaviest necks tend to win the violent mating contests, ensuring their genes are passed down to future giraffe generations.

But long necks have their downside, too. Our brains control our bodies, and a giraffe's brain is up to 6 feet away from his beating heart. So a giraffe's heart must pump extra-hard to push blood up to his tree-house brain.

Bend over or hang upside down, and blood rushes to our heads. Stand up too quickly, and as blood leaves the head, we may faint. But when a giraffe dips his head to the ground, then raises his neck 15 feet in the air, he doesn't faint—even though his heart is much farther from his head.

How come? Scientists note that giraffes' hearts are much heavier than ours, weighing in at up to 26 pounds. Still, for a body tipping the scales at a ton or more, giraffe hearts are relatively small.

But a 2009 study found that the walls of a giraffe's heart are incredibly thick. This allows the heart muscle to contract strongly enough for blood to reach a giraffe's faraway brain. Normal human blood pressure with each heartbeat is about 120 mm Hg or less. In a giraffe's upper body, the pressure with each beat can reach 260 mm Hg—a force that might cause blood vessels to burst in humans.

In addition, when a giraffe lifts his head from ground to treetop, blood vessels channel blood away from his face and into the brain. Special muscles in a giraffe's neck veins also keep blood from draining too quickly to his distant heart. Which is why you're unlikely to encounter a woozy giraffe: Giraffes have evolved to be virtually faint-proof.

Fast Fact

Along with its very long neck, the giraffe has a very long tongue— more than 18 inches long. It uses its tongue to pick the smallest leaves off thorny plants.

I'll be with you in a minute—I'm all tied up.

Tie Dept.

Measure FOR Measure
20 feet = 6.1 m
6 feet = 1.8 m
600 pounds = 272.2 kg
3,500 pounds = 1,587.6 kg
15 feet = 4.6 m
26 pounds = 11.8 kg
18 inches = 45.7 cm

Why do zebras have stripes?

A zebra is an almost mythical looking creature, but it's actually a member of the horse family, along with donkeys and true horses—the kind we see on farms.

Zebras live in Africa, and they stand about 4 feet (1.2 m) tall at the shoulder, which is the way horses are measured: from the shoulder to the ground. Zebras usually live in families, with a stallion, several mares, and some foals. These families often travel together in herds of up to 1,000 zebras. Sometimes, zebras join forces with antelopes and roam around with them, searching for grasses to eat.

All striped zebras, scientists say, evolved from a common horse ancestor, which was probably a solid dark color. One clue: A now-extinct zebra called the quagga had a solid brown rump. And we know that a zebra developing in its mother's womb starts out dark (black or brown). But as the little zebra grows, he or she develops light stripes.

Scientists say the stripes appear where genes suppress the production of dark pigments. The skin pigments are inhibited in a pattern determined by the zebra's species (Grevy's, Mountain, or Plains) and by his or her particular parents.

So by the time zebra babies are born, they are already covered in stripes. And scientists have suggested a number of ways in which a zebra's bold stripes make good survival sense.

Surprisingly, camouflage—blending in—is the oldest argument for the stripes' usefulness. A herd of milling zebras creates one big, shifting, dizzying pattern. Result: The optical interference of moving stripes may make it harder for predators (like hungry lions)

to pick out and chase down individual animals.

Next, there's zebra social life. A zebra's stripes help other zebras identify it by its species (the number, width, and pattern differ) and as a unique (attractive) individual.

Then there's the fly theory. Yes, zebras are indeed stylin' horses. But here "fly" refers to the nippy insects that plague horses, from tsetse flies (which carry the encephalitis virus) to horseflies. Scientists say that biting flies are especially attracted to large, dark-colored animals. Stripes, some think, might act as a kind of fly repellant.

The "fly" theory got a boost from a 2012 study. Researchers knew that blood-sucking female horseflies are drawn to polarized light (light that vibrates in a flat plane). Dark-colored horses, they say, reflect horizontally polarized light, and flies find them very attractive. On the other hand, flies land less often on all-

Fast Fact

The quagga zebra got its name from its neighing cry. So many were hunted that by the early 1900s, quaggas had disappeared.

white horses. So, the scientists devised experiments using dark, light, or striped boards, and striped plastic horses, setting them up on a fly-ridden horse farm in Hungary. They found that horseflies were even less attracted to black-and-white stripes than to solid white surfaces. And the more narrow and zebralike the stripes, the more flies took a pass.

Why? Black-and-white stripes, according to the researchers, are very good at reflecting light in alternating polarized/nonpolarized patterns. Making zebras visually confusing to dive-bombing horseflies, as well as to prowling lions.

Why do some animals, like bears, hibernate in winter?

When spring arrives after an endless winter, we can look forward to the first blooming daffodils, hopping robins . . . and stirring bears.

When winter winds down in the north, bears come out of hibernation. We think of hibernation as a kind of extra-long sleep, but it's actually more like the suspended animation of a science-fiction movie. A bear can go seven cold months without eating a bite, drinking an ounce, or taking a bathroom break.

Hibernation is one

answer to the question "How can I survive when nearly all the food is gone?" For most animals, frigid winter is a dangerous time. Days are short and cold; nights are long and colder. Plants and their fruits are in short supply. Small animals that were the prey of larger animals may be hibernating themselves. And searching for what food remains can burn more calories than an animal obtains from eating it.

Some, like migrating birds, go south for the winter. Others tough it out, and many die. Warm-blooded animals

By hibernating, an animal reduces its body's energy needs to a bare minimum.

must maintain their body temperature at its normal level—say, 98°F. But among those that hibernate, body temperature and metabolism both drop, allowing an animal to get by on far fewer calories.

Besides bears, other hibernators include rodents like prairie dogs and ground squirrels (including chipmunks and woodchucks), as well as three kinds of primates (all of them dwarf lemurs). A small hibernator's heart rate may drop from 300 beats per minute to just 7; body temperature may drop from 100°F to near freezing (32°F).

Hibernating bears lower their temperature less drastically, from around 91°F to about 80°F. However, a bear's heart rate drops from about 55 to 9 beats a minute. And his metabolism slows to just 25 percent of normal.

To prepare for their Big Sleep, bears spend the late summer pigging out. Each

Fast Fact

A bear preparing to hibernate eats the human equivalent of 10 breakfasts, 10 lunches, and 10 dinners a day in late summer.

day, a bear may gorge on 20,000 to 50,000 calories of food, from berries and nuts to birds' eggs, insects, field corn, and sometimes mice or other small animals. The bear may gain 3 to 16 pounds every 24 hours, building an enormous layer of fat to live on over the winter.

A dormant bear requires far less energy than usual to stay alive. So instead of eating for energy, the bear's

Measure FOR Measure
98°F = 37°C
100°F = 38°C
32°F = 0°C
91°F = 33°C
80°F = 27°C
3 to 16 pounds = 1.4 to 7.3 kg

WINTER BREAK

Every few weeks, or even every few days, small hibernators like ground squirrels swim up from their hibernation like a patient coming out of anesthesia. They sip water, perhaps grab a bite to eat, and go to the bathroom. Their bodies warm up, and they may be awake for an entire day and night, before sliding back into their barely-alive hibernating state. Small hibernators may lose about 40 percent of their body weight over the winter.

body slowly burns its extra fat. When fat is burned completely, carbon dioxide and water remain. During hibernation, a bear doesn't urinate, and his body doesn't lose much water. So even without drinking, a bear can get the water he needs to sustain blood and body tissues, simply by burning fat.

During hibernation, a bear's kidneys mostly shut down; toxins build up in his bloodstream, and the kidneys themselves suffer damage. Somehow, bears survive, their kidneys quickly healing and resuming their work in the spring.

Unlike very overweight humans, a bear's body stores all its extra fat in fatty tissue just under the skin, and none in the muscles or the liver. This allows a bear to stay temporarily obese, but healthy. As hibernation ends, a bear's body restarts its metabolism, raising his heart rate and temperature— prompting the much-skinnier bear to sniff the first spring breeze, and lumber out of his den.

How can dinosaur bones still be on Earth after millions of years?

After death, the remains of plants and animals usually decompose. Bacteria break down tissue, and as the months and years pass, the tissue disintegrates.

But once in a while, when the remains are in the right place at the right time, some parts—usually bones, shells, and teeth—get preserved. When a paleontologist,

digging in the dirt, is excited to turn up a 3-million-year-old tooth, what she's found is called a fossil.

A fossil may be an animal's actual tooth or bone

or shell, preserved over the centuries. Or it may be a cast, or impression, of the original: a tiny sea creature's skeleton, carved into stone. Still other fossils are replicas of the original bony parts, sculpted by the Earth from minerals.

For the Earth to create a fossil—allowing us to see part of a creature from the enormously distant past—the conditions must be exactly right. Most importantly, the remains must be protected from wind and rain. This can happen if the plant or animal is buried by sediment—rock fragments such as sand or gravel. Ash also makes a good cover.

Remains are sometimes protected by sediments in places like lakes, swamps, and caves. The best spots, however, are sites where the Earth is (or once was) "geologically active"—near a volcano that has spewed ash, or near growing mountains. The already towering

Himalayas are growing mountains, created from the slow-motion collison between the plate carrying the landmass of India and the Eurasian plate. Such mountains shift bits of rock and dirt from their sides and into rivers, which carry the sediments into oceans.

Most fossils are found under bodies of water (or where water once flowed), nicely covered by sediments and safe from the bacteria that live on dry land.

Fossils are made in several ways. Minerals may seep into the pores of a slowly decaying shell or bone and preserve it from further decay. Or acids may dissolve a shell, leaving an impression or cast of the shell in the rock it was pressed against. Sometimes, the Earth creates a duplicate shell. Minerals fill the mold carved into the rock, forming

Fast Fact

Most fossils are sea creatures, since they are buried much more quickly than land animals.

a replica of the original shell.

Fossils come in every size, from the humongous *Tyrannosaurus rex* thigh bone—to the exquisitely tiny. Scientists have even found fossils of dinosaur embryos— unborn baby dinosaurs. One fossilized embryo, found by a geology student in Colorado, was 135 million to 150 million years old. It included tiny foot bones and part of a little backbone and jawbone. Two baby teeth were poking up from the jaw. Scientists think the tiny dinosaur probably died just before it was about to hatch.

How can insects be preserved in amber?

Think "fossil," and you probably imagine an animal's shell, bones, or teeth, re-created in rock. But in fossilized amber, we often find a tiny animal's actual body, from eyes to wings to antennae, perfectly preserved.

Amber allows us to see with our own eyes what ancient, now-extinct life actually looked like (such as a praying mantis, trapped 87 million years ago in Japan).

How does it work? Amber is fossilized resin, which once oozed from the bark of a living tree. Picture an insect crawling on the trunk of a tree, only to get caught in a glob of sticky resin. Centuries pass, the tree dies and decays, but the chunk of dried resin hardens. Sediment covers it, and over time, buries the resin inside the Earth.

Over time, many animals and plants disappear— including the insect's own species, vanished into the dust of Earth. Meanwhile, the resin hardens into a fossil. Sediments carrying the fossilized resin are pushed up by the movements of landmasses. And one day, scientists, digging for fossils, find a chunk of smooth, translucent amber. Inside, the insect waits, held in its golden prison for millions of years.

Scientists have even unearthed amber containing thousands of long-extinct ants. But insects aren't the only things imprisoned by amber. Tiny frogs, hair and feathers, leaves and fruit, spiderwebs, bacteria, and other remnants of the ancient Earth have also been found.

So far, the oldest creatures found in amber are two tiny mites, discovered in Italy. The mites lived around 230 million years ago, when most of Earth's land was united in one vast supercontinent called *Pangaea*. Scientists speculate that the mites may have unknowingly engineered their

The oldest creatures found in amber are two 230-million-year-old mites.

own end, by feeding on a tree and releasing its gluey resin.

And sometimes, amber preserves a scene from the past. Spring flowers, bursting into bloom. A brood of baby spiders, emerging from a white cocoon. And, in one of the most startling amber images, a predator about to pounce on its prey.

The fossil was found buried in a mine in Burma (Myanmar). It shows a small male wasp, unluckily caught in a spiderweb. Looming above it is a young orb-weaver spider. The wasp appears to be staring at the spider, who is about to make him lunch. Nearby, a second spider lurks in the web.

But before the spider could make its move, all were caught in a flow of tree resin—and frozen forever. Researchers say the confrontation took place between 97 million and 110 million years ago, when dinosaurs roamed our planet.

Famous Last Words . . .

I told you not to touch that.

How and why does a chameleon change colors?

Chameleons have always been a mystery. Do they change color mainly to match their surroundings, a kind of lizard-y disappearing act? Or do a chameleon's colors shift, as French scientist Paul Bert suggested in the 19th century, with his shifting emotions?

A recent study weighs in on Bert's side, finding that chameleon colors reflect mood like the reddened face of an angry human. But unlike a red-faced man, a chameleon can access an artist's palette of colors, signaling other chameleons to go away or come closer.

True chameleons—more than 130 different species—

Chameleon colors often reflect mood, like the red face of an angry human.

live mainly in Africa, India, Pakistan, and Spain. More than half live on one island—Madagascar, off Africa's east coast.

The basic, everyday colors and patterns of chameleons do help them blend in nicely with their local habitats. (Some look

like chameleon-shaped leaves, down to a pattern of leafy veins.) But scientists say chameleons don't automatically change color to match their backgrounds, as was once thought; they are already well camouflaged.

But many kinds of chameleons can and do shift through a rainbow of colors—reds, blues, purples, greens, yellows, pinks—in mixed patterns of swirls, splotches, stripes, and chevrons. And each species has its own signature range of colors.

Color tricks are coordinated in a chameleon's layered skin. Underneath a

Pickpockets...

Professional Chameleons...

Undercover police

...Hungry lizards!

transparent outer layer is a layer with red and yellow pigments. Next comes a layer of light-reflecting cells, some bouncing back blue light, others white. At bottom are cells containing brown melanin, the pigment that makes human skin brown or tan. A chameleon's hormones and nervous system send chemical and electrical messages telling pigment cells to expand or contract.

This creates a shifting array of colors and patterns visible through the skin's see-through surface, like an electronic billboard.

To figure out what's most important to chameleons—blending in or standing out—scientists at the University of Melbourne in Australia studied more than a dozen species of dwarf chameleons. The chameleons' home turf ranges from rain forests to

grasslands. The researchers found that species from drab local environments displayed colors just as conspicuous as those of chameleons from brightly colored habitats.

Chameleons change color in response to changing temperature, light, and, especially, mood. The scientists watched as dueling chameleons cycled through dizzying color changes in just milliseconds. Two hostile males would morph into their brightest colors as the fight began. But the loser in each contest soon faded, shifting into dark, dreary "I give up" colors.

Male chameleons also change colors to attract females, like a male peacock unfurling his iridescent tail. Females also color-shift, to signal interest (or disdain). Besides hues visible to us, chameleons display colors stretching into the ultraviolet spectrum, an extra range of color appreciated by other chameleons.

So like a TV wrestler donning an intimidating outfit—or a man changing into the latest fashion to impress a date—chameleons seem to color-shift mainly to intimidate or attract. What if the dramatic color changes attract someone other than a cute chameleon—say, a hungry hawk? Researchers say that the shifts are so quick—a flash of orange here, a stripe of pink there— that predatory birds don't have time to notice.

However, a 2008 study in Australia found that chameleons shown models of two of their most fearsome predators—a venomous tree snake or a bird that uses thorns to snare the lizards— ramped up their camouflaging colors. Faced with the bird (which has better color vision) the chameleons' color shift matched their background better than when threatened by the snake. But the chameleons also presented a paler color to the snakes, which usually slither up from below. Researchers say a lighter shade may help the lizards blend into the bright sky above.

Why do elephants have such big ears?

Do Your Ears Hang Low ?

Do they wobble to and fro?

Can you throw them over your shoulder, like a Continental soldier...

Do your ears hang low?

Can you tie them in a knot? Can you tie them in a bow?

When you see a big, wrinkly gray elephant, what's the first thing you notice? Probably its long, curling trunk, like an animated water hose in place of a nose. The second thing you notice is probably those enormous, flapping ears. No wonder Dumbo could fly.

The truly giant, Dumbo-esque ears only belong to one kind of elephant—African elephants. An African elephant's ears can measure up to 4 by 6 feet, and weigh more than 110 pounds each. The ears of Asian elephants are less than half as big, but still impressively outsized.

Big, flappable elephant ears come in handy for doing things humans do with their hands, like swatting bugs away. Elephants also use their ears to appear more formidable when faced with a threat. Just as animals from cats to birds puff out fur or feathers to look larger, elephants spread their ears. By extending each 24-square-foot ear, an annoyed African elephant makes himself look almost four times wider from the front—and much more intimidating.

Best of all for elephants, who live in very warm places, large ears are a kind of built-in air-conditioning. Elephants have massive bodies, but not-so-massive surface areas. Compared to their volume, elephants just don't have enough skin surface to efficiently radiate all the heat built up internally. Elephants don't have sweat glands, either, so they can't

Fast Fact

Whatever their ear size, elephants are the largest mammals outside the oceans. If it weren't for certain whales, elephants would be the largest animals on the planet.

perspire to cool down on hot days. Instead, they flap their enormous ears.

But waving big ears does much more than waving a fan on a wooden stick. While the skin on an elephant's body can be a tough hide, an inch thick, elephant ears are built of more delicate stuff. A thin layer of skin barely covers a visible network of crisscrossing blood vessels, in a pattern as unique to each elephant as a fingerprint. These blood vessels swell in hot weather and shrink in cold. So on sweltering days, elephants gently flap their

ELEPHANT LIFE

Elephants live in places like Africa, India, and Ceylon, as well as other regions in Asia. Their large heads give a hint of their enormous intelligence and highly emotional makeup. Preferring to live in groups of 25 or more, elephants are nomads, traveling hundreds of miles to forage for food—grasses, leaves, fruits, and nuts. Every 18 hours, an elephant must chow down on about 600 to 700 pounds of food, leaf by leaf, nut by nut. They wash down all that roughage with 20 to 40 gallons of water a day.

Besides ear size, there are other differences between elephants. The African elephant's skin is rumpled and wrinkled, while Asian elephants' skin is smoother. The African elephant has two "fingers" on the end of its trunk, like our thumb and forefinger, and can use its "fingers" to grasp objects. Asian elephants have only one "finger," requiring a neat curl of the trunk to pick up an object.

ears to pass air over their enlarged ear veins, cooling the blood flowing through them. In a good breeze, an elephant will simply unfurl his or her ears.

Since a single ear can measure more than 4 feet across, a lot of blood can get cooled as it passes through the road map of blood vessels on the ear's surface. The cooler blood flows back through the elephant's body, helping it chill out. In fact, elephant ears are so good at cooling that the temperature of the returning blood may be lower by more than 9°F.

BIG EARS = BETTER HEARING?

Having big ears doesn't mean that elephants have superior hearing at the frequencies we humans hear. But elephants can make—and hear—sounds we can't even imagine. Humans can hear low-pitched sounds only down to about 20 hertz (or cycles per second). What does that sound like? The lowest note on a piano resounds at 27.5 hertz. Rolling, booming thunder may be pitched at 15 to 40 hertz.

Like thunder, calls made by elephants can drop down to a rumbly 15 hertz (which we humans can't hear). These super-low bass sounds can travel on and on across clear spaces. When atmospheric conditions are just right, the "infrasonic" calls can be heard by other elephants in a range of 110 square miles (284.9 square km) or more. Likewise, elephants are among the animals that can hear the very low, threatening sounds made by an impending earthquake or tsunami.

Measure FOR Measure

4 by 6 feet = 1.22 by 1.83 m
110 pounds = 50 kg
24 square feet = 2.23 m²
600 to 700 pounds = 272 to 318 kg
20 to 40 gallons = 76 to 151 l
11.5 feet = 3.5 m
lower by 9°F = lower by 5°C

Is it true that camels store water in their humps?

One Hump or Two?
Great for Storage of fat...
Easy Access Snacks 24/7...
and collapsible when empty...

Camels, unlike people, fit into dry lands like a hand into a glove.

A camel's body is ideally suited to the extreme dryness and the extreme temperature swings of desert living: daytime heat, nighttime cold, fiercely blowing sand, and little access to water.

We think of camels as plodding through the deserts of countries like Saudi Arabia. But surprisingly, the (rabbit-size) ancestors of modern camels evolved in North America, around 45 million years ago. Over millions of years, goat-size and larger camels evolved. Camels lived all over North America, from Canada to Mexico.

In fact, eight different kinds of camels lived in what is now California. One of these was the towering *Titanotylopus*, which stood 11.5 feet tall at the shoulder and foraged for food along the California coastline 3 million years ago. Scientists have also discovered fossils of another giant camel who lived in the Arctic forests of northern Canada.

Camels spread out from North America into South America and across the Bering Land Bridge, which then connected North America

with Asia. By 7 million years ago, camels had spread all the way to what's now Spain.

But by 10,000 years ago, camels in North America were extinct, perhaps as a result of changing habitat, human settlements, and hunting.

Today, there are only two living species of true camels. Two-humped Bactrians live in Central Asia. One-humped dromedaries roam the Horn of Africa and the Middle East.

All camels have long, thick, curling eyelashes, no mascara required. The fringe neatly catches blowing sand, keeping it out of a camel's big brown eyes. Camels also have a third eyelid, which slides closed from the side. In air full of blowing sand, a camel can shut her (very thin) third lid, and still see well enough to trudge on.

A camel's jutting brow bones and bushy brows shade her eyes from blinding desert sun. Her flaring nostrils can

shut tight against windborne sand. And her small, furry ears help keep out annoying ear sand.

Next, a camel's temperature automatically adjusts to the air temperature, falling as low as 93°F during cold desert nights, then rising to nearly 106°F during the searing days (when the temperature can soar to more than 125°F). With the difference between body and air temperature minimized, the air doesn't heat a camel's body as much as it would a cooler body, like ours.

Water is essential to all life on Earth, and camels can't survive without it. Blood is 91 percent water. If water is lost—through sweating and urination, for example— and not replaced, the blood thickens. Instead of streaming through blood vessels, it moves like molasses.

That's dangerous, because quickly flowing blood helps cool the body. How? As

Measure FOR Measure
93°F = 34°C
106°F = 41°C
125°F = 52°C
80 pounds = 36.3 kg
120°F = 49°C
25 pounds = 11.3 kg
100 pounds = 45.4 kg

the body converts food into energy, heat is produced. Blood heats up from these reactions deep in the body, carrying this heat as it streams up to and through the skin. Presto: The skin radiates the heat into the air. Result: The body stays cool. But honey-thick, dehydrated blood can't get to the skin fast enough. Heat builds up; death may follow.

Even in the coolest weather, human beings can live only a few days without water. Camels, however, can survive for up to 17 days between drinks.

A camel's metabolism—the speed at which its body burns food—slows during hot weather, making for less body heat.

Camels have also evolved a way to recycle water from their kidneys, funneling it to one of three stomach compartments and then back into the blood. But there's more: If you look at a camel's blood under a microscope, you'll see that the red blood cells are oval rather than round like those of other mammals. The streamlined shape allows oxygen-carrying cells to ease through vessels—even when a camel is dehydrated.

Finally, there are those humps. Although a camel's hump isn't actually full of water, it does keep a camel cooler in hot weather. Packed inside the humps are fat, up to 80 pounds in a single mound. How does all that extra padding help on an afternoon when it's 120°F? The hump acts as a protective hood. Baking in the desert sun, the mound of fat absorbs and traps heat, slowing its descent to the camel's vital internal organs. Meanwhile, the rest of a camel's body— especially those thin, spindly legs— radiates heat into the air.

But above all, the hump is a camel's emergency food supply, like a hiker's backpack

stuffed with trail mix, turkey jerky, and energy bars. A hump (or two) allows a camel to survive for several weeks without actually eating. As the fat is burned for energy, the hump gradually shrinks, becoming flabby and floppy.

Why do raccoons have black masks?

Raccoon Body Language Unmasked...

Cool stuff in here!

Thanks for leaving the door open!

Mom?

With their black masks and their convict-striped tails, raccoons can look like bandits—or like guests at a masquerade party. Raccoons also have short, stubby legs; pointy noses; small, stand-up ears; and a waddling walk. From the end of its nose to the tip of its bushy tail, a raccoon may measure nearly 3 feet long and weigh about 22 pounds.

Raccoons, native to North America, now roam throughout Europe (and Japan). They often sleep in snug nests in hollow trees. But they can also camp out in a dugout in the ground, snooze in an old barn or shed, or curl up in the crawl space under a porch.

Usually, about three or four baby raccoons (called kits) are born at a time. Little raccoons make a twittering sound when they are upset, rather like baby birds. Kits depend on their moms for milk for about 10 weeks, when they begin sampling solid food.

What do raccoons eat? Anything and everything. Raccoons, like bears, are omnivorous—they take what food they can get, depending on the time of year and where they happen to be camped out. On the menu any given day might be some tasty crayfish, a crunchy cricket, a sloppy raw egg, a handful of sweet blackberries, and an ear of yellow corn. Raccoons do much of their foraging at night. That's when you might catch a raccoon in the beam of your flashlight, looking like a masked robber going through your garbage can.

Raccoons have five toes on their feet and five fingers on their front paws, including a "thumb." And raccoons use their "hands" in much the same way we do—picking up and turning over objects and prying open lids (especially trash can lids) to get at what's inside.

Anyone who has been around raccoons knows that they are very smart and very curious. Raccoons, like little kids, are attracted to bright, shiny objects like mirrors. And they've been known to open back doors to get into well-stocked kitchens.

Raccoons sometimes appear to wash their food before they eat it, dunking it in water until it's nice and wet. But according to scientists, getting the food clean may not be the point. A raccoon may douse his food, they say, because it reminds him of the pleasures of eating out of a lake or river. After all, a raccoon's favorite foods—crayfish, frogs, and crabs—are water creatures.

Kits sport their little black masks by two weeks of age. Raccoons use their faces (as we do) to communicate with other animals, both of their own and other species. They also use their ears and tails.

According to scientist Dorcas MacClintock, the mask and other markings make certain behaviors, such as being threatening or showing meekness, more obvious to other animals. How? It's easy to see exactly what a face, tail, and ears are doing when they're colored so distinctively. In addition, the mask, rings, and other markings help raccoons identify one another (much as you might identify an approaching friend by his red baseball cap).

But there is another reason black masks may make good evolutionary sense. Like the black smeared under the eyes of a football player to reduce the sun's glare, a raccoon's black mask may cut the glare of light from water—sunlight during the day, moonlight at night.

Measure FOR Measure
3 feet = 91.4 cm
22 pounds = 10 kg

How do porcupine quills work?

Porcupines may look odd, but their quills are part of a long tradition of animal defenses. Animals don't walk around with knives and guns to protect themselves, like some humans. But each animal has evolved its own unique safeguards. Skunks spray. Electric eels jolt. Porcupines jab. While the porcupine is unique among animals, its defenses are very similar to a plant we all know and love—the cactus. (In fact, the porcupine has been called a walking cactus.)

Some fast facts: There are 43 different kinds of porcupines. Porcupines live in North and South America, Asia, Africa, and southern Europe. They hang out in trees or on the ground, foraging nightly for everything from twigs and bark to apples and dandelions. A porcupine can weigh up to 25 pounds (11.3 kg). They don't move very fast; they waddle.

But what it lacks in speed a porcupine makes up for in armor: about 30,000 quills, ranging from the very short, very sharp quills on a porcupine's tail to the quills that are 4 inches (10 cm) long on its back and flanks. The quills are actually hairs, but hard as shards of clear plastic. And quills are barbed rather than smooth, so they'll catch and lodge in their victim's skin.

Before a porcupine resorts to quills, however, she gives fair warning—gnashing her teeth, rattling her quills, lashing her tail, and even, skunklike, giving off a foul odor. But when push comes to shove, porcupines don't send their quills zinging through the air like darts, as we've seen in countless cartoons.

How it really works: A threatened or angry porcupine uses muscles in her skin to makes her quills bristle all over. The quills fit so loosely in the porcupine's hide that, when touched, they easily dislodge and jab into the victim. Of course, a porcupine may speed the process by rushing at an intruder or smartly slapping him with her tail, releasing many quills into his skin or clothing.

Once lodged painfully in the skin, a quill can work

its way farther in, often disappearing under the surface. Sometimes, the quill will pierce an organ inside the body, even causing death. More often, quills are very painful but cause no lasting harm. Quills can be slowly pulled out, and they often work themselves out on their own, pushed forward by contracting muscles. For example, biologist Uldis Roze, of New York City's Queens College, watched a quill stuck in his upper arm retreat under the surface, slowly travel under his skin around his elbow, and finally exit near the wrist—three days later.

Quills may keep porcupines safe in more ways than one. Roze discovered that hidden in the greasy coating of each quill is a natural antibiotic. When the quill emerged from Roze's arm, he found that the wound, unlike a splinter puncture, was clean and uninfected. Analyzing the fats found in quill grease, Roze discovered that they could kill six kinds of bacteria, including *Staphylococcus* and *Streptococcus*.

Why would porcupine quills be coated with bacteria-killing substances? Porcupines can sometimes impale themselves or other porcupines by accident. Built-in germ killers can prevent such injuries from becoming serious, helping the porcupine and its kind survive.

Porcupines may look fearsome, but they are actually like most animals— if they get to know and like you, they'll take care not to hurt you. Another biologist, Richard Earle, found this out when he raised a male porcupine (called Tubby) from babyhood.

Tubby liked to play a sly game with Earle. The porcupine would start to spin around and around. Then he would stop abruptly and slap his tail against Earle's leg. The idea, apparently, was that Earle would know the slap was coming but would be caught by surprise by exactly when it occurred—rather like the game of musical chairs.

What added excitement, of course, was that a slap of a tail is exactly how one gets a legful of quills. But when Tubby walloped Earle, he would make sure he twisted his tail so that only the soft underside slapped the biologist's leg.

Can some squirrels really fly?

Flying Squirrels Airline

"Spiders or the baby bird entree?"

Eclectic Cuisine...

Flight Departures
9:00 – Down the tree
9:01 – Across the yard
9:02 – Up on the roof
9:03 – Down the chimney

Frequent Service...

Cartoons available on longer flights!

Flying squirrels don't actually fly; they don't have wings to flap, like birds or bats do. But they are expert gliders that can turn, brake, and come in for a soft landing on the hard side of a tree. And as anyone knows who's seen a hang glider or a glider airplane pass overhead, gliding can be even better, more effortless, than true flying.

Flying squirrels have their very own group in the squirrel family. Far from being rare, there are at least 44 species gliding around Europe, Asia, and North America. The two species that swoop around North America are about 8 to 12 inches long. The northern flying squirrel makes its

THE FAMILY SQUIRREL

Flying squirrels, like other members of the squirrel family, are rodents. In addition to the 44 species of flying squirrels, there are also 230 kinds of tree and ground squirrels, from the gray squirrels we see in the park to eastern fox squirrels, European red squirrels, and tassel-eared squirrels. Surprise: Other animals in the squirrel or Sciuridae family include chipmunks, prairie dogs, and woodchucks.

home in Canada and the northern United States. The smaller southern flying squirrel stays mainly in the east and south, from Ontario to Mexico.

If an ordinary squirrel decided to take a flying leap from the top of a tree, it would probably be in the daytime. And he could expect to land in the branches of a nearby tree—or on the roof of your garage. But if a flying squirrel took the same leap, he would probably do it in the dark. And he could expect to land on the trunk of a not-so-nearby tree—say, 50 feet across the yard—after a graceful sail through the cool night air.

Flying squirrels do most of their traveling under cover of night. As darkness falls, they go looking for dinner, which might include an appetizer of acorns, a main dish of spider, and a lovely fruit dessert. Flying squirrels are also partial to leaves, flower buds, sweet maple sap, insects, birds' eggs, and, alas, baby birds. Meanwhile, the squirrels themselves must watch out for hungry hawks and owls, raccoons and coyotes, and bored house cats.

For gliding, a flying squirrel has a loose flap of skin like a tarp connected from his wrist to his ankle on each side. Stretching out all four legs and taking the leap, a flying squirrel looks like a mini hang glider or furry kite, floating on a current of air. As he glides along on a gradual downward arc, a flying squirrel pilot turns or changes his angle of descent by using his wrists to tighten or loosen the flaps, and his flat tail as a handy stabilizer.

A flying squirrel can even use his side flaps to execute banking curves like an airplane, or to make a sharp right or left turn in midair. The distance he

There are at least 44 kinds of flying squirrels gliding around Europe, Asia, and North America.

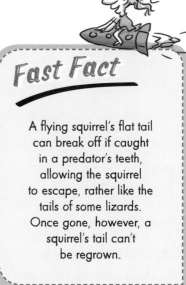

glides depends on the height he jumped from, and the direction and strength of the wind carrying him. Like a swimmer pushing off from the side of a pool, a squirrel uses his powerful hind legs to push off a branch into a forceful glide.

To come in for a landing, the flying squirrel lifts his body, relaxes his flaps, and drops his tail, letting the air act as a brake. Landing on all fours on the tree trunk, the squirrel usually scampers around to the other side, in case something was following.

Then, if the journey isn't done, he runs to the treetop and flings himself into the sky again, making quick progress through the woods. The longest recorded single glide of a flying squirrel measured nearly 300 feet.

Fast Fact

A flying squirrel's flat tail can break off if caught in a predator's teeth, allowing the squirrel to escape, rather like the tails of some lizards. Once gone, however, a squirrel's tail can't be regrown.

Measure FOR Measure
8 to 12 inches = 20.3 to 30.5 cm
50 feet = 15.2 m
300 feet = 91.4 m

How come dogs bark, even when it's quiet?

Dogs fit their barks to the situation. A fire engine screams by in the distance? A coyote howls and yips? An alarmed bark. A skunk ambles by the fence? An interested, excited bark. (And, perhaps, a regret or two a second later.) And then there's that random, monotonous, I'm-lonely-out-here bark.

Dogs may growl at a threatening stranger, whine excitedly when a beloved person approaches the front door, or let out an excited short yip during a play tussle with another dog. But barking is an all-purpose vocalization.

Scientists who study dogs note that their closest wild relatives, the wolves, rarely bark as adults. Wolf puppies, on the other hand, bark quite a lot. Which is a clue, researchers say, as to how domesticated dogs became such enthusiastic barkers.

Human beings shouldn't complain so much about barking, since in a real sense, we're responsible for the racket. By 30,000 to 50,000 years ago, evidence shows that people often brought wild wolf puppies into their nomadic camps. Raised

 As docile dogs evolved, they essentially became overgrown yappy puppies.

around people from a very young age, the grown-up wolves tended to be tamer than normal. And the friendlier and less fearful the wolf-dog, the more successful she or he was at coexisting with us, gaining access to tossed-out scraps of food.

As these tamer animals bred with one another, even more docile offspring were born. Dogs helped humans become better hunters. They were used to drag loads of belongings from camp to camp and to guard settlements. Later, they were trained to herd other animals, like sheep. And, of course, dogs also became beloved companions.

But why all the barking? Most baby animals (think

The Evolution of Arf!

bear cubs) are more docile and people-friendly than their (scary) grown-up parents. Scientists who bred extra-docile foxes discovered that friendlier foxes sounded less like foxes, more like dogs. Tamer adults, it turns out, act like big babies. So as wolf-dogs evolved into the equivalent of overgrown puppies, they were more friendly. More playful. And way more bark-y.

Barks convey both emotional states and other information, and vary in pitch, loudness, and timing. In one study, scientists recorded dogs barking, then played the barks for other dogs. Dogs reacted strongly to "uh-oh, a stranger!" barks, but paid much less attention to "I'm all by myself!" barks.

And after tens of thousands of years, we humans understand our doggy friends pretty well, too. One study found that even six-month-old infants could match a friendly or angry bark to pictures of a happy or threatening dog.

Even babies with no exposure to dogs were able to decode the barks. An affinity for dogs, it seems, is hard-wired into our human brains.

How come cats purr?

In Translation...

Purrrrr*

What a sweet Kitty!

* How 'bout some chow?

Purrrrrrr*

You are the cutest!

* I haven't eaten for 3 days, I'm starving!

I could eat you up!

Meow!*

* uh-oh!

Like meowing, hissing, and yowling, purring is a way of (kitty) communicating. Newborn kittens purr by the second day of life, vibrating loudly as they find mom and latch on to nipples for feeding. And mom purrs back, creating a comforting bond. Between two cats, purring may signal friendliness and a desire to play. But cats may also purr when they're tail-switchingly angry, scared, or in pain. And, of course, cats purr when they're petted—and when they want something from an easily manipulated human.

In fact, scientists in the United Kingdom have discovered that cats can vary the sound of their purrs, trading in a contented rumble for an irritatingly urgent sound when the need arises. Like, say, at six a.m., when you'd rather sleep in.

How cats purr at all is still something of a mystery, but we do know that there is no "purring organ" that kicks into gear. Most researchers think cats make purring sounds using the muscles and folds of the larynx (voice box), causing inhaled and exhaled air to vibrate like a mini-motor.

Annoyed by her own cat's rather frantic early-morning purring, a U.K. researcher designed a study to see if purring really comes in several varieties. Karen McComb and her research team at the University of Sussex in England asked cat owners to record their own cats' everyday purring. Then her team played back the recordings for both cat owners and the cat-naive.

What the team found: Listeners tended to have a positive reaction to the agreeable low rumble of between-meal purring. On the other hand, they found mealtime purring rather urgent-sounding, and unpleasant.

What triggered the opposing reactions? According to the researchers, the I-want-food purring contained high-frequency sounds mostly missing from the contented, low-pitched purring. And the higher the number of high-pitched interludes in each purr, the more frantic and urgent-seeming the sound. According to McComb, the high-pitched segments resemble hidden meows and cries, and may even remind people of a crying infant—or a whining child.

In a sense, the "soliciting purr" is a cat's version of a subliminal tape, with an embedded message custom-designed for an easily hypnotized human. There's the rumble-y comfort of the low purr: "Remember how warm and cuddly I am?" And then there are the hidden cries: "Don't you get it? I'm starving!" The entire message: "I'm trying to be nice here, really I am. But just get out the can opener, lady!" Obligingly, we obey.

Cats can vary the sound of their purrs, from a slow rumble to a more urgent sound.

Waking up a handy human with amped-up pillow-side purring is a favorite feline tactic. But McComb notes that not all hungry cats employ nuanced purring to get what they want from their human companions. In a household with multiple pets and people, cats seem to rely more on outright frantic meowing near mealtime—a more annoying but less subtle way to get the message across.

Why do cats' eyes shine in the dark?

Have you ever seen a cat pass by in an alleyway or darkened hallway? As it turns toward the light to look at you, its eyes gleam for a moment before it slinks off.

Shining eyes are a side effect of a cat's excellent night vision. Domestic cats evolved to do much of their hunting at night. Today that may mean nothing more than locating the bowl of cat chow in a dark kitchen. Still, it's a handy ability to have—in a power failure, a cat could navigate near-darkness much better than you or I.

First, a little about how eyes work: When light bounces off an object it zooms into the cornea, the clear shield covering the eye. The cornea helps to

 Cats have excellent night vision and can see objects in near darkness that we would miss.

focus the light, which zips on into the iris, the colored part of the eye, through a black area called the pupil.

The little black pupil gets bigger in the dark to let more light in, and tiny in bright sunlight. (Watch your pupils do a rapid shrink by standing in the dark in front

of a mirror, and then flicking a light on.) Muscles in the iris push and tug on the pupil to make it behave.

Light that is allowed through the pupil passes into the lens, a rubbery membrane that focuses the light once more. Then, as the light streams through the eye's dark inner chamber, it hits a screen called the retina. The retina's nerve cells, the rods and cones, send signals to the brain through the optic nerve, and the brain registers an image. You see something. And it all happens in a split second.

Cat eyes work like human eyes, with a difference: Cats have a special layer of cells in the rear of their eyes, called the *tapetum lucidim* (Latin for

"bright carpet"). This carpet of cells reflects light like a mirror back to the cells in the retina. So in near darkness, a cat's eyes collect and magnify every bit of light that enters them. This means that cats have excellent night vision and can see objects in near darkness that we would miss. And it's also why cats' eyes shine so brightly in reflected light at night.

Cats can't see in absolute darkness, however. Shut up in a windowless room in pitch-blackness, a cat would find her cautious way by sniffing everything around her and listening carefully. As she crept through the room, her sensitive whiskers would brush against unseen objects, telling her how much space she had to navigate.

Because her eyes work so well in dim light, capturing every bit of light, you might expect that very bright sunlight would hurt a cat's sensitive eyes and make it hard for her to see. The round pupils in our eyes react to bright light by shrinking to let in less. The special pupils in cats' eyes, however, narrow to a long slit in bright light. This lets cats' eyes control the light exactly.

How? If we humans begin to close our eyelids in bright light, we soon cut off all light entering the tiny, round, pinpoint pupils. But in cats, the pupils become narrow, vertical slits—up and down, rather than side to side. So cats can use their eyelids to hide more or less of the slit, like a shade partially pulled down over a window. This gives them more precise control over the amount of light entering their eyes than nearly any other animal. On a blindingly bright day, cats can avoid letting in too much light, while still being able to see perfectly well.

EYES ALL AGLOW

Besides cats, who has glow-in-the-dark eyes? A surprisingly long list of animals, many (but not all) fond of hunting or foraging at night. Proud tapetum owners include raccoons, dogs, owls, deer, crocodiles, harbor seals, dragonflies, zebras, ferrets, moths, sharks, elephants, spiders, whales, and even cows.

Glowing eyes come in a rainbow of colors. Some dogs' eyes shine yellow or green, others blue. Owls usually have red eyeshine. And some possum eyes glow pink.

Scientists say the tapetum is usually designed to reflect the wavelength of light an animal is most likely to encounter. So some deep-water fish, for example, have tapeta that selectively reflect the blue-green light of their murky underwater home.

Biologists think that the differences in animal tapeta show that these handy light boosters evolved independently in many different species, starting some 350 million years ago. We humans, however, must make do with flashlights, headlamps, and night-vision binoculars.

How come so many animals have tails (but we don't)?

Why the Devil still has a tail?

To let people know where they're going... *Ready or not...*

To help them get there... *Here we go...*

To assist in an eternity's worth of paperwork. *Send 'em down!*

Where did tails come from? We could imagine some ancient cosmic game of Pin the Tail on the Donkey (and the elephant, and the crocodile, and so on). But the fact is, tails came from the sea.

Scientists think life started in the oceans. Long before there were any land animals, there were primitive fish. Fish evolved with tails because tails allowed them to move easily through the water. A flipping tail provides a nice forward thrust, as anyone who's worn flippers in a swimming pool knows. Over millions of years, amphibians evolved from fish, reptiles evolved from amphibians, and birds and mammals evolved from reptiles.

But before we are born, each human embryo repeats some of our evolutionary history. Tiny embryos start out with gill slits like fishes, our most distant ancestors. And by their fourth week of development, human embryos have little tails, remnants of their mammal ancestors. The tiny tails grow for about two weeks before gradually disappearing. All that's left of the tail is a fused-together lump of bone at the end of the spine, called the coccyx.

Tails come in all shapes, sizes, and colors, and are equipped with different features. A tail can aid in balance; act like a rudder, an extra hand, a weapon, or a warm blanket; come in handy as a fly swatter; communicate feelings; or provide a beautiful adornment, as in the male peacock.

Burrowing animals (like groundhogs) tend to have short, stubby tails; longer ones would just get in the way. But animals that climb trees or run along the ground often have long tails (like lemurs and lions).

Tree-dwellers like squirrels use their tails for balancing on limbs. In some animals, like opossums, chameleons, and many monkeys, the tail is "prehensile," meaning that it functions as a spare hand. A spider monkey can wrap her tail around a branch like a rope, and hang on for dear life.

When menaced by a predator, many lizards drop their tails, like you would drop your wallet in front of a mugger. In some species, the tail is designed to break off between two vertebrae if the lizard is captured by his tail. Other lizards can contract the tail muscles, fracturing one vertebra along a built-in weak spot. As the tail wriggles on the ground, the predator is momentarily distracted. If the lizard escapes, he may regrow part of his tail.

Fast Fact

Surprise! The animal with the longest tail—up to 8 feet (2.4 m)—is the male giraffe.

Porcupines use their tails like weapons, releasing a raft of sharp quills. Some dinosaurs may have wielded their heavy, spine-studded tails like armored clubs.

Tails can also be used in body language. A cat whips her tail back and forth, warning that she's annoyed or angry. A dog's crazily wagging tail shows excitement, like a little kid jumping up and down. A tail held up high may mean "I'm top dog," like a man pulling himself up to full height in an attempt to intimidate. Tucking a tail under and cowering communicates "Okay, you win; I'm afraid. Now please leave me alone."

How do snakes move (and even climb trees) with no feet or hands?

FAMOUS SLITHERING SNAKE MOVES

Garden of Eden... *The slow crawl was effective—I didn't want to frighten Eve.*

Your Basic Western *I switch to the serpentine method to chase cowboys.*

And Action Movies *Doing the concertina makes climbing ice walls a snap. Indiana Jones eat your heart out!*

Slithering snakes look like they're slip-sliding away. But snake locomotion actually depends on friction, just like walking. (Ever try strolling across a smooth patch of ice? It's a slippery reminder of how the friction between your feet and the sidewalk keeps you moving forward.)

Snakes move themselves along a surface mostly by squeezing and releasing muscles around their hundreds of ribs. These muscles are attached to skin covered with belly scales, which grip the ground like tire treads.

While snake species move in a variety of ways, all snakes can do the undulating crawl known as slithering. This familiar S-shaped motion is actually the speediest of snake movements, with the fastest-known snake gliding forward at about 12 miles per hour (19.3 km/h).

Slithering snakes use their flanks to push off of objects on either side—say, pebbles in a driveway. Snakes can even undulate through a pond, by pushing against the resistance of the water around them.

But snakes also slither nicely across a piece of rough cloth. Scientists have known since the 1940s that snakeskin is good at generating friction with surfaces, helping a snake move steadily along. But it wasn't until the last few years that they figured out how a snake's hundreds of scales help propel it across your lawn—and then up the nearest tree.

Scientists knew that the scales—shaped like tiny clamshells, and overlapped

> Snake scales act like hooks, catching here and there on uneven surfaces.

like mini-blinds—helped a snake move along by catching here and there on an uneven surface. In 2009, a study found that the friction between a snake's belly scales and a surface was highest when a snake was traveling forward, while sliding from side to side. By slithering and shifting its weight, allowing for more or less contact (and thus friction) with the ground, a snake could move quickly across a rough surface.

Then, in 2012, researchers at the Georgia Institute of Technology and New York University made a startling discovery: A snake can apparently control each of its belly scales, varying the scale's angle to the ground. By deliberately moving each tiny skin flap, researchers say, snakes can double the amount of resistance between scales and the surface they're moving across—substantially increasing grip strength.

The researchers also found that snakes on a bark-covered wall used their muscles to push on the bark with a force equal to nine times their body weight. Add angling their scales to catch on nooks and crannies, and snakes are able to slither up tree trunks—rather like a climber using hands and feet to scale a vertical cliff.

How did dinosaurs get their long names?

Bibliotops...

"That's Bookface to you!"

Jurassic Inventus...

Hors d'oeuvre-o-saurus...

Watch out at cocktail parties!

... Autoraptor...

I love stick shifts!

Their names are tongue twisters: *Archaeornithoides. Dachongosaurus. Megacervixosaurus.* But it seems fitting, somehow, that long, weird names should belong to the biggest, weirdest creatures ever to walk or fly over planet Earth: the dinosaurs.

It all starts with the word dinosaur itself. An English scientist named Sir Richard Owen coined the word *dinosauria* in 1841. He combined two Greek words, *deinos* and *sauros. Deinos* means "terrible"; *sauros* means "lizard." And some (though not most) dinosaurs were terrible lizards indeed.

One of the most terrible was the familiar *Tyrannosaurus.* This big-headed, long-toothed, 39-foot dinosaur (11.9 m) is a favorite movie monster. The Tyrannosaurs, armed with heavy claws and massive jaws, attacked and ate other animals, including other dinosaurs. *Tyrannosaurus rex*

(*T. rex*) lived in what is now the western United States, Canada, and East Asia, and weighed up to 15,000 pounds (6,804 kg). The name fits: *Tyrannosaurus* means "tyrant lizard" and *rex* means "king."

It has been scientists—mainly biologists—who have named the dinosaurs whose bones have been unearthed over the years. Each name has its own story.

Some names refer to how scientists believe the animal behaved, as with ferocious *Tyrannosaurus*. Take *Oviraptor* ("egg stealer"); scientists who named it thought it snatched and ate other dinosaurs' eggs. Then there's *Segnosaurus* ("slow lizard"), whose long thighs, short shins, and short feet probably made it one of the pokier dinosaurs.

Some names refer to a dinosaur's physical features, especially those that set it apart from other kinds of dinosaurs. For example, *Triceratops* means "three-horned face." *Triceratops* had a long horn mounted above each eye and a short, stubby horn atop its nose. And *Deinonychus* ("terrible claw") had large fangs and claws, including two longer claws shaped like scythes.

Other names identify where the dinosaur was found. *Minmi* was an armored dinosaur named after Minmi Crossing, a place in Australia near where its first skeleton was discovered. *Danubiosaurus* ("Danube lizard") was first found in Austria, where the Danube River runs.

And a few dinosaurs are named after people, some of them scientists, some of them not. *Herrerasaurus* ("Herrera's lizard") was a flesh-eater that was 10 feet (3.05 m) long. It was named after Victorino Herrera, a goat farmer who found the skeleton in the Andes Mountains of South America.

While the average person may have heard of a handful

Fast Fact

The dinosaur with the longest name—*Micropachycephalosaurus*—was one of the smallest, a mere 20 inches (51 cm) long. Its name means "small, thick-headed lizard."

of dinosaurs, hundreds of kinds of dinosaurs have been identified and named. These include *Abrictosaurus* ("awake lizard"), *Anatotitan* ("giant duck"), *Barapasaurus* ("big-leg lizard"), *Chindesaurus* ("ghost lizard"), *Daspletosaurus* ("frightful lizard"), *Fulgurotherium* ("lightning beast"), *Phaedrolosaurus* ("gleaming lizard"), *Seismosaurus* ("earth-shaking lizard"), and *Vulcanodon* ("volcano tooth").

Here's an idea: Why not create, describe, and name your own dinosaur?

Why do the hearts of small animals beat faster than those of big animals?

My beatin' heart...

It beats for you!

Mine beats faster, my love is true!

Their pulses pound as slow as goo! So let them go 'cause I love you!

Boing Boing Boing Boing

Thud Thud

TickTick Tick Tick Tick

Your heart may beat faster when a certain card or box of chocolates is delivered on Valentine's Day. However, if you were a squirrel, your heart would beat faster still if a box of assorted acorns arrived.

The pace of our own human hearts—about 60 to 80 beats at rest—seems normal to us, but other creatures skip to different beats. A resting rabbit may have a heart rate of 130, which speeds up to 300 when the bunny darts across the lawn. But the silence between a blue whale's heartbeats may last 20 long seconds.

Hearts beat, of course, to send blood pulsing through the body, from heads to distant toes and tails. With each squeeze of your heart, up to half a cup of freshly oxygenated blood is pushed along through your arteries, nourishing cells as it goes.

Among mammals, from humans to squirrels to whales, heart rate varies according to size: The bigger the mammal, the slower the heart. So an elephant's heart, weighing 26 to 40 pounds, thumps about 30 times a minute. But a resting bat's small heart races along at more than 300 beats a minute.

It seems like a mystery. A larger body requires more blood, so we might expect a big animal's heart to beat faster. And isn't it easier to circulate blood throughout a tiny body?

Measure FOR Measure

26 to 40 pounds = 12 to 18 kg
12,000 pounds = 5,443 kg
1 ounce = 28.4 g

HEART RATE EXTREMES

The slowest heartbeat of all belongs to the blue whale, whose heart is the size of a Volkswagen Beetle. When the whale is swimming near the water's surface, its heart is beating about six times a minute—once every 10 seconds. But if the whale dives, its heart, conserving oxygen, slows to three beats a minute. Compare that to the fluttering heart of a hummingbird, racing at 1,200 beats a minute as the bird executes such aerial acrobatics as flying backward and upside down.

But it turns out that the mass of a large animal is packed into a proportionately smaller body suit than the mass of a small animal. Which is why, compared to its mass, a mouse's body actually has more surface area than an elephant's. And since animals lose heat through their skin, the body of a smaller animal must work even harder to maintain its internal temperature. The result? Small animals burn calories very quickly; big animals have slower, thriftier metabolisms.

The average elephant tips the scale at more than 12,000 pounds. A typical field mouse weighs just an ounce, about as much as a Valentine requiring just one stamp. But thanks to its slower metabolism, an elephant weighing 200,000 times as much as a mouse will need only 10,000 times the calories.

Result: The faster metabolism of smaller animals requires that their hearts supply oxygen at a higher rate, beating extra-fast to keep up with the demand. Which is why, at about 400 beats a minute, a mouse's tiny heart beats more than 10 times faster than an elephant's.

If human beings evolved from apes, why don't apes in jungles turn into humans?

Although we are closely related to modern apes, they didn't turn into us. It's similar to your relationship to a distant cousin. You and your cousin descended from two of the same great-grandparents. We and the apes descended from a common relative, too.

We don't have to look into the distant past to see evidence for evolution. Evolution is a process going on all around us. Bacteria that were once easily killed by penicillin have evolved new forms that are resistant to that antibiotic, and to many others.

Animal species change over time, becoming better suited to their environments. And new animal species appear, live for thousands or millions of years, and then vanish.

 Evolution is a process going on all the time, all around us.

Evolution needs time and happy accidents to work its changes. Features that may help a species survive better—such as unusual but more efficient teeth, or a larger brain—can show up in newborn animals accidentally, as random variations. If new features are truly helpful to survival, the fortunate animals that have them may live longer and survive where some others won't. They will live to have offspring, and the changes will be passed along over generations. If the features are great aids to

survival, the animals with them may gradually crowd out the animals without them. Over many years, a whole species will look different.

Human beings are primates, as are more than 100 other species, including monkeys, apes, and gorillas. We primates are more alike than different. We have hands with five fingers and feet with five toes. We have teeth that are good for eating a wide variety of foods—from tearing off a chunk of meat to grinding up a succulent plant. We give birth to one or a few children at a time. And our children take a long time to grow up.

Our closest primate relatives are the "great apes"—chimpanzees, gorillas, and orangutans. We are related not because we evolved from them, but because we share a common ancestor with them.

The first mammals, the ancestors of dogs and whales, chimpanzees and humans, and all of the other creatures that feed their young milk, evolved about 225 million years ago. They were tiny,

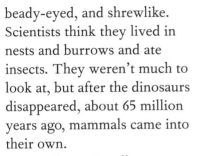

beady-eyed, and shrewlike. Scientists think they lived in nests and burrows and ate insects. They weren't much to look at, but after the dinosaurs disappeared, about 65 million years ago, mammals came into their own.

By about 60 million years ago, the first true primates, the early prosimians, had appeared. Small and rather ratlike, they scampered through the treetops in forests that covered much of the solid ground on our planet. By 30 million years ago, they had been joined by monkeys and small apes, who eventually crowded out the prosimians. Later, apes and monkeys evolved in separate directions, and bigger-brained apes evolved—orangutans, gorillas, and chimpanzees.

Human beings, common chimpanzees, and bonobos (a kind of chimpanzee) share a recent common ancestor, an animal that lived about 7 million years ago. But then we all went our separate ways. One evolutionary line led, step-by-step, to us. Another led to the chimpanzees.

Not only are chimpanzees our closest relatives, but we are *their* closest relations as well. We share about 99 percent of our genes with them (although there are some genes we share only with common chimpanzees, and some only with bonobos). We can see some of the similarities ourselves: Chimpanzees are sociable animals who use simple tools (modifying twigs to dig out tasty ants), make primitive weapons (spears, used to hunt smaller primates), and share food with each other.

The key to our own human evolution was the grasslands, or savannas. Some groups of our primitive, apelike ancestors left the forest and began to try making their living on the grasslands. During the wet

All mammals share a common ancestor that evolved about 225 million years ago.

season, the grass is green and thick, trees are leafy, and bushes burst forth. But when the rains stop, the trees lose their leaves, and the grasses dry into hay.

Animals that live on the savanna must learn to cope with these changes. Sometimes, there is plenty to eat. Other times, favorite foods nearly disappear. So being able to reach into bushes and comb the ground for nuts and berries can mean the difference between death and survival.

By about 4 million

years ago, a new creature could be glimpsed roaming the savanna. It looked much like an ape, but it walked on two legs, which left its hands free for gathering food scattered on the grasslands. Its brain was larger. It wasn't human, but it wasn't quite an ape, either.

These first hominids—humanlike primates—appeared about 9 million years ago. Fossils show what they looked like. In Ethiopia, scientists found a nearly complete skeleton of a female, which they nicknamed "Lucy." Less than 4 feet (1.22 m) tall, Lucy lived and died millions of years ago. She walked upright, but was probably quite hairy and apelike.

Lucy and her kind eventually died out. Scientists think that they lost the competition for food to later hominids even better adapted to grassland life. These hominids had even bigger brains and made specialized stone tools. They were able to hunt large game as well as gather fruits and vegetables.

Modern humans (*Homo sapiens*) first appeared at least 200,000 years ago. We walk upright, use our hands to make complex tools, and have devised language to communicate through symbols. We live in complicated social groups. And we have developed a shared culture of ideas and ways of acting that we teach our children.

Today, we are not confined to the grasslands. We live everywhere on Earth, even in places where we could not "naturally" survive, such as in the bitter cold of the far North. The apelike creatures that were our ancestors are long gone. We, and the modern great apes, are separate but related animals, sharing the Earth.

How do birds know where south is?

Imagine you're on a long car trip. It's night, and you take a wrong turn onto a dark country road. With a sinking feeling, you realize that you have no idea where you are.

Then you glance up at the sky, and the answer is written in light: a glowing compass face, with north, south, east, and west at the four points, and a big needle pointing at north. What a relief! You turn your car around and head in the right direction, guided by the sky.

For migrating birds, finding their way over long distances through the darkest nights is second nature. And they do it in part by reading directions in the sky—directions written by light and magnetism.

Some birds journey thousand of miles in their twice-yearly journeys. Familiar landmarks, like mountain ranges and rivers, play a part. But birds may also navigate using the stars, and by sensing—or even "seeing"— the Earth's magnetic field, arcing out from the poles.

For many years, scientists have been studying what's

behind the uncanny ability of migrating birds to find their way to their winter and summer homes. One thing that they agree on: Migratory baby birds are already equipped with a kind of preset inner compass. This compass leads them to make their very first autumn flight in the direction long-traveled by the rest of their species. So scarlet tanagers, cerulean warblers, and purple martins are born knowing which way home is.

To travel hundreds or thousands of miles— perhaps to a place they've never been— birds use the whole planet and sky as a natural map.

HOW FAR DO THEY FLY?

Some migrating birds don't go very far, making the short hop from a mountain home to the warmer valley below. Others cross several states. But some make much longer trips. Prompted by the change in seasons, blackpoll warblers soar into the sky over the eastern United States and fly to spots in Puerto Rico or the Lesser Antilles in the Caribbean, or to northern South America. The small black-and-white birds weigh less than 1 ounce (28.4 g). Equipped with radio transmitters, the birds have been found to fly 1,200 miles (1,931 km) from the southeast United States to Venezuela—nonstop.

The most epic journey is made by the Arctic tern, which can live 30 years, and experiences two summers each year. The birds can travel 50,000 miles (80,467 km) in their wending flights from the Arctic north to bottom-of-the-world Antarctica and back again, chasing summer.

However, if fledgling birds are moved far away from their usual starting point, they never reach their warm winter homes in the south. Experienced adult migrators, however, remember their routes, making corrections as needed.

How do migratory birds develop such remarkable inner maps? Some tantalizing clues have emerged from decades of studies. During the daytime, birds may use the position of the Sun in the sky as a compass. For example, a bird flying north from the equator can stay on course by keeping the Sun behind and to his right in the morning, behind and to his left in the afternoon. And birds may figure out where they are, latitude-wise, by the exact height of the Sun in the sky at a particular time of day. Most migratory birds, however, don't even take off until dusk; they do most of their traveling overnight.

A bevy of birds, winging silently across the sky on a clear moonless night, are like sailors on a boat in the middle of the sea. Although they might be unable to see familiar landmarks in the dark, they can check the stars. Polaris, the North Star, glows directly over the North Pole. Studies show that birds seem to use the Pole Star and star groups like the Big Dipper to determine which way north and south are, just as we humans do.

But the most important navigational tool of all, many scientists say, may be magnetism. The Earth is one enormous magnet; magnetic field lines loop out and connect the North and South Poles. To migrating birds, the planet's magnetic field may be like a map of the world,

SILENT SPRINGS?

More than 380 species of birds that nest in eastern U.S. forests go far south for the winter, to places in Mexico, Central America, and South America. Their final stop is usually a tropical rain forest. But each year, they find less and less forest standing as trees are cut down for lumber, burned down to build cattle ranches, or cleared for mining or agriculture. According to the United Nations, 18 million acres (7.28 million hectares) of forest disappear every year—and half of the planet's dense tropical rain forests are already gone.

And yet, the rain forests are where nearly half of all the species of life on Earth live. Scientists estimate that more than 135 species of plants and animals, including insects, vanish every day from the tropical forests—some 50,000 species a year.

It's very difficult to count birds and figure out how many are surviving year to year, but around the world the number in many species of migratory birds is dropping steadily. Some species have lost more than 90 percent of their member birds. And habitat loss, according to researchers, is the number one reason.

Saving the tropical rain forests is crucial for many reasons, not the least of which is that trees clear the air of carbon dioxide and supply Earth's air with its vital oxygen. Most of the world's remaining trees live in the rain forests. If too much carbon dioxide accumulates in the atmosphere, more heat is trapped on Earth, creating a greenhouse effect. The rise in temperatures can disrupt weather systems and melt the polar glaciers, with flooding in some places, droughts and famines in others.

Climate change sometimes seems too complicated to imagine, but it's not hard to imagine exhausted, hungry birds—those that survived the flight south, because many do not—finding their winter homes a smoking ruin. Saving the rain forests will ensure we have no birdless "silent springs" in the north or the south.

readable even on the darkest, stormiest night.

How do birds sense the force fields of magnetism? Studies point to a combination of built-in detectors. Iron-tipped nerve cells in a bird's upper beak may sense the direction, angle, and intensity of the earth's magnetic field at a particular location. Other magnetic detectors may be hidden in a bird's eyes. Some scientists think that shifting magnetic fields trigger tiny chemical changes involving a blue-light receptor in the eyes called cryptochrome. Scientists think that birds may actually see the Earth's magnetic field, perhaps as patterns of light and shade. The ability may be tied to a bird's right eye and the left brain that receives its input. So clear vision in the right eye may be essential for good navigating.

And a 2006 study found that birds may calibrate their inner magnetic compass using sunlight. The scattering of sunlight by gas molecules causes invisible polarization patterns in the sky. (Polarized means that the light vibrates in only one direction, in a flat plane.) At sunset and sunrise, an intense band of polarized light extends across the sky at a 90-degreee angle from the Sun. (So when the Sun is due west, the band lies north-south.) Birds may see this polarized band, and use it to orient themselves before departing.

Seeing magnetic force lines may be yet another enviable bird ability, trumped only by the ability to fly, which we humans can only do

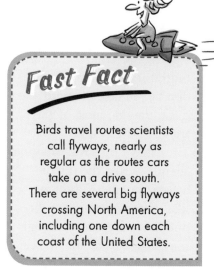

in dreams. But a 2010 study suggests that a sense we can relate to—smell—may also be important to navigation. Researchers found that smell-impaired birds chose a due-south route when they should have flown southwest, unlike birds that could follow familiar odors.

How can hummingbirds fly upside down and backward?

Hummingbirds are probably a little tired of being called nature's helicopters, but that's what they are. Or, rather, since hummingbirds came first, helicopters are technology's hummingbirds.

Surprise: While many people may have seen only one or two kinds of hummingbird, there are actually more than 300 different species. Most live in the tropics of South America. But hummingbirds buzz around Central and North America, too, as far north as Alaska. The tiniest is the bee hummingbird, at about 2 inches long; the biggest is the giant hummingbird, whose body, at about 8.5 inches long, is the size of a large sparrow's.

All hummingbirds have patches of iridescent feathers, which shimmer like the rainbow colors on an oil slick. Hummingbirds use their needle-slim bills

---

A hummingbird combines a bird's body with the flying tricks of insects.

---

to nose deep into flowers, using forked tongues to lap up the sweet nectar hidden inside. For protein, they may swallow tiny insects lurking in the flowers' fragrant depths or snatch bugs caught in the nearest spiderweb.

Hummingbirds use enormous amounts of energy simply being themselves. When a hummingbird is sitting quietly on a branch, its heart races at 550 times a minute, or more than nine beats a second. But when a bird is engaged in aerial acrobatics, its heart goes into overdrive, accelerating to more than 1,200 beats a minute. A person whose body burned energy at the rate of a hummingbird would have to eat about 155,000 calories a day. (That's about 1,550 bananas—or 281 Big Macs.)

But hummingbirds prefer nectar to burgers. So instead of hovering at the nearest drive-through window, a hummingbird helicopters alongside a flower. Just as a helicopter can perform feats that put ordinary planes to shame, hummingbirds can fly rings around other birds—including upside down and backward.

Most birds fly by flapping, moving their wings forward and downward with great force to achieve "lift" in the air. A bird's flight muscles are specialized chest muscles (pectorals), souped-up versions of human pecs. But

Measure FOR Measure

2 inches = 5.1 cm
8.5 inches = 21.6 cm
180 pounds = 81.7 kg
60 pounds = 27.2 kg
one-tenth of an oz = 2.84 g

TRY IT FOR YOURSELF

Biologists say hummingbirds can beat their wings so quickly mainly because of their body size and wing length. In general, the bigger and longer the body part, such as an arm, the slower it moves.

Pretend your unbent index finger is a wing, and flap it up and down as you watch a clock tick off the seconds. Now try flapping your arm. While your finger can flap speedily, your arm is a relative slowpoke. But a hummingbird puts your finger-flapping to shame—its tiny wings beat up to 80 times a second, in a blur of motion.

the average bird's upstroke muscles are weak, weighing only 5 to 10 percent as much as its powerful downstroke muscles.

The hummingbird difference? First, its flight muscles make up nearly a third of its body weight, compared to 15 to 20 percent for other birds. (Imagine a 180-pound bodybuilder—with 60-pound pecs). Second, its upstroke muscles are more powerful than those of other birds. Like a regular bird, a hummingbird flaps its wings to fly forward. But a hummingbird's wings can

rotate nearly 180 degrees at the bird's flexible shoulders.

So by slanting the angle of its wings and using its powerful chest muscles, a hummingbird can tip up and fly backward. And by spreading its tail and doing a quick backward somersault, a hummingbird can also fly upside down (a position in which its powerful upstroke is now transformed into a downstroke).

Finally, a hummingbird can hover. It does so by tilting its body nearly straight up and down, while moving its wings forward and

backward in a too-fast-to-see figure-8 pattern. This allows it to suspend its body weight over a delicate flower, while it sips the flower's nectar. In addition, like a helicopter, a hummingbird can lift straight up into the air. This comes in handy for doing a quick turnaround in a nest.

During the airshow-style maneuvers, the tiny bird's wings beat about 18 to 80 times a second. (Compare that to a vulture's once-a-second flap.) In fact, it's the sound of those tiny wings beating that put the "hum" in hummingbird.

Hummingbirds combine a bird's body with the flying tricks of insects, like the hover-and-dart motions of dragonflies. Insects move their flat wings in a figure-8 pattern that creates nearly equal lift during downstrokes and upstrokes. But bird wings are more like human arms than insect wings. Even a hummingbird is no match for an insect, since about 75 percent of its weight support, according to research, still comes from the downstroke.

However, other birds' in-flight weight support comes almost 100 percent from the downstroke. It's the 25-percent lift on the upstroke that helps give hummingbirds their insectlike hovering advantage. Studies have found that hummingbirds get their extra upstroke lift from inverting their wings as they fly.

Alas, all the fancy flying feats come at a price. Try as they might, hummingbirds cannot soar, surely one of the high points of possessing the ability to fly. So the next time you see a sparrow soaring into a deep blue sky, don't feel sorry for it because it can't fly backward.

How come some birds fly in V formations?

Geese Yappin' on Formation Flappin'

Some birds make alphabet letters in the sky, no Wicked Witch exhaust broom required. But instead of SURRENDER DOROTHY, we just get the random V, J, or W.

Think of birds flying in a V, and you might imagine ducks or geese, winging across town to a lake, or across the state line to somewhere warmer. But other large birds that fly long distances—pelicans and swans, cranes and cormorants—also travel in letter-shaped packs.

No one knows for sure why these birds fly in a V (ever try to interrogate a goose?), but scientists have good theories.

In a 2001 study in France, researchers partnered with filmmakers who had trained pelicans to fly behind light planes and motorboats for a movie. For the experiments, the pelicans were outfitted with heart rate monitors, and filmed as they flew in formation. What the researchers found: The V shape helps birds save energy, critical on long flights.

Just as a car uses more gas to drive 500 miles than 15 miles, birds use more energy and need more food to fuel long hauls. How does flying in a V help? Each flapping bird leaves roiling, turbulent air behind itself. Flying directly behind another bird, scientists note, would be like trying to swim behind a motorboat. But by lining up behind and to one side, a follower bird gets a boost from the resulting slipstream.

How? Each bird's wing tip rests on the rising air streaming from the wing of the bird just ahead and below it. The result: a free lift and reduced air drag, with birds drafting like cyclists in a road race.

Behind the lead bird, pelicans spent less time energetically flapping, more time gliding. Their heart rates dropped, too. By flying in the V, pelicans enjoyed an energy savings of up to 14 percent.

And by expending less energy, pelicans and other birds can fly farther without stopping to rest or eat. In fact, one study showed that geese flying in a V may be able to fly 70 percent farther than if each were flying solo.

Birds like geese may also like the V for the same reason bomber planes flew in V formations in World War II. The V shape, with each bird slightly higher than the one in front of it, lets each goose keep track of the whole bunch, allowing the best view and quickest head count. Plus, an open V allows geese to see what else might be approaching through the air, a feat that would be more difficult if the birds were bunched up in a mass.

Why don't smaller migrating birds use Vs? Researchers say their flapping wings don't create enough up-rushing air to help other birds glide for long.

Although the V shape may be optimal for long trips, birds like geese still get a bit of a boost (and keep the group together) flying in a less-organized J. And then there's the W, two linked Vs of birds, flapping and gliding into the sunset sky of autumn.

How do birds sleep?

MULTITASKING, BIRD STYLE...

Sleeping while Grocery shopping...
Must get corn FLAAAAKES!

Sleeping while Flying...
The wrong side of his brain is awake!

Sleeping while studying...
Half a brain is better than none!

During a long day at school or work, do you ever feel half asleep? Half asleep for a human means "drowsy." But at night, that blue jay in your backyard may really be half asleep.

Unlike us, many birds can enter a state of true half-sleep. In a half-sleeping animal, one side of the brain is slumbering, while the other side is wide awake. Scientists call this kind of sleep unihemispheric, because only half of the brain is sleeping.

During half-sleep, one eye will often be open and one eye closed, corresponding to the sleeping and non-sleeping halves of the brain. Besides birds, aquatic mammals like whales, dolphins, and seals often do the half-sleep, as may some reptiles.

Why not simply drift off to sleep, both eyes blissfully shut? Unihemispheric sleep allows birds to stay on guard, keeping an eye (and half a brain) peeled for threatening predators.

Like mammals, birds sleep in cycles of so-called slow-wave sleep and rapid-eye movement (REM) sleep, where most dreams occur. While birds spend part of their sleeping time only half-asleep, they also spend time with their whole brains asleep, both eyes closed. It's only when both hemispheres are snoozing that a bird's brain will enter short periods of REM sleep and enjoy a few brief dreams.

Scientists say that both half-sleep and extra-short bouts of dreaming sleep help protect vulnerable birds from other animals. Unfairly, it's usually predators like cats that have the luxury of enjoying lots of deep, dream-filled sleep, two eyes closed to the world.

Like us, most birds sleep during the night. The only birds that sleep in nests are baby birds and the adults taking care of them. When not nesting, most birds sleep perched on branches in trees or bushes, or in handy tree-trunk holes.

How do birds doze without falling? When a bird alights on a branch, bending his legs and settling his weight down, his leg muscles shorten. When the muscles contract, attached tendons pull on the toe bones, which curl into a tight grip. Toe tendons also have a rough underside that adheres to the tendon stretching down from the ankle, creating a built-in latch.

Unihemispheric sleep is especially useful when birds flock together to snooze. Studies of mallard ducks found that ducks sleeping on the edge of a row—a particularly vulnerable spot—spent most of their sleeping time half-awake, one eye open and facing out. Ducks in the more protected center, however, were more likely to sleep with their whole brains. Every so often, ducks on the edges turned 180 degrees and switched eyes, allowing the alert side of the brain to snooze, while the other side took up guard duty.

But even birds can't resist the power of deep sleep if they're truly sleep-deprived. When scientists kept chickens awake long enough, they found that the birds spent

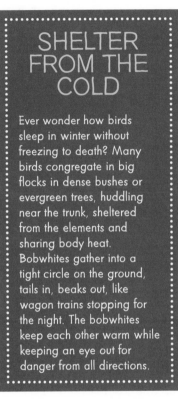

SHELTER FROM THE COLD

Ever wonder how birds sleep in winter without freezing to death? Many birds congregate in big flocks in dense bushes or evergreen trees, huddling near the trunk, sheltered from the elements and sharing body heat. Bobwhites gather into a tight circle on the ground, tails in, beaks out, like wagon trains stopping for the night. The bobwhites keep each other warm while keeping an eye out for danger from all directions.

less time with one eye open, half-asleep, and increasing amounts of time fully, deeply asleep, both eyes firmly shut.

How can birds sit on electrical wires and not get electrocuted?

In the spring, when birds come back to roost, it's like a high-tension convention. Birds of all sizes, from hummingbirds to sparrows to turkey vultures, find wires or poles a convenient spot to take a rest. Why? High above the ground, smaller birds feel less vulnerable to stalking predators like cats. Meanwhile, raptors like red-tailed hawks find a pole top a handy vantage point for hunting field mice far below.

Thankfully, most birds are never injured by their wire- or pole-perching behavior. When, say, a sparrow alights on a live wire, her body does become charged, rather like your hair when it's brushed in a dry room. But since the bird and the wire are at the same "electric potential," no current flows into the bird's body.

How does it work? An electric current is a movement of electrons, which jump from atom to atom in a material that can act as a conductor, such as copper or aluminum. Like water falling over a cliff and into a river below, tugged by gravity, electrons flow from a region of high electrical potential to low potential.

Compared to the aluminum wire carrying the current, a bird's body is a poor conductor. So the flow of electrons takes the path of least resistance, continuing on through the wire, rather than taking a detour through the bird. More importantly, electrons flow from a region of high potential to one of low potential. And the feet of a perching bird are at the same potential as the wire they're holding onto. Result: The flowing current ignores the resting sparrow.

Small birds are usually safe on their highly charged perches. However, a bird can be electrocuted if, while in contact with a single electrified wire, she also touches a second wire with her leg or wing. Now the bird has made herself into a part of an electrical loop or circuit, and the current will take the new, shorter path through her body.

The base of the electrical pole holding up the wires is buried in the ground. So if a bird sits on a pole and touches a wire (or vice versa), current will flow from the high-potential wire, through the bird, and down to the low-potential ground.

Larger birds of prey, with their greater wingspans, are especially likely to be killed by power-line perches. In the open plains and deserts of the western United States, power poles and their transformer boxes are often the only high perches for miles around. Raptors like golden eagles use them to scan the landscape for prey, before soaring off into rising wind currents.

The California condor, with a wingspan of more than 9 feet (2.7 m), can easily connect a live wire and a transformer box while settling onto a pole. Their huge wings can also connect two live wires. Sadly, thousands of raptors are killed by power lines each year.

Some power companies have taken steps to protect large birds by widening the gap between conducting wires and grounds, insulating metal parts, and moving wires farther away from pole tops. In some cases, perch guards are mounted on poles, keeping raptors and other large birds from sitting in hazardous spots.

Where do bugs go in the winter?

Winter Survival Guide for Insects...

Create a bug beach in the basement

Hot water heater

Fly with friends to a secret hideaway...

Have a hive party and dance till spring!

Get down!

...with your bad bug self!

Recipe for a snowman (besides the snow): hat, carrot, charcoal, corncob pipe, scarf, flea collar . . . Wait, what? You say your snowman doesn't have fleas? Look closer, and you may see a few tiny, jumping specks: snow fleas, one of the few bugs active in winter. But here's the rub—snow fleas

aren't really fleas. And they're not full-fledged insects, either.

The true insects—the flies, mosquitoes, ants, bees, butterflies—are either long gone or lying low. Many adult insects don't survive the freezing cold of winter. But many migrate, and others hide and hibernate.

Flies often crawl into the nooks and crannies of a warm house or barn, venturing out to flit around only on milder winter afternoons. Some adult mosquitoes look for dark, damp hiding places—like your basement—to spend the winter months. Other mosquito species do things differently. In summer, they lay their eggs, and the adults die off. Through fall and winter, the eggs lie dormant, actually freezing when the weather turns cold. In the spring, the eggs thaw and hatch.

Besides surviving as eggs, some insects make it through the winter in their immature forms, as larvae, nymphs, or pupae. Caterpillar larvae may wait, buried under leaves; the larvae of cicadas, June bugs, and fireflies burrow into the soil. Dragonfly and mayfly nymphs live in streams and ponds, even when the water is topped by ice. And the pupae of certain moths stay attached to branches, just waiting for spring. Meanwhile, tomato hornworm pupae rest several inches underground.

But adult insects look for warm(ish) spots to hibernate, like holes in tree bark; under rocks, leaf piles, and fallen trees; and in barns, attics, basements, and the walls of houses. (Think ladybugs and

DO BUGS SLEEP?

At a summer picnic, with flies soft-landing in the potato salad, ants swarming the coconut layer cake, and mosquitoes dive-bombing Uncle Harry, it's easy to assume bugs never nap.

Scientists once thought bugs rested, but never really slept. But research indicates that many insects may have periods of sleep remarkably like ours. So far, scientists have found that bees, fruit flies, cockroaches, moths, paper wasps, locusts, and scorpions all enjoy (and require) a good snooze.

Of the known bug sleepers, honeybees and fruit flies have been studied the most. Fruit flies, after all, have been the subject of heredity and gene research since 1910. Scientists say honeybees make good subjects because hive living makes them so social, and because their elaborate social life has been studied for so long.

Studies found that fruit flies are still for a total of about 6 to 12 hours a night. Tired flies find a resting spot and then snooze face down. And the longer they sleep, the harder it is to wake them up by tapping on their cage.

Honeybees may sleep about 8 hours a day, including naps. Like us humans, bees tend to sleep mostly at night. Inside the hive, they crawl into empty cells or simply crash on the hive floor, lying on their sides, antennae slumping. Just like sleep-deprived people, bees kept up one night tend to sleep more the next.

And as in a dreaming dog—or person—a bee's legs (and antennae) may jerk in its sleep. The idea of a slumbering, dreaming bee makes the world seem like an even richer place. It might even be time for a new adage: "Let sleeping bees lie."

wasps.) Honeybees stay warm in their hive homes, snuggling up in a tight ball, using their wing muscles to generate heat.

And like many birds, some insects migrate in the fall, escaping the cold for warmer places. The most widespread species of locusts are migrators. So are some kinds of butterflies, moths, wasps, and other insects. The orange-and-black monarch butterfly, found across the United States and Canada in summer, is one of the most famous insect migrators. Hundreds of millions of monarchs leave in the fall, flying up to 3,000 miles to their winter home in Mexico's Sierra Madre Mountains.

Meanwhile, some species that stay put, including some beetles, bees, and butterflies, protect themselves from the cold by changing their body chemistry—allowing a kind of natural antifreeze called glycerol to build up in their tissues. But these insects also try to remain as still as possible, to conserve energy and stay warm.

Snow fleas, on the other hand, stay active throughout the winter. These "fleas" are actually springtails, tiny bouncing bundles that look like dark specks on the snow. (Springtails were once considered insects, but are now classified as insectlike hexapods, since their eyes and abdomens don't match those of true insects.)

Springtails range into the polar regions, and their bodies have evolved to survive the frigid cold. When the temperature drops to about 28°F, Arctic springtails begin making hydrogen peroxide (just like the peroxide bleach in those brown drugstore bottles).

Fast Fact

Honeybees may eat up to 30 pounds of the honey stored in their hives over a long winter.

The peroxide helps the springtails' bodies slowly dry out as their pores open to the dry, cold air. Meanwhile, they also begin to produce a sugar called trehalose, a natural antifreeze. Hidden under rocks, springtails survive Arctic winters as shriveled-up versions of their former selves. In the spring, warmer, more humid air causes dehydrated springtails to plump up again, like mite-size sponges.

Measure FOR Measure
28°F = −2°C
3,000 miles = 4,828 km
30 pounds = 13.6 kg

How can a fly walk across the ceiling?

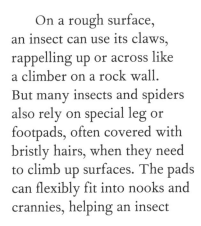

If we could look closely at our ceilings, we'd see the crisscrossing paths of thousands of tiny footprints, left by flies, ladybugs, and other insects (as well as by spiders). In fact, the problem for flies and other bugs may not be holding onto the ceiling, but breaking free from it. Turns out, a fly strolling across a ceiling is a bit like a person walking across a field of wet mud.

How do flies walk upside down, apparently effortlessly? Being tiny helps. Very-low-mass animals like wall-walking insects and spiders feel less of a pull from gravity. So it's easier for a fly than, say, a pig to stick to the ceiling.

On a rough surface, an insect can use its claws, rappelling up or across like a climber on a rock wall. But many insects and spiders also rely on special leg or footpads, often covered with bristly hairs, when they need to climb up surfaces. The pads can flexibly fit into nooks and crannies, helping an insect or spider keep its footing. In addition to using its sticky silk, a spider climbing a wall can grip tiny bumps in the plaster or wallboard with its microscopic hair "feet."

Scientists once thought that rough, bumpy foot hairs allowed flies to cling to tiny imperfections on smooth-looking surfaces. A substance secreted by the hairs helped, adding a bit of Post-it style adhesion.

But in 2006, scientists discovered that the substance secreted by the hairs on a fly's feet is a surprisingly sticky glue, tailor-made for striding confidently upside down across the ceiling.

The glue-y stuff oozing out of a fly's footpad hairs is a mixture of oils and sugars. Researchers say that all insects may secrete the glue, since all 300 species of wall-climbing insects studied left a trail of tiny, sticky footprints.

The adhesive is strong enough to keep each foot planted on the ceiling, with the fly standing still. Walking, however, is another matter. The journey across the top of a room may look effortless from our perspective, but it's a struggle for the fly.

To get a foot unstuck and moving again, flies use at least four different maneuvers. Watching slow-motion tapes of each foot detachment, scientists found that a fly sometimes pushed a foot away from himself, popping the footpad off the surface like a freed suction cup. Flies also twisted their footpads until they loosened from the wall. Or they jerked them quickly, like yanking off a Band-Aid. Flies also used the handy, built-in claws on their feet to pull their own footpad off the ceiling, like a person tugging off a boot.

According to the scientists, the techniques that involved peeling the pad off

a ceiling or wall work best, because they require less energy.

Using four of six legs as they crawled across the ceiling also helped the flies make their gravity-defying journeys. On the ground, scientists say, flies often use just three legs at a time to move around: two legs on one side and the middle leg on the other, forming a stable triangle, alternating sides with each step.

How do fireflies glow?

On a warm summer night, fireflies wink on and off in a field like distant lightning. Catch one in a jar, and you can see the firefly's lantern signal in a ghostly, green-yellow light. The light looks strangely cold, and it is: Firefly light, unlike sunlight, produces almost no heat.

Fireflies—surprise—are beetles, and there are more than 2,000 firefly species on Earth. Grown-up fireflies are brown or black and are about half an inch (1.3 cm) long.

Baby fireflies hatch out of eggs hidden in the soil. Like many other newborn insects, they are called larvae. The larvae don't look much like adult fireflies. Like adults, they are brown; unlike adults, they're quite flat.

Some species of firefly larvae glow all the time.

There is an old song about glowing little glowworms that "glimmer, glimmer." Well, "glowworm" is another name for a baby firefly.

Firefly light is made in the insect's abdomen, or lower belly, which contains cells called photocytes. Two chemicals in the photocytes, luciferin and luciferase, react with each other, releasing energy. (*Lucifer* means

REALLY? NO LIGHTNING BUGS IN CALIFORNIA?

Surprise: Kids (and adults) who've never traveled outside of California may have seen winking fireflies only in books, movies, and TV commercials (and at the Pirates of the Caribbean ride at Disneyland). Lightning bugs are noticeably absent from California lawns and fields.

According to entomologists (scientists who study bugs), there are different kinds of fireflies in California and other western states. There are the so-called dark fireflies, in which adults don't fly and only larvae glow, and the glowworm fireflies, in which babies and wingless adult females glow.

Lightning bugs—the firefly species in which adults flash *and* fly—prefer warm, moist places. They have never crossed the dry, geographical barrier of the eastern Rocky Mountains or the deserts of the Southwest. So flying lanterns won't be seen at night in California, Washington, Oregon, Nevada, Wyoming, Idaho, New Mexico, Arizona, Colorado, or western Texas.

And even in places where lightning bugs are abundant, they prefer the country and suburbs to big cities. Which is why you probably won't see any fireflies competing with the neon lights in Times Square.

"light-bearing" in Latin.) The energy excites the atoms in luciferin, which give off photons of light.

Behind the photocytes, another layer of cells, filled with a white chemical, reflects the light out at us, like the reflector on a bike.

Other animals (and plants) give off cold light, too. On a dark night in the woods, you may see a patch of toadstools, scattered like glowing lampshades across the ground. In the ocean, squids squirt out glowing clouds of chemicals to cloak themselves from prey. And jellyfish flash.

But *why* do fireflies light up? Scientists think the insects blink their lights mainly to attract mates. Each kind of firefly blinks with its own rhythm, so female and male fireflies can make sure they're hooking up with a member of their own species.

Some species, known as synchronous fireflies, can coordinate their blinking, so that a large group lights up or goes dark at the same instant. Fireflies gather in trees, or across a hillside, blinking randomly. Soon, a pair begins to flash together. The pattern spreads; larger and larger groups send out bursts of light at the same time. Soon, an entire tree may be winking on and off, as fireflies blink in unison.

Synchronous fireflies can create waves of light across a hillside. Scientists aren't sure how they coordinate their twinkle-light flashing—or why.

Why do bees die after they sting someone?

To Bee or...(pending loss of Stinger) Not to Bee...

Whether 'tis Nobler to Suffer...a bunch of bad luck...

or to take arms against a Sea of troubles...

and by opposing end them? Bummer...

Boxer Muhammad Ali once said that in the ring he would "float like a butterfly and sting like a bee." Actually, Ali stung more like a wasp than a bee. After delivering its own version of a sharp punch, a honeybee is down for the count.

The world is full of bees; up to 30,000 different species buzz around the flowers of Earth. Bees belong to the Hymenoptera order, which also includes wasps, hornets, and even ants.

Surprisingly, most bee species are solitary, with female bees laying eggs in individual nests. Honeybees and bumblebees, on the other hand, are wildly social, living in a complex tribe. A single queen does all the egg laying. A community of thousands of female workers clean, tend to the larvae (baby bees), and make nectar runs. Meanwhile, hundreds of male drones lounge about, their only job being to mate with the queen. Up to 50,000 individuals live in a hive, a small humming city of bees.

Most bees are "live-and-let-live" creatures. It takes a lot to provoke the average bee—like stepping on a worker sipping water from a blade of grass, or, especially, threatening its hive home. After all, the hive is full of everything a bee holds dear—bee queen, bee children, bee friends, and a pantry full of food.

The only weapon the average bee has to defend itself and its tribe is its stinger. Only female bees have stingers. Workers, which don't usually lay eggs, have an egg duct modified into a stinger and connected to a venom sac. The stinger's end is barbed like a fishhook. So when a female bee projects her tiny harpoon, it embeds in the skin. Once hooked in flesh, muscles around the venom sac continue to pulse out poison for up to a minute.

A female bee uses her stinger only as a last resort, since in trying to pull away, she rips the organ from her abdomen. Sacrificing herself for her fellow bees, the bee soon dies of her injury.

Not all bees sting, however. Some species are stingless, defending themselves by biting. (Interestingly, stingless bees produce a tiny fraction of the honey of their lancet-equipped cousins.)

Then there are the members of the Hymenoptera order that can sting again and again, living to tell the tale. Wasps and hornets have smooth stingers that deliver a shot of venom and then neatly retract. These pollinators

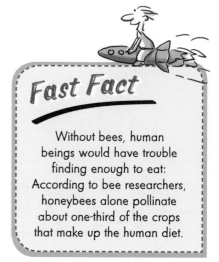

Fast Fact

Without bees, human beings would have trouble finding enough to eat: According to bee researchers, honeybees alone pollinate about one-third of the crops that make up the human diet.

seem to be on a hair trigger, stinging with less provocation than the average bee.

Bumblebees also have non-barbed stingers, but they are the gentle giants of the bee world. All queen bees are likewise exempt from carrying a suicide stinger. Since the queen is so important to the future of her clan, she carries a smooth stinger, the better to kill off rival queens and reign another day.

Why do mosquitoes bite people? And why do the bites itch?

Not all mosquitoes bite. Male mosquitoes spend their days peacefully drinking nectar from flowers. Female mosquitoes like nectar, too. But in most mosquito species, females must also drink blood before they can lay their eggs. And large, lumbering human beings are a good source of a blood meal.

Mosquitoes notice people by our movement, by the heat our bodies radiate, and by the way we smell. When a hungry mosquito flies near your ear, the humming sound you hear is the beating of her tiny wings. Scientists say the buzzing—so maddening to us on a hot, sleepless night—

Only the female mosquito bites.

is very attractive to male mosquitoes. And it's not your imagination—many species of mosquitoes do most of their blood hunting at night. After dark, hosts tend to be conveniently asleep, and far less likely to respond with a killing swat.

Landing lightly on your skin, the mosquito taps with the tip of her proboscis, like someone knocking at a door. (The proboscis is rather like a snout.) Then folding back her hairy lip, she neatly pierces the skin with her feeding stylets (named after a tool used in surgery).

Probing in the skin for blood vessels (small veins and capillaries), the mosquito searches for blood. In less than a minute, she is usually successful, sucking blood through one strawlike mouthpart while injecting her saliva into you with another. Special substances in the saliva keep your blood from clotting while she feeds.

A mosquito can swallow about four times her own weight in blood before her stomach bloats unbearably. If you have the stomach to watch her dine on your arm, you can see the blood through the wall of her abdomen. A full mosquito, one scientist said, looks like a tiny red Christmas tree light.

> A mosquito can swallow four times her own weight in blood.

However, it's a better idea to knock the mosquito away. Along with their saliva, mosquitoes may accidentally inject you with one of more than 100 different viruses or parasites. (Since they travel from host to host, they pick up infections as well as blood.) One of the most serious is malaria, with about

MIGHTY MITE

Other insects make skin itchy, too. One of these is the itch mite, which causes a skin condition called scabies. Like the mosquito, only the females are interested in us. But don't blame them—they're just trying to find a warm, safe place to lay their eggs.

The tiny female mite crawls around on the host's skin, looking for sheltered places—between the fingers, or under a fold of skin. Once she finds a spot she likes, the mite digs a trench, burrowing under the top layer of skin. In the little dark tunnel she has made, the mite lays her eggs. Days pass. Then the secret spot where the mite has taken up residence becomes very itchy.

Most people can't help but scratch, and all that scratching injures the skin. So although the mite did little damage herself, the skin around the burrow becomes cut and crusted.

What causes the itchiness? Scientists believe it's the body's allergic reaction to the mite's feces, which accumulate in the tunnel under the skin.

A mosquito drinks blood for its amino acids—the building blocks of protein. She needs lots of protein to make eggs: After a blood meal, a mosquito may lay 100 eggs. Without blood, some mosquitoes still produce fertile eggs, but usually less than 10—and perhaps only 1.

While we may feel we are being "eaten alive" on a warm evening, humans are not actually the female mosquitoes' favorite food. Human blood contains little of the amino acid isoleucine, which mosquitoes need to build their egg proteins. They might prefer to take a drink of buffalo or rat. But as humans elbow out other animals and their habitats, many mosquitoes have come to depend on us. We give them places to live (old bottles, spare tires) and warm bodies to feast on. We're not buffaloes, but we'll have to do.

300 million people infected around the world, mostly in tropical climates.

Once she is full, the mosquito pulls her mouthparts out of the wound and flies off. If this is your very first mosquito bite, you won't even know you were briefly someone's meal. But if you've been bitten before, your body has become sensitized to the proteins in mosquito saliva. The bite will swell and itch—an allergic reaction. If you get bitten many, many times, your body may get used to the proteins. For example, some researchers who study mosquitoes have been bitten so often that they are desensitized, and their mosquito bites no longer itch.

Are ants really stronger than humans?

Notice any tiny visitors at your summer picnic? Cartoon ants march in and carry off sandwiches, fried chicken, and pieces of chocolate cake. But real ants can also perform seemingly amazing feats of strength, hoisting up to 100 times their own weight in breadcrumbs, grass blades, and dead bugs. And then carrying them for hundreds of feet.

That certainly sounds like the equivalent of a 150-pound person lifting a 15,000-pound farm tractor above his or her head. But before you try hoisting, say, the nearest SUV overhead, consider this: Scientists say that when it comes to size versus strength, it's all a matter of scale. Make an ant 6 feet tall (er,

> Asian weaver ants can hold objects weighing 100 times their own weight— while hanging upside down.

long), they say, and it would actually lose its ability to lift outlandish loads. So instead of stealing a truck, a giant science-fiction ant would promptly collapse under its own weight.

How come? Make an organism larger, and its mass—the amount of matter it contains—increases much more than its strength. Similarly, make an organism smaller, and its strength decreases much less than its mass.

An animal expanding to 5 times its normal size, increasing in size by a factor of 5, will weigh not 5, but 125 times as much as before. That's because its volume has ballooned by 5 x 5 x 5.

When it comes to muscles, strength depends on cross-sectional area. Result? A muscle that is 5 times wider might be only 25 times stronger. So an ant that increased in size 100 times would actually be about a million times heavier—but only about 10,000 times stronger. Which

is why a human-size ant couldn't stand on its own six legs, let alone lift an SUV.

But scale an animal down, and it can perform what appear to be impressive feats of strength. The average ant's body mass (a mere 1/500th ounce or so) makes its perfectly normal muscles proportionately much stronger than those of a bigger animal. Which is why ants (and many other insects) can lift or drag objects weighing 5 to 50 or more times their own bodyweight.

A 2010 study by Cambridge University researchers found that Asian weaver ants could hold objects weighing 100 times their own weight—all while hanging upside down.

How do they do it? Surface tension between the ants' damp footpads and the surface they're walking on keeps them in place. Researchers say that when an ant is carrying a lightweight object, it folds up its feet, resulting in less contact (and less stickiness) with a surface. But when toting a heavier load, an ant will spread out its feet, creating extra surface tension. That enables the ant to safely crawl along upside down, even when a weight is tugging it toward the ground.

Measure FOR Measure
150 pounds = 68 kg
15,000 pounds = 6,804 kg
6 feet = 1.83 m
1/500th ounce = 0.57 g

How do crickets and cicadas make their loud sounds?

♫ CICADA SONGS ♫

Ooohhh, say can you see by the dawn's early light...

Don't cry for me, Argentina!

Living La Vida Loca!

Crickets and cicadas have a lot in common (besides the "c"). Both insects begin making their music in summer. Both are loud. And in both insect families, the noisemakers are mostly male.

But there the resemblance ends. If there were an insect orchestra, crickets would be seated up front in the string section. Cicadas would bring up the rear, assigned to percussion. And while the crickets would

happily perform at night, cicadas would stick mostly to matinees.

It wouldn't be midsummer without the dog-day cicadas, their plaintive chorus rising and then dying away. (There are also the cicadas that

A chorus
of cicadas
can be as loud as
a vacuum cleaner.

appear in waves every 13 or 17 years, emerging in late spring and early summer.) Cicadas, whose racket rises during the daylight hours, are the loudest of the world's insects. (In fact, a chorus of cicadas can be as deafening as a running vacuum cleaner.) But it's not that cicadas have big mouths; the average North American cicada is less than 2 inches (5 cm) long.

Cicadas have only a short window to find a partner and create a new generation of nymphs before their life aboveground is over. So when you hear a cicada chorus so loud you're prompted to shut

your window, think "speed-dating."

Male cicadas make most of the noise, their music filling the few weeks the insects have to mate. The males serenade the females using a pair of ridged membranes, called tymbals, in their lower abdomens. Strong abs are a must: A cicada contracts his ab muscles around the tymbals, causing them to cave in like

a drum struck with sticks. Then, in the cicada's nearly empty abdominal cavity, the percussive sound resonates, like a musical note in a concert hall.

Next, a cicada's portable sound system ramps up the volume. The insect's angled-out wings form a natural megaphone, amplifying the sound as it exits his body into the air. The result: A noise that can reach 90 to 100 decibels, as

CICADA SONGS

In North America, male 17-year cicadas make at least five categories of sounds. Ever hear a cicada make a short, harsh buzz as you approach? Entomologists call that an alarm call; males make it when they feel threatened.

The calling song attracts other cicadas to a group chorus (often in the highest tree branches). The song often consists of one to three calls separated by

several seconds of silence.

Once upon a time, a man leaving for a date with flowers and candy was said to be "going courting." And it's the sound of his court call (which comes in three varieties) that will win a male cicada a mate. While flirting female cicadas don't have hair to flip, they do flick their wings, making a come-hither rustle or pop in response to a male's noisy overtures.

loud as a nearby lawnmower or passing subway train.

When the male cicadas have settled down for the night, the crickets take their place. Like the cicadas, it's the males doing the singing. But a cricket's chirping doesn't come from the gut. Instead, it's all in the wings.

Crickets have four wings, two front and two back. To begin the serenade, a cricket raises his front wings about 45 degrees. Then, like drawing a bow across the strings of a violin, he draws the thick, ribbed vein on one wing over a ridge of wrinkles on the other. The result is a kind of music. And as with the cicadas, the music's volume is turned up by the wings: Acting like a violin's sound board, the wings amplify the notes produced by the rubbing ridges.

Scientists think that male crickets, like male cicadas, sing mainly to attract females. The male crickets also have threatening songs, warning off rival males. And crickets may chirp out alarms when predators, such as mice, frogs, and lizards, are nearby.

So why don't the loud chirps and buzzes of male crickets and cicadas damage the insects' own hearing?

Fast Fact

Ever hear a cicada make a short, harsh buzz as you approach? Male cicadas make the alarm call when they feel threatened.

Scientists say that a cricket's brain can temporarily turn down his hearing, muffling the sound of his own singing. Likewise, male cicadas also apparently disable their own hearing as they launch into their earsplitting routines.

How do jumping beans jump?

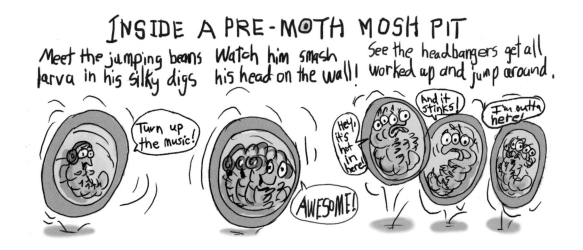

While they aren't jumpy from too much caffeine, jumping beans do have a secret that makes them very jittery.

It starts with a flowering shrub that grows only in the deserts of Mexico, Central America, and the southwestern United States. Next, add a special jumping bean moth, which is attracted to the flowers.

The shrub *Sebastiania pavoniana* blooms in the summer. The gray moths, smaller than dimes, lay their eggs among the tiny flowers, directly on the seed capsules. Now, the fun starts.

Each capsule has three sections, or carpels, with a seed lurking in each one. When the moth eggs hatch, tiny larvae emerge and worm their way inside the carpels. Warm and safe, they begin nibbling away at the tasty seed.

Late in the summer, the carpels split up and drop to the ground. Not every carpel was visited by a moth, so some spill out healthy seeds to grow more shrubs. Others shelter wriggling larvae.

Here comes the jumping part: Propelled by their wormy tenants, the carpels jerk and roll around on the ground, like brown beans come alive. Despite their name, they don't really leap into the air. But what's amazing is that the "beans" move at all, since each weighs as much as the larva propelling it.

How do the larva budge their beans? The answer, surprisingly, lies in home renovation. Once a larva has gobbled up its seed food, the inside of its carpel is empty. So the larva gets busy decorating, spinning comfy silk to line the walls of its brown house.

> Larvae seem to move their beans more when it's hot, perhaps angling for a shadier spot.

When it wants to move, a larva grabs the silk webbing with tiny legs, snapping its body (and even slamming its head into the wall). This sends the bean house skidding across the ground, where it may roll for some distance. Larvae seem to move their beans more when it's hot, perhaps angling for a shadier spot. As a fringe benefit, the jumping may spook hungry birds. But mostly, the idea seems to be to maneuver the beans into a safe, secure location, such as a crack beneath a rock. There, a larva can spend the winter transforming into a perhaps undreamed-of future version of itself.

As the weather turns chilly, the larva wraps itself in a thick cocoon. Its bean lies still now, as the larva changes into a mummylike pupa. But just before it enters pupadom, the larva does one last bit of remodeling: It etches the outline of a perfect, circular trapdoor into the wall of its house, slicing through most (but not all) of the circle.

As summer comes around again, the pupa has become moth. With the rains that make desert shrubs bloom thrumming on its carpel, the moth takes the wake-up call and pushes against the escape hatch cut months before. The door swings open; the moth flies out into the warm air.

After mating, a female moth looks for the shrubs where it all started—and creates a brand-new crop of jumping beans.

ALL ABOUT ME (AND YOU)

Stare at yourself in a mirror, and, after a moment, you'll have the unsettling sense that *we* are the aliens. Those long, dangly arms. The small, rounded ears, set so close to the head. The expanses of hairless skin. We humans are as peculiar-looking as any creature that ever swam, crawled, or walked across this planet.

Inside, our bodies work feverishly, around the clock, with no breaks—manufacturing sweat that seeps from our skin; pushing hair out of holes in our head; pumping 1,800 gallons of blood a day through hundreds of miles of arteries and veins strung through our bodies. All that and much more is going on, while we're busy doing other things.

No one knows your body better than you do, but it's still pretty mysterious. Why do your fingers get wrinkled after soaking in water? How do arm hairs know to grow only so far, and then stop? Are identical twins really identical? Where does the fat go when you lose weight? Why does blood look blue in our veins, but red coming out of a cut? Look into the bathroom mirror—this section's all about you.

If you keep your fingers underwater, why do they get wrinkled?

Washing dishes. Washing your dog. Taking a long bath. You pull your hands out of the water, and there it is: the heartbreak of pruney fingers. And they don't just look funny—they feel funny, too.

A study suggests that finger and toe wrinkles aren't just a random (weird) effect of soaking in the tub, but an evolutionary advantage: Crinkled digits may help us make our way across wet surfaces—such as tiled bathroom floors.

What happens when you submerge your fingers and toes for at least five minutes? Whether in tub or pool, or

> Crinkled digits may help us move across wet surfaces.

so one theory goes, keratin protein in the skin's outer layer (epidermis) quickly soaks up 6 to 10 times its weight in water. Blood vessels in the fingers and toes constrict. As the vessels shrink, the negative pressure tugs down the plumped-up (but flexible) epidermis. Result: furrows.

However, some researchers say that absorbed water should cause fingers and toes to simply swell up, remaining wrinkle-free. And it's been known since the 1930s that when nerves to the fingers and toes are damaged by injury or disease, the wrinkling effect vanishes. In a 2006 study, researchers found that fingers reattached after a nerve-severing accident remained smooth after submersion in water.

Evolutionary biologist Mark Changizi was intrigued by such studies. Since the prune effect is orchestrated by the body's nervous system, he said, there must be a reason for the wrinkles. Changizi and his colleagues note that most of the wrinkling occurs on the tips, which are the first part of our digits to make contact with a surface.

Studying images of wrinkled fingertips, the research team found that finger furrows closely resemble the branching channels carved by rivers running down the sides of mountains. This suggests that the wrinkles on our digits are channels, too—the body's way of draining water off our human "gripping points."

Changizi says finger and toe wrinkles are like the treads on a tire. On a dry surface, a smooth tire can function fairly well. But on a wet, rain-slick road, a tread-less tire will cause a car to hydroplane, dangerously skimming the surface rather than gripping the pavement.

Changizi thinks our built-in treads were an adaptation preserved from our evolutionary past. Like the ridges and furrows on our sneakers, ridges on fingers and toes keep us from slipping on a wet surface. So when our bare feet and hands get wet enough, the gripping tips wrinkle up, channeling water away. And unlike shoe treads, Changizi says, our finger and toe treads are pliable, allowing more complete contact with a wet surface—such as the cement surrounding a swimming pool.

The Heartbreak of Prune Hands

Transatlantic swimmers...

your hands are a mess!

Dishwashers...

oh! disgusting!

Lovers of very long baths

yuk!

Why does the Sun make our skin darker, but our hair lighter?

It takes two products to do the trick: self-tanner for the skin, plus a bleaching dye for the hair. But the Sun does it all in one step, even as you stroll outside on your lunch break on a summer afternoon. And instead of reading instructions on a box, just check the weather: The higher the day's UV index, the more likely your (unprotected) skin will darken, even as your hair mysteriously lightens.

Why the mismatch between skin and hair? Skin is actually an organ, stacked layers of living cells fed by tiny blood vessels. Hair, on the other hand, isn't living tissue. Strands of hair are about 97 percent keratin, the protein that also sculpts fingernails, toenails, and many animal horns. The remaining 3 percent? Mostly fats (lipids), along with water, traces of minerals, and the pigment melanin.

But melanin is something hair and skin have in common: It gives both their color. And it's melanin that undergoes a change in bright summer sunlight.

Here's how it works: Packed between ordinary skin cells in the skin's epidermis are octopus-shaped cells called melanocytes. These cells churn out the pigment melanin, tinting the skin. Genes passed down by our parents determine our own skin color. But no matter what the base color, skin that contains working melanocytes will darken when exposed to sunlight.

However, it's not visible sunlight that does the tanning. Light from the Sun comes in all frequencies. Visible light is medium-frequency, but both lower- and higher-frequency light are invisible to us humans. One kind of high-frequency light is ultraviolet (UV), and it's mainly UV that darkens skin.

Skin darkening helps protect the body against the damaging effects of high-energy radiation, which can include skin cancer. How? First, dead surface skin cells absorb some of the UV. Then, melanocytes ramp up their production of melanin, which also soaks up UV. The more UV light we're exposed to, the more pigment piles up, making skin darker and darker. But even a dark tan only stops about half of UV light from penetrating the skin.

But while skin color deepens, hair fades fast. Hair's melanin is made in the living skin cells at its roots. But once in the hair shaft, melanin isn't replenished. As UV radiation penetrates each strand, it causes a chemical reaction that destroys the hair's stored melanin. So when hair bakes in strong sunlight, it begins to bleach out—like bones in the desert, or a faded window awning. The result: Hair lightens, even as skin darkens. Black hair may develop red tones, brown hair may sport blonde streaks, and blonde hair may bleach to platinum.

Lower layers of hair may remain darker, even as outer layers fade in the noonday sun. Likewise, skin that's usually under wraps will stay close to its original color. Skin that's nearly always exposed to sunlight, such as the backs of the hands, may remain darker, even in winter.

Why do our ears pop when we fly on a plane?

The Pressures of Travel...
An ear-ie experience

Awful snacks

Teeny seats...

It's a pain in the Eustachian tube!

Imagine you are the passenger in a car going up and down steep mountain roads. At some point, your ears may seem to fill up with an invisible substance. Noises may sound muffled. Or perhaps you don't notice any change in your ears until you feel them *pop*. Then, all of a sudden, all the sounds around you—the chirping of birds in the woods, the irritating whine of your little brother—become clearer and louder.

The same thing happens in a plane—your ears seem to close up. The noise of the jet engines is muffled and far away; voices in the cabin are low. Then, suddenly, your ears pop open. The engines drone loudly; the hustle and bustle in the plane rises. Your hearing returns to normal as mysteriously as it left.

How come? The answer has to do with air pressure. Ears are very sensitive to changes in pressure. They must be, since ears are able to hear by reacting to fluctuating sound waves in the air, pressing against eardrums and then releasing.

Ears pop when the air pressure changes dramatically. Imagine the air surrounding Earth as a blanket of gas molecules. The closer we are to Earth, the more air there is above our heads. So a maximum amount of air presses on us when we are standing on flat ground.

But the higher we rise, the less air presses on us. High up, air gets thinner and thinner, until it fades into the airless vacuum of space. That's why air pressure is lower on top of a mountain—or around a high-flying plane.

Although a passenger jet may fly 35,000 feet above Earth, where the air is very thin, cabin air pressure is kept higher, so that passengers can breathe easily. Even so, as you climb into the sky, the pressure changes from that at ground level to what you would find on top of a mountain 5,000 to 8,000 feet high.

This is a quick and dramatic change for your ears. The air normally in your middle ear, now under less pressure, relaxes and spreads out. Some of this air may escape into the Eustachian tube, which is the tunnel connecting your ear to your nose. This can cause that "popping" feeling.

When the plane begins to descend, pressure once again increases. Air in the middle ear is squeezed smartly back into place. There may even be a partial vacuum created in your ear—a place where there is no air at all, since the bloodstream tends to absorb stray gases.

If there is a tiny airless space in your ear, air should flow up the nose and through the Eustachian tube to fill it. But if the tube is closed by mucus—as it may be when you have a cold or allergy—air can't flow through. Did you ever hear the phrase "Nature abhors a vacuum"?

If there's no air available, fluid may begin to fill the empty space in the ear instead. That can cause a stuffed-up feeling in your ears, which can last for hours, or even days.

You won't be able to hear well until the fluid drains away. If the clogged condition lasts too long, the eardrum may be damaged. That's why doctors may tell you not to fly if your nose is very stuffed up.

However, for temporarily clogged ears on a plane or in a car, try one or all of these: Swallow hard, take a big yawn, or chew gum as you are descending. This can help clear the Eustachian tube and equalize the air pressure.

Measure FOR Measure
35,000 feet = 10,668 m
5,000 to 8,000 feet = 1,524 to 2,438 m

Why do I see wiggly white shapes when I look into a bright blue sky?

Have you ever looked up into the blue sky on a sunny summer day and then noticed that it was covered with a moving field of bright paisley shapes? You may have wondered if there was something wrong with your eyes. But when you see the blue-sky motion, you are actually watching something moving in your own body. This something is part of the defense system our bodies use to protect us from infection: the white blood cells.

The blue-sky effect was first officially described by a German scientist in 1924 and is sometimes called Scheerer's phenomenon. It is also known as the blue field entoptic phenomenon (entoptic means "originating in the eyeball"). But it wasn't until 1989 that scientists figured out exactly how it worked.

Crisscrossing the eye's retina are many small blood vessels, the capillaries, ferrying the oxygen-rich red blood cells that feed our eyes. But we don't see dark red lines crisscrossing our vision. That's because the brain helpfully edits out the image of the blood-filled capillaries when it processes the images we see.

While it's mostly red blood cells moving through the capillaries, there is also the occasional leukocyte, or white blood cell. When we look up at a bright blue sky, the red blood cells strongly absorb the blue light. But the red cells are packed so closely together that they don't show up as individual dark spots. And our visual processing system edits the (darker) capillaries.

But the white blood cells that pass through *don't* absorb

much blue light. They are also much bigger than the red cells. So as the white cells pass by, they act like moving holes in the capillaries. And we see bright, moving white shapes in the sky.

Why do the shapes seem to wriggle and dart? Many of the retina's capillaries are S-shaped. So with each beat of the heart, the white cells move jerkily through the blood vessels, causing us to see bright shapes moving along a snaky path in the sky.

The wiggly spots are fish-shaped, with what appear to be little tails. Leukocytes are, in fact, naturally knobby. But some researchers say that the tail is just an afterimage, the glowing image we see after we stare at something very bright, like a lightbulb.

Seeing the white squiggly shapes can actually be a sign that your eyes are healthy. In fact, the blue-field effect is sometimes used to see whether blood flow to the eyes is impaired. Ophthalmologists create the paisley effect using blue light, and then ask the patient to match the shapes they

Fast Fact

Noticing blue-sky squiggles is different from seeing "floaters." Floaters are debris in the eye's vitreous humor, often appearing as dark shreds that move slowly or not at all. These spots call for a visit to the eye doctor.

see (and their speed) to a computer-generated screen of moving dots.

LEUKOCYTE: THE MUSICAL

Why are yawns so contagious?

Monkey see, monkey do? Just watch as someone's head tilts back, mouth drops open, eyes squint, and forehead furrows. Now add the familiar, drawn-out *YAAAWN*-ing sound. Chances are, you'll yawn in response, even if you felt wide awake a second before. In fact, just reading about yawning—or thinking about it—can trigger a yawn. Thankfully, just thinking about the flu won't cause you to come down with a case. But when it comes to behaviors, yawning is about as contagious as they come.

Over the past several years, studies of yawning have come to the conclusion that this familiar (uncontrollable) response is a

> Just reading about yawning can set off a yawn.

sign of empathy, our capacity to identify with the feelings and actions of others. And we humans aren't the only contagious yawners on the block.

In a study of gelada baboons, researchers found that the monkeys yawned when they saw other individuals yawn, especially if the monkeys were socially close. So if a baboon being groomed by a fellow baboon

yawned, the groomer often yawned, too.

And a 2009 study of chimpanzees found that cartoon yawning worked as well as real-life yawns. Researchers showed computer animations of yawning chimps to a group of 24 chimpanzees. While watching the animated yawning, most of the chimps yawned right along with their cartoon counterparts. The chimps seemed to know the animated chimps weren't real, since they didn't react in either a friendly or aggressive way. But the yawning part proved irresistible.

Many dogs apparently yawn when they see a human yawn, too. In a U.K. study published in 2008, researchers

A Three-Volley Yawn...

visited with 29 dogs in the pets' familiar surroundings. After making eye contact with the dogs and calling them by name, the experimenters yawned realistically. In another part of the test, the experimenters simply opened their mouths wide.

None of the dogs responded to the open-mouth test by yawning. But an astonishing 72 percent of the dogs yawned after watching the testers' realistic yawns. This indicates, the researchers said, that dogs may feel an empathic connection with human beings, even those they've never met before.

In fact, scientists think that contagious yawning may be one of the earliest examples of empathy and social awareness in some species. While our primitive ancestors may have started with yawning in concert, we humans soon evolved higher levels of empathy—such as identifying with others who are hurt or sad, and feeling distressed ourselves.

But whether you catch a contagious yawn may depend on what part of the yawner's face you happen to see. Studies with people and animals show that making eye contact or at least glancing at a yawner's eyes seems crucial to feeling the urge to yawn yourself. And if you find it impossible to stifle a yawn when thinking about yawning or watching other yawners, pat yourself on the back. Studies indicate that people who are more likely to "yawn along" scored highest on other tests of empathy, too.

WHY YAWN AT ALL?

Is yawning just another way to take a deep breath? Not according to researchers. It's not low oxygen, or the need to stretch, that prompts a yawn, they say. Instead, yawning may be a kind of low-tech air-conditioning—for the brain.

In one experiment, researchers at the State University of New York (SUNY) in Albany asked volunteers to breathe normally—but only through the mouth or nose, not both. In another experiment, volunteers held warm-, cold-, or room-temperature packs on their foreheads.

Meanwhile, all watched a video of people yawning, laughing, or doing nothing.

The researchers found that those who breathed only through their nose or held cold packs to their foreheads yawned very little or not at all as they watched others yawn. But more than 40 percent of those who breathed through their mouths or had warmer foreheads found the videotaped yawning very contagious, yawning right along with it.

What's the explanation? The SUNY researchers say that both nasal breathing and cold compresses help the brain chill out, by sending cooler blood its way. Which may be why the mouth-breather/warm-forehead groups yawned more: Yawning may be another way for the body to boost blood flow and lower the temperature of the brain. And a cooler brain, the researchers say, is able to think more clearly.

So if you yawn when you're bored, it may be your body's last-ditch attempt to keep you awake and alert.

What causes "brain freeze"?

Chillin' With Frozen Treats! May Lead to: Frosty Tooth! Esophagus Freeze! or Popsicle Brain!

Have you ever come down with a case of sphenopalatine ganglioneuralgia? If you've ever slurped down a Slurpee, chugged a milkshake, or bitten off a mouthful of ice cream from a cone, chances are you've had it: brain freeze. It's a headache with a twist, pain accompanied by a freezing feeling. The pain usually peaks in 30 seconds to several minutes, and fades just as quickly.

In fact, some researchers say that ice cream may actually be the most common cause of head pain. But any frozen concoction or very cold drink will do: At least 40 percent of people occasionally get "brain freeze" after eating or drinking something frigid.

(And while we're not really in danger of our brains becoming icky gray popsicles, studies show that head temperature does drop when we eat something very cold very quickly.)

Just a minute or two of milkshake sipping may be enough to trigger the creepy sensation: a freezing ache spreading across forehead and temples, sometimes advancing to the top and sides of the head. (Some unlucky people also get a frosty toothache, or painful "esophagus freeze," as the milkshake plummets to the stomach in an icy avalanche.)

In one brain freeze experiment in Japan, participants chomped 12 ounces (340 g) of shaved ice in 10 minutes. At a little more than two minutes into the ice swallowing, the volunteers began to get headaches— some of them severe. While they didn't get to eat ice cream, they did come down with an ice cream headache.

What causes the painful sensation? Some say the ache is referred pain from chilled nerves in the roof of the mouth and throat. Consuming icy-cold food or drinks may also overstimulate the trigeminal nerve, which runs through the cheeks and temples. Others say the pain is due mainly to cold-responding blood vessels in the mouth and head.

A 2012 study found some

 Just a minute of milkshake sipping may be enough to trigger brain freeze.

answers. Volunteers sipped ice water through a straw, aiming it at their upper palate, raising their hands at the first twinge of brain freeze.

Using ultrasound equipment, researchers monitored blood flow in the participants' brains. As the icy headaches began, scientists found that the anterior cerebral artery expanded rapidly, "flooding the brain" with blood. When the artery returned to normal, the pain receded, too. While the maneuver may ensure that the brain stays warm, the researchers say, the sudden rush of blood raises pressure

in the head, triggering pain.

Even though brain-freeze pain peaks in seconds and quickly fades, it can put a real damper on that I-scream/you-scream ice cream excitement. Besides giving up ice cream (and even ice-cold water on hot afternoons), there are simple steps we can take to lessen or avoid brain freeze.

Scientists say that the quicker we down icy concoctions, and the more contact the frigid stuff makes with the roof of the mouth, the higher the chances of getting a headache. So sip slowly, point straws away from your upper palate, and don't bite off huge chunks of an ice cream cone.

If brain freeze hits, try touching your warm tongue to the roof of your mouth, or sipping a warm drink. Ice cream, after all, should make you scream with happiness, not pain.

Why do we get hiccups?

Hiccups, the International Language

GERMAN   FRENCH   ENGLISH   CANINE

One slice too many of that birthday cake and pepperoni pizza? Startled by your little brother leaping from behind a door? Laughing so hard you can't stop? Next up: Hiccups crash the party.

Most people blame the diaphragm for those annoying, staccato *hic* sounds. But according to

William Whitelaw, professor of medicine at Canada's University of Calgary, hiccupping involves the whole upper body, in a kind of coordinated spasm.

Take the diaphragm, the domed muscle under the lungs. The diaphragm helps us breathe, expanding upward to shove used air out of the lungs, then collapsing

downward to allow fresh air in. When we hiccup, the diaphragm suddenly contracts strongly.

But the diaphragm isn't alone. Other muscles that help your body import air from the atmosphere—the intercostal muscles running through your ribs, along with muscles in the chest and neck—squeeze at the same instant. As the muscles spasm in concert, the vocal cords in your throat also snap shut—making that annoying *hic* sound.

Hiccups are repetitive, and the brain has circuits that generate patterns for the body's other repetitive actions (think breathing, sneezing, coughing). The brainstem, where the brain connects to the spinal cord, is home to these pattern generators. So along with a Sneeze Center, there may a Hiccup Central lurking in the brainstem, too.

The brain, like a lighthouse, sends out a repeating signal telling breathing muscles to contract, and the vocal cords (aka glottis) to snap shut. But something must set off the hiccup generator to begin with. A common trigger seems to be eating and drinking. When the stomach expands too far, stomach acid climbing into the esophagus, irritated nerves probably set off the brain's hiccup circuit.

The brain's blueprint for hiccups may have come from our ancestors who breathed using gills.

While the *hic*-ing pattern is set by the brain, it seems to be tied to the beating of the heart. In a study, Whitelaw found that in most hiccupping volunteers, each hiccup struck in mid-heartbeat. So just as the heart muscle is contracting, the glottis clamps shut: *hic*-cup. And when hiccups continue, they follow a regular pattern in each person, with a certain numbers of heartbeats—say, four—between each *hic* and the next.

Researchers think the brain's blueprint for hiccups came from our ancestors who used gills for breathing. Just look at modern tadpoles. A half-grown tadpole has both gills and lungs. When a tadpole breathes underwater, its glottis snaps shut as its mouth fills with water. The water is then pushed out through the gills, its dissolved oxygen absorbed into the tadpole's bloodstream.

But above the surface of the water, a tadpole can open its mouth and fill it with air. Then, since tadpoles don't have diaphragms, it shuts its mouth (and nose); the gill passageway closes, too. Squeezing its mouth down, the tadpole actually forces the air into its lungs. These choreographed, hiccup-like moves seem to originate in a central pattern generator in the tadpole brain, much like Hiccup Central in the human brain.

What makes your stomach growl?

Your Stomach Speaks

isten to your own (or someone else's) growling stomach, and it sounds like there's something alive in there, rumbling like distant thunder and creaking like a rusty door hinge.

Your stomach is most likely to make a growling sound when it is very empty, and you feel very hungry. When the stomach is empty (except for a little air and some stomach juices), it contracts and expands rhythmically. These contractions really get going when you smell food, or even think about it. That growling you hear is your stomach rippling and squeezing. You may feel hunger pangs, too—dull to sharp pains that urge you to eat, right now.

But the stomach also makes noises when it's full of food and working hard—and so do the intestines.

Have you ever eaten a huge meal and then sat back

BUTTERFLIES IN YOUR STOMACH?

Have you ever had to speak in front of a group and felt a fluttering in your stomach, like butterflies beating their wings?

What causes stomach "butterflies"? According to scientists, your anxiety over what you are about to do causes your body to release a surge of adrenaline, the hormone that prepares us to fight or flee in a truly dangerous situation. Adrenaline makes your heart beat faster. Blood flow may be increased to your muscles, and away from organs like the stomach. And your stomach may feel queasy and fluttery.

But there may be more to such "gut feelings" than was previously thought. When people are upset, they may experience more than butterflies or mild stomach pains. Some people get diarrhea; others vomit. Scientists say that the gut is like a second brain. The esophagus, stomach, and intestines are connected in an elaborate nervous system, using the same chemicals to communicate as the brain in our heads. So the digestive tract can react on its own to all the events in our lives, by speeding up, slowing down, breaking down—or even, in happy times, by working exceptionally smoothly.

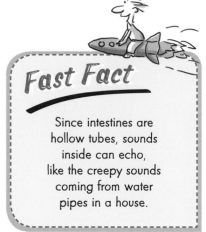

Fast Fact

Since intestines are hollow tubes, sounds inside can echo, like the creepy sounds coming from water pipes in a house.

to relax, only to hear your stomach gurgling and your intestines rumbling? Digesting food is hard work. Imagine your stomach, stuffed with food after a holiday feast. Dumped down into your stomach sac might be a sweet potato, a lump of stuffing, a mound of peas, several dinner rolls, some turkey, and a piece of pumpkin pie. It's no wonder that your body gets a little noisy as it goes into overdrive like a food processor, liquefying the food by squirting it with acidic juices, then extracting nutrients.

Adding to the din may be air swallowed along with food and drink. Air, a mix of gases, creates turbulence as it mixes with liquids in the stomach.

Noises in the intestines likewise come mainly from gas—the gas produced by bacteria as they further digest food. Think of the noises coming from stomach and intestines after a meal like the noises of a radiator as it starts to heat up, clanking, hissing, and rumbling from trapped water and steam.

What causes the popping sound when you crack your knuckles?

It ain't just at breakfast anymore...

SNAP! *oooh!*

Crackle! *Feels good!*

Pop! *Yeah*

It can feel like the hand's version of a satisfying yawn. Human beings have probably been lacing their fingers together, stretching out their arms, and cracking their knuckles after a long session of toolmaking (or homework writing) for many thousands of years. Yet it wasn't until the 1970s that scientists began to figure out how the popping worked.

Take a look at the top of your hand: The knuckles are the joints linking your hand bones (the metacarpals) to your finger bones (the phalanges). The knuckles allow us to grip objects between our fingers, from pencils to pliers to pennies, using a system of ligaments and tendons.

Inside the knuckles, just as in knee, elbow, and shoulder joints, there are spaces between bones. In these spaces, providing helpful cushioning and reducing friction, lurks a thick liquid called synovial fluid. Synovial fluid, which is the consistency of raw egg, contains dissolved gases like carbon dioxide and oxygen. This slippery, gassy fluid is trapped in a fibrous capsule surrounding the joint.

But when you pull your fingers back, you widen the space between the joints, stretching out the fluid-filled capsule. Result? With its holding tank expanding like a balloon, the synovial fluid is suddenly under a lot less pressure.

Stretching and pulling on your knuckles is a bit like shaking a can of soda pop. As the synovial fluid's pressure swiftly drops, its trapped gases begin forming scattered pockets of vapor. Presto: downright bubbly joint fluid. As you stretch the joints to the max, the pressure drops so low that the bubbles burst. Mini shockwaves race through the synovial fluid. And we hear a *crack* or *pop*—a tiny sonic boom, finger-style.

But even as the bubbles burst with an audible *pop*, the gas doesn't immediately re-dissolve in the joint fluid. Small, lingering bubbles keep the joint capsule expanded. In fact, knuckle X-rays show that it takes up to 30 minutes for the tiniest bubbles to completely disappear. As the gas gradually dissolves, the capsule shrinks back to its normal, compact size.

That's why it's nearly impossible to crack your knuckles twice in a row. The

Fast Fact

Finger joints may feel temporarily looser after knuckle cracking, just as other joints feel looser (and better) after a good stretch. However, too much knuckle cracking may injure soft tissue around the joint, causing swollen ligaments and reduced grip strength (making it harder, for example, to open stuck jar lids).

synovial fluid capsule can't form big, *pop*-tastic bubbles if it hasn't first shrunk back to normal. In fact, impatiently pulling on your fingers while the capsule is shrinking back only makes the dissolving bubbles re-expand a bit. But let the gas fully dissolve, and the stage is set for another loud *POP*.

How come tears come out of our eyes? Why do they taste salty?

Above the outer corner of your eyes, just below your eyebrows, are the lacrimal glands—the tear glands. They are only the size of almonds, but these tiny factories can churn out a flood of tears. The lacrimal glands are always making tears— even as you read this.

It's no accident that tears taste like the sweat that runs down our face on a hot day. Our flowing blood is salty, too. In fact, about 55 percent of the salt in the body is dissolved in fluids outside our cells, like blood plasma. Another 40 percent of the body's salt is inside our bones. The remainder is found in

Leftover tears flow away through handy drains in the eye's inner corner.

other cells and organs. The salty total? According to researchers, each human adult body contains about 8 ounces (227 g) of salt.

All day long, our eyes are wetted by a film of salty tears, each time we blink (some 900 times an hour when we're

awake). These "basal" tears wash away dust and bacteria, and keep eye surfaces moist. If irritating pollen particles, wind-blown dirt, or stinging onion fumes intrude, a flood of "reflex" tears streams to the rescue.

Leftover tears flow away through handy drains in the eye's inner corner, through another passageway, and into the area behind your nose, where they are absorbed into the body.

Get a lot of dust in your eyes, however, and it's a different story. Tears start flowing faster, to keep up with the cleaning job. There may be so many tears that they begin to overflow your bottom lid, instead of neatly draining away. "My eyes are watering," you complain.

Tears are about 98 percent water. In addition to sodium, tears contain other minerals, like potassium, manganese, calcium, and zinc. There is also glucose (sugar) in tears, plus enzymes and antibodies that protect eyes from infection. Oils and mucus in the fluid lubricate eyes and help retain moisture.

Also in the tear ingredient list are hormones like corticotropin, made by the brain's pituitary gland when we're stressed. Scientists have also found at least one natural painkiller, leucine enkephalin. Both seem to show up in greater amounts in "crying"

Fast Fact

The actual concentration of salt in our tears is a little less than 1 percent. By contrast, seawater is about 3.5 percent salt by weight.

Tears, A few Alternative Uses...

Seasoning for cakes

Window Cleaning

Birdbath water source

tears, the kind that spill out of our eyes when we're sad, or after a bruising fall.

Why do we cry when we're hurt, distressed, or even very happy? Most researchers think emotional tears evolved as another way to signal our feelings and needs to other people. Babies cry when they're hungry, tired, in pain, or just want to be held—showing a parent that they need help. We may cry, psychologists say, when we want to appease someone else—to defuse their anger. Tears may increase empathy in others, and they—even strangers—may reach out to help. Seeing someone cry over the death of a loved one can move us to tears, too. And sharing an uplifting moment with others—from watching the rescue of a dog caught in a flood to "Our team finally won!"—can produce (contagious) tears of joy.

HOW COME CHOPPING ONIONS MAKES OUR EYES WATER?

Onions are a vegetable that seems to resist being eaten. Cut into an onion, and it's like a mini-mace attack: stinging, watering eyes, which you struggle to keep open as you (valiantly) keep chopping. But hold an uncut onion to your face, and . . . nothing. Little to no scent. Zero tear gas.

How—and why—does an innocent-looking onion launch its tiny assault? Broken onion cells release molecules called amino acid sulfoxides, along with a special enzyme. The enzyme changes the sulfoxides into sulfenic acids. And the acids rearrange themselves into a chemical called syn-propanethial-S-oxide (C_3H_6OS)—which stealthily spreads as a gas into the air. C_3H_6OS is the lachrymatory factor in onions, since the tears it induces flow from the lacrimal glands.

About 30 seconds after being cut, an onion's out-gassing reaches its peak. Wafting up, the lachrymatory factor reacts with the eyes' thin film of tears. One chemical produced in the reaction is a mild form of sulfuric acid—the corrosive acid our stomachs use to break down food.

Result? Irritated nerve endings fire off messages to the brain, and the eyes begin to sting. Meanwhile, the nerve signals cause tear glands to up production, releasing a flood of tears to dilute and wash away the acidic chemical.

The onion's chemistry seems designed to protect it from other threats—invading bacteria, viruses, and fungus. The irritating gas, scientists say, may just be a by-product of a kind of chemical "bomb," designed to kill microbes invading through a cut.

Try these anti-tear techniques: Chill the onion before cutting; cold tames the lachrymatory factor. Cut it under running water, which dissolves the chemical. Or set up a fan, and blow the onion vapors away from you.

Why does scratching make an itch go away?

Everyone knows what it feels like. But what, exactly, is it? Science defined the itch in the 1600s, when a German doctor named Samuel Hafenreffer pronounced that an itch is "an unpleasant sensation that elicits the desire or reflex to scratch." In other words, Question: What is an itch? Answer: Something that can be relieved by a scratch.

But before you mouth a big "duh," think about it: Do you ever want to scratch a spot that's just been slammed by a softball, scraped on the sidewalk, or cut on a piece of paper? Much research has focused on pain and ways to treat it, with many fewer studies done on itching. In fact, until the last 25 years or so, scientists thought that itching was a kind of low-level pain, transmitted by the same nerves as ordinary pain. Then, experiments discovered that itching has its very own nerve pathways. But compared to pain, itching is still a bit of a mystery.

Like pain, itching can have many causes: dry skin, foot fungus, mosquito bites, allergies, measles, eczema, psoriasis, diabetes, kidney disease, even cancer.

Pain can be felt both on the skin and in the muscles, organs, and bones underneath. But no one ever complains about an itchy gallbladder. However, even though itching happens in the top layer of the skin, scientists say that it's really the brain that itches.

How? Peripheral nerves in the skin carry signals through the spinal cord and on to the brain for processing. The sensation of itching, researchers say, is formed in the central nervous system, and then projected into the area of skin where we feel the itch.

So why do we itch? Scientists say that itching probably evolved as a protective mechanism. Skin comes into contact with irritating or thorny plants, crawling bugs, searing summer sun. If our skin feels itchy, we may knock off that potentially poisonous spider, step away from the poison ivy tickling our bare ankles, brush off sand and dirt, and go indoors for some cool shade.

Brain scans show that when we feel itchy, a part of the brain is activated that plans motor activities, such as reaching for a cookie. But in this case, the activity the brain is gearing up for is—you guessed it—scratching.

Still, scientists aren't sure how and why scratching works. One theory is that scratching creates slight pain. Itch nerves transmit impulses much more slowly than ordinary pain nerves.

So the minor pain created by scratching may simply overwhelm the itching feeling. (Interestingly, the prick of a pin near an itchy spot can also sometimes make an itch go away.)

But newer research shows that itching has not only its own nerves, but its own molecules and cell receptors, too, distinct from those involved in pain. And scratching lights up parts of the brain identified with

reward, motivation, and pleasure, like other activities we love to do.

Researchers say a good scratch can make itching fade for 15 minutes or more. Experiments show that scratching your own itch is more effective than having someone else do it. But overdo it, and the scratching simply inflames and injures the skin, leading to even more itching: the maddening itch/ scratch cycle.

Why do we get colorful bruises?

Bruise Control...

Cuts are red, bruises are blue—and purple-black, sea green, even mustard yellow.

When you get cut, blood seeps from the body and out through the wound until clotting seals the cut dry. But a bruise is an injury in which the blood is going nowhere fast. Bang your knee on a coffee table, and tiny injured capillaries spring leaks and spurt blood under the skin. The spilled blood collects at the spot where you were hurt.

But a green bruise doesn't point to a long-lost Vulcan ancestor. Pay close attention the next time you're unlucky enough to get a bruise, and you'll see that it gradually changes color, from red to purple to green to a sickly yellow. And then? Gone.

Bruises are the body's injury chameleons. Their colors depend on the age of the bruise. The first sign of a forming bruise may be an angry red blotch. A bump or fall injures tiny blood vessels under the top layer of skin. The blood's clotting agents, such as platelets, work to stem the tiny hemorrhages before too much damage is done.

The more blood that leaks from capillaries, the bigger the bruise. Apply some cold pressure right away (try a bag of frozen peas wrapped in a washcloth), and you may minimize the eventual size of the bruise—and perhaps even shorten its colorful stay. Pressure (even with the heel of your hand) can stop the bleeding, and ice constricts the blood vessels so that further bleeding and swelling are reduced.

Still, even quick thinking probably won't stop your injured knee from going mood ring over the coming days. Overnight, your plain red blotch will be replaced by the deep scarlet, blues, and

A bruise's stormy-day colors are actually a trick of light.

purples of a scary-looking bruise.

The red in a bruise comes courtesy of hemoglobin, the pigment in red blood cells pooled under the injured skin. The stormy-day colors—the dark blues and deep purples—are actually a trick of light. How? When light strikes the bright red hemoglobin, it's not only reflected back but refracted (bent), as it travels through multiple thin layers of skin.

So when white light emerges from its brief trip

into the skin and back, its wavelengths are shifted toward the blue and violet end of the rainbow spectrum. Presto: purple.

What about the rest of the bruise rainbow? Red hemoglobin is gradually broken down by scavenger cells called macrophages, leaving the pigment called biliverdin. Biliverdin adds a greenish tint to the bruise. Over time, biliverdin is broken down into orange-yellow bilirubin, and your bruise yellows and browns.

Finally, the brownish-yellow fades into the background of your skin, as cells carry off remaining colored pigments from the wound. Depending on its size and depth, it may take from two days to several weeks for a bruise to change from purple to yellow, on its way to disappearing altogether.

Why do we get goose bumps?

Recipe for goose bumps: Take one dark room. Add yourself, standing behind a half-closed door. Wait for your sister or brother to enter. Jump out. Voilà: instant goose bumps, accompanied by screaming, followed by shouting (possibly of parent).

In Great Britain, goose bumps are called goose flesh. People have been using "goose" words for temporarily bumpy skin since at least the early 1800s. What do the bumps have to do with geese? People used to eat a lot more goose than they do now, especially on holidays. After a goose has been plucked of its feathers, its body is covered with little bumps where the feathers once sprouted. So when little bumps rose on

> Goose bumps are part of the "flight-or-fight" response.

someone's arms, people thought their skin looked like goose flesh or goose bumps.

What causes goose bumps? Goose bumps spring up when small muscles around hair follicles suddenly contract. This pushes up a bit of skin and hair, making a bump. Have you ever seen your cat's tail puff out suddenly, or a porcupine's quills suddenly spring up? These are forms of goose bumps, too.

Animals, us included, get goose bumps when they are startled or threatened. Scientists say goose bumps are part of the "flight-or-fight" response. A surge of stress hormones makes muscles contract. In a cat, this causes hair to stand on end, and may make the cat look big and scary to another animal threatening it. Our goose bumps are an echo of this evolved response; our ancestors had more hair, and goose bumps made good evolutionary sense for them.

Goose bumps also break out when we get an abrupt chill. Why? Because our distant ancestors had fur. And for animals, fluffing their fur up in the cold provides better insulation.

The Faces of Goose Flesh!!!

Goose bumps can break out in any thrilling circumstance, not just frightening ones. Hearing your country's anthem play at the Olympics, learning of a strange and wonderful coincidence, or witnessing a selfless act of courage may make the hairs on your arm rise. Even the memory of a thrilling event or encounter may bring on a rash of goose bumps. In such cases, our bodies may not be threatened, but our spirits are deeply moved.

Why can't we tickle ourselves?

Are you ticklish? Do you giggle uncontrollably, squirm away, run screaming? The sound of two kids in a tickling war, laughing so hard they can't stand up, can make anyone within earshot start laughing, too. In fact, even the verbal threat of being tickled ("Coochie-coo!") can provoke a giggling fit. And the sight of wiggling fingers coming your way, scientists say, can produce the same reactions in your brain as actually being tickled.

What is it that makes tickling so frantically funny? Scientists say the tickling effect depends crucially on the element of surprise. Even if you expect to be tickled—even if your sister is approaching menacingly from the other side of the couch— you don't know the exact instant it will happen. It's a lot like someone jumping out from behind a door in a dark room—or a spider suddenly dropping from the ceiling onto your shoulder. Despite the fact that it drives us crazy, studies show that most people like being tickled and see tickling as a playful way to express affection.

If tickling is so fun, then why can't we just tickle ourselves, provoking gales of our own giggles?

Researchers say it's because the brain is so good at screening out sensations of what it knows we ourselves are doing. If it weren't, we'd have a hard time just getting through an afternoon.

Why? All day long, our senses are besieged by incoming sensations from the world at large. There is also the constant drumbeat of sensations arising from our own actions: the pressure of the floor on our feet as we walk, the feeling of our own arms resting against our sides as we sit, the movement of our tongue as we speak or chew. The brain mostly ignores these and many other expected sensations.

But if, during lunch, someone sneaks up behind you and lightly touches your shoulder, you may literally jump out of your chair. Your brain is programmed to react on full alert to such unexpected, not-coming-from-you sensations. Reacting to surprises helps keep us safe, since a surprising touch or encounter (think poisonous spider) can mean danger.

So try to tickle yourself, and it's a ho-hum situation for the brain. Scientists doing tickle research (publishing papers with titles like "Central Cancellation of Self-Produced Tickle Sensation") have looked at the brains of people being tickled. On an MRI, a self-tickle causes very little activity in the brain's somatosensory cortex, which lights up when the tickling is being done by someone (or something) else.

Studies show it's the cerebellum, located at the rear of the brain, that predicts the consequences of a self-tickling movement, sending out the signal to cancel a ticklish response when it's "only you." Researchers have also found that the response to outside tickling was more intense when an expected tickle was delayed by a split second, producing a surprise similar to real-life tickling. The more unpredictable the

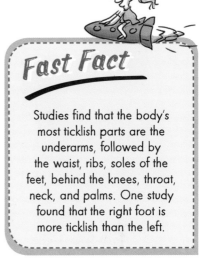

Fast Fact

Studies find that the body's most ticklish parts are the underarms, followed by the waist, ribs, soles of the feet, behind the knees, throat, neck, and palms. One study found that the right foot is more ticklish than the left.

tickle, the more delicious the panic we feel.

How come I feel cold when I have a fever?

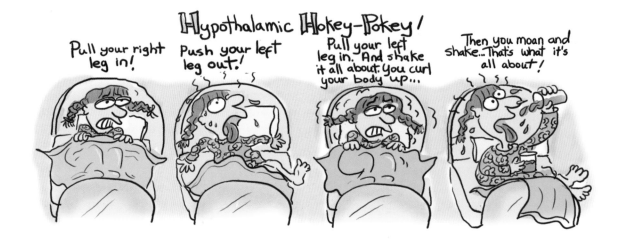

Lie in the sun on a summer day and as your skin heats, you feel warmer and warmer. But come down with a fever, and while your skin feels burning-hot, you feel icy cold. Your temperature rises, but you have the shivering chills, even as you pile on the blankets.

Our normal body temperature ranges between about 97°F and 99.5°F. If our temperature is too high, we get the signal to sweat and feel like changing into lightweight clothing. Hidden in the center of the brain, the hypothalamus gland keeps our body temperature in a narrow range by comparing the temperature of the blood to its thermostat set point. If our temperature drops too low, our bodies may shiver to make heat, and we'll feel like putting on a sweatshirt or getting under the covers.

When we get sick, however, our inner thermostat can be reset, the heat turned up to fight the infection. Immune system cells become activated during an infection and float through the blood, targeting bacteria and viruses. Some of these immune cells produce proteins called cytokines. These particular cytokines are pyrogenic—they cause fever. Floating through the bloodstream, the pyrogens come in contact with nerve cells around the outside of the brain, which send messages to the hypothalamus and brain stem.

In a fever, messenger hormones cause blood to flow away from the skin to deeper layers in the body, minimizing heat loss. Sweating dwindles to a minimum, and the body's temperature may rise 2 to 7 degrees. The extra heat seems to make immune cells better at killing bacteria, as well as making it harder for invading microorganisms to reproduce.

So why do we feel so cold, when we're actually heating up like a slice of toast? Once its set point has been raised—say, to 102°F—the hypothalamus sends a message to the 98.6°F body: "Too cold!" Shivering and chills ensue. And until your temperature rises to the new set point, you feel teeth-chatteringly cold and dive under the nearest blanket. Once your body's temperature has reached it new set point, you will no longer feel so chilly.

Just as you paradoxically felt cold as you heated up, so will you feel hot as you cool down. When your body has decided it doesn't need to be baking at 102°F anymore, your set point may be reset to, say, 99°F. Now the hypothalamus is telling the body that it's too hot. So as your fever breaks and your body begins to cool, you suddenly feel too warm. You begin sweating and throw off the covers. Once your temperature matches your set point again, you'll feel just right.

Fast Fact

Our body temperature is usually lowest in the morning, higher in the late afternoon and evening. But the temperature doesn't vary much, since the body has its own thermostat.

Measure FOR Measure
97°F to 99.5°F = 36°C to 37.5°C
102°F = 39°C
a rise of 2°–7°F = a rise of 1.1°–3.9°C
99°F = 37°C

How come it hurts so much when I hit my "funny bone"?

Bump your shin on the coffee table, and you feel a sharp pain in the front of your leg. Ouch. But bang your inner elbow on your desk, and the pain is searing, buzzing, electrical—and may extend down your arm and into your fingers. Double ouch.

And just what makes that funny? Some say the dreaded spot is called the funny bone in honor of the humerus bone, which runs from shoulder to elbow. ("How humorous.") But the real reason is probably because the feeling we get from hitting it is not only painful, but downright weird.

> The ulnar nerve is mostly defenseless.

If the funny bone were actually a bone, the pain we'd feel would be a lot like shin pain. Instead, what we experience is, in a way, worse: pain from a dinged nerve.

The culprit is the ulnar nerve, named after the ulna bone it runs near in the forearm. The ulnar is one of three big nerves (the others are the radian and the median) that run from the spine, down our arms, and to our hands. The ulnar nerve's main function is to control muscles in the forearm and hand, as well as enable our pinky and ring fingers to feel sensations.

Our body's large nerves are usually protected by bone and muscle. But the ulnar nerve is mostly defenseless. In fact, you may be able to actually (creepily) feel it, by pressing on the grooved space on the inside of your elbow.

What's not so funny: All that stands between this exquisitely sensitive nerve and a hard tabletop is a thin layer of fat and skin. Bump your inner elbow on a desk, and the big nerve is slammed between solid bone and solid wood. The result: a starburst of searing, electric pain in your elbow, which shoots down your arm, and into the fourth and fifth fingers of your hand. (Are we having fun yet?)

The pain from your so-called funny bone only lasts a few seconds. But the unprotected ulnar can also become compressed and irritated by everyday activities. Like lying half-propped up on your elbow to read. Holding your phone to your ear for many minutes. Or sleeping for hours on your bent arm. Chronic elbow pain, or tingling numbness in the pinky and ring fingers, or along the outside of the hand, can result. Remembering that the ulnar has no armor can

Fast Fact

The ulnar nerve runs through several grooves on its way to the fingers: the cubital tunnel, in the elbow, and the ulnar, or Guyon's canal, in the wrist.

help us to protect our funny-bone nerve from long-term injury.

How does hair grow?

Hair is high maintenance, and not just because we all want to avoid bad hair days. There are those aisles and aisles of hair products— shampoos, conditioners, blow-dryers, flat irons. And then there's what the body needs to do to maintain a head full of hair, day after day, year after year.

Look at a hair under a magnifying glass, and you'll see a long, spaghetti-like cylinder. A hair shaft is constructed mainly of keratin, the tough protein that also makes up fingernails and toenails. Inside the shaft is a spongy core. The sponginess makes the hair flexible, so that it can bend without breaking.

Follow a hair down into the skin, and you'll eventually find its root. Under the skin, each hair is encased in a slim tube called the follicle. The follicle's bulb-shaped end is rooted in the dermis, the lower layer of skin, like a tulip bulb is embedded in the ground.

Hairs don't last forever; besides becoming damaged and broken, they eventually fall out. On average, we each lose about 50 to 100 each day. To keep churning out new hairs, a follicle cycles its production: years of growth (the anagen cycle) followed by a few-week transition phase (the catagen cycle), and finally a follicle vacation, the rest (telogen) phase.

Thankfully, the follicles on our heads are not in lockstep. Otherwise, we'd lose all of our hairs around the same time, and then slowly begin growing them back. Whatever its current phase, each follicle takes about two to seven years to complete its cycles, with nearly all of that time spent in the growth phase.

At the bottom of each follicle bulb is a ring of rapidly dividing cells, supplied with nutrients and oxygen by a tangle of small blood vessels. The new cells pile up in a tube, pushing through the follicle. Cells on the inside of the tube die and harden into a hair shaft. Cells in the outer layer harden into a covering sheath.

Once a hair nears the skin surface, chemicals secreted by the follicle walls remove the sheath, uncovering the hair beneath. At the surface, the hair is coated with protective oil courtesy of the sebaceous glands, and emerges from the skin into the light of day. A newborn hair will continue to grow about a half-inch (1.3 cm) a month—or about 1/100,000th of an inch (0.00025 mm) each minute—until it's cut off from its nutrients by the follicle (or pulled out by accident).

Although a hair looks smooth to the naked eye, it is really covered with scales, resembling the shingles on a roof. (This layer of keratin scales is called the cuticle.) Scales get ruffled up when hair is dry and damaged,

Fast Fact

A human being has about 90,000 to 150,000 hairs on his or her head.

usually from overbrushing, hot blow-drying, or harsh hair coloring. For hair to be shiny—to reflect light—the scales must lie flat, like the surface of a mirror.

Recent studies show that hair growth cycles are regulated by genes that control the body's 24-hour circadian rhythms. But in the case of hair, the genes operate on longer time scales, signaling follicles to alter their cycles according to season. In one study of Northern Hemisphere men, the number of hair follicles in the growth phase was highest in March, lowest in September.

How does arm hair know to stop growing?

Arm hair —and other body hair—is a lot like the silky fur on your dog or cat: It grows to a preset length and then obediently stops. Human head hair, on the other hand, can cascade down to the ankles.

How does it work? The hair on our head grows, on average, about a half-inch (1.3 cm) a month, month after month. Still, even head hair can't grow forever. Each follicle has a set growth phase, the length of time it will continue to churn out new hair cells. For a head hair follicle, the growth phase lasts, on average, about two to seven years. Then the follicle stops making new cells. Eventually, its hair breaks off at the scalp. After a few months' rest, the follicle revs up production, and a new hair sprouts.

The growth phase varies from person to person, and also changes as we age. If your follicles have a long growth phase, and your hair grows quickly, you can grow your hair to knee length or longer if you choose. It all depends on the genes you inherited from your parents.

The length of the hair on the rest of the body is determined by genes, too. But there's a twist when it comes to the hairs that stay stubbornly short. Scientists studying hair growth noticed that follicles from head and body hair looked similar under a microscope. But when they transplanted head hair to the leg, researchers found that newly rooted head hairs grew much faster than nearby leg hairs.

Meanwhile, body hair transplanted to the head

Armhair Alert...

An arm hair grows at a snail's pace for just a few months.

simply refused to grow past a certain length. Body hair, it turns out, grows like fur, to a roughly predetermined length. Which makes sense, since our patchy body hair is all that remains of the fur coat that protected our primate ancestors from the elements.

So how does body hair know when to stop growing? The follicle cells that produce abbreviated hairs from eyebrows to legs are programmed by genes to grow extra-slowly—and to have extra-short growth cycles. A head hair can grow a half inch a month for a maximum of about seven years. But an arm hair grows at a snail's pace for just a few months before stopping. Result: Body hair ranges from the short (like arm and leg hair) to the very short (eyebrow hair).

But the exact growing cycle of body hair varies

Fast Fact

There's always that rogue hair that has its instructions scrambled, which is why a weird, longer-than-normal hair may sprout somewhere on your body.

from person to person, just like head hair. Take eyelash length, for example. According to scientists, human eyelashes come in "short" or "long," and we inherit our eyelash length from our parents.

Why do we have eyebrows?

BROW TALK

Hi! Good to see you!

Not really...

What did I do?

you Never called me back.

I'm sorry...

Forget it, Let's go have lunch.

Two slim patches of hair, one above each eye, like twin caterpillars: Eyebrows are one of evolution's more clever uses of body hair. The brow bone juts out above eyes, protecting them. And the multitasking brow hairs act as handy-dandy filters and as conveyers of emotion.

Spend any time in the sun, and you'll realize your forehead is rich in sweat glands. A sweating forehead helps keep the head (and brain) from overheating as sweat evaporates into the air. And as sweat rolls down the forehead, the eyebrows help trap this salty, stinging liquid before it can drip into our eyes.

Likewise, eyebrows help keep rain out of our eyes when we are caught in a downpour. Like the gutters on a house, angled eyebrow hairs

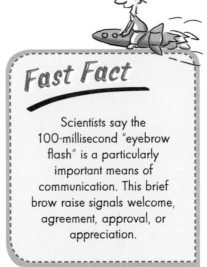

 Eyebrows  can warn of an insect approaching the eye, since a crawling bug causes hairs to move to and fro like grass.

direct liquids away from the eyes and down the temples.

Eyebrows may also warn of an insect approaching the eye, since a crawling bug causes hairs to move to and fro like grass. These little hair strips also catch dust and dirt, like two doormats positioned above the eyes.

Eyebrows, like head hair, are also a kind of adornment.

Like dirt-catching eyelashes, eyebrows accentuate the eyes and make us more attractive to other people. Which is why there's a market not just for mascara but for eyebrow pencils, gels, and tweezers to create just the right thickness, shape, and arch.

Fashions in eyebrows come and go, from the pencil-thin flapper look of the 1930s to the bushy brows of the 1980s. But shaving off the eyebrows has never been as popular, since it deprives us of a key element of facial expression. One of the main functions of eyebrows, scientists say, is to convey emotion.

Other animals have eyebrows, but human eyebrows stand out on otherwise almost hairless skin. Think of eyebrows knit in concentration . . .

Fast Fact

Scientists say the 100-millisecond "eyebrow flash" is a particularly important means of communication. This brief brow raise signals welcome, agreement, approval, or appreciation.

raised in surprise . . . or set in a stern frown. Even from some distance away, we check out other people's facial expressions—and especially their eyebrows—to figure out their mood. This has obvious survival value, whether you are being approached by an angry member of another tribe or an angry teacher from across the room.

Why does hair turn gray as we get older?

It may start as soon as your 20s: a glint of silver hidden in a forest of dark strands. The first gray hair can be shocking. But whether you yank it out or call it a highlight, the strand will eventually be joined by a host of silver siblings.

Where does our natural hair color come from? Unlike dye in a bottle, designed to spread across a whole field of hairs, the body has no Central Color reservoir, feeding the scalp a stream of colored liquid. Instead, each strand has its own dedicated pigment factory near its roots, in cells called melanocytes. Which is why one hair may be chocolate brown, while the strand a quarter-inch away is palest white.

The master pigment tinting both hair and skin is melanin. Melanin is made mainly from an amino acid called tyrosine, a building block of the proteins we eat. But instead of a Crayola range of colors, melanin comes in just two main varieties. Pheomelanin comes in shades of gold to red; eumelanin is brown to black. Granules of pheomelanin are shaped like little round balls, while eumelanin granules are egg-shaped. Bigger or smaller granules mean stronger or weaker hues.

Like pots of paint, eumelanin and pheomelanin in every combination create the astonishing variety of hair (and skin) color found in human beings. Our own unique melanin recipe is determined by the genes we inherit from our parents.

The melanocytes that give each hair its color are located mainly in the hair's bulb at the bottom of each follicle. Hair-making cells called keratinocytes, which surround the melanocytes, pull in a load of melanin. Since hair strands receive different amounts, not all are exactly the same color. The result: a mix of natural highlights.

With aging, more and more hairs lose their melanin supply. Hairs receiving only a fraction of their usual pigment look dull and faded. When melanocytes die off entirely, the emerging hair is colorless, and we see white.

Going, Going ... Gray!

Scientists haven't worked out all the details of the color loss. But by looking at the hair follicles of aging mice and people, researchers have found that the stem cells destined to become melanocytes were themselves dying off, and cells that remained were making more errors.

In 2009, researchers found that compared to normally colored hairs, gray hairs have accumulated hydrogen peroxide, from root to tip.

Sounds familiar? Diluted, hydrogen peroxide makes a handy antiseptic for wounds. But it's also good at bleaching and whitening, which is why peroxide is an ingredient in many tooth whiteners.

When we're young, an enzyme called catalase breaks up hair's excess hydrogen peroxide into oxygen and water. But as we age, catalase production drops. And so do levels of enzymes that repair hydrogen peroxide damage.

More hydrogen peroxide plus low levels of repair enzymes means less tyrosinase, the enzyme needed to make melanin. The result: hair that has less pigment *and* that makes its own bleach—a perfect recipe for whitening.

If blood is red, why does it look blue in our veins?

On a winter's day, walking to school in a frigid wind, your nose turns Rudolph-red. Later, embarrassed by something you did in class, you feel a rosy blush spread across your face. After lunch, the teacher hands out a pop math quiz. Turning over the test sheet, you manage to get a paper cut—and a single scarlet drop wells out of your fingertip.

From these rather obvious clues, we might guess that the blood inside our bodies is red. But look at the underside of your wrist, and all bets are off. What about those blue veins, crisscrossing like tiny tree branches? Isn't it blood that tints them purplish-blue?

As it turns out, blood's natural color is red. The red comes courtesy of the erythrocytes, or red blood cells, which make up some 40 percent of our blood volume. It's the job of red blood cells to ferry oxygen into all the body's nooks and crannies, to cells in the brain, liver, kidneys, skin, and other organs.

Red blood cells collect oxygen in the lungs, after we inhale it from the air. Toting their oxygen cargo, the erythrocytes move through the body's arteries like train cars on branching tracks.

Inside each erythrocyte are some 250 million hemoglobin molecules, composed of proteins and iron. Hemoglobin is naturally dark red. But when oxygen gloms onto hemoglobin's iron, the hemoglobin brightens to fire-engine red, the true color of oxygen-rich blood.

When the oxygen is delivered to cells throughout the body, hemoglobin's job isn't done. Cells receiving oxygen give up carbon dioxide (CO_2), the waste product of their energetic activity. Using the body's back roads, the veins, hemoglobin obligingly carts the CO_2 back to the lungs.

Without thinking about it, we exhale the carbon dioxide into the air.

Having given up its oxygen to other body cells, blood traveling through the veins is a moody dark red.

However, when dark blood from a vein spills out of a cut, it may absorb enough oxygen from the air to brighten up to a clear red.

So why do the veins in our wrists, arms, and legs look blue, rather than, say, maroon? It turns out the blue hue is just a trick of light.

Scientists in Toronto solved the blue blood conundrum by using blood-filled glass tubes as artificial veins. They immersed the tubes in a fatty, milky fluid to simulate light-colored skin. The "veins" appeared red before their milky dip. But submerged to a certain depth, the tubes of blood suddenly turned blue.

Why the color change? The researchers say that when light falls on our skin, longer-wavelength red light travels further into the skin than shorter-wavelength blue light before it's reflected back out. So when a vein is at least two one-hundredths of an inch (0.05 cm) below the skin's surface, blue light reflects out before it can be absorbed by the vein. Presto: The vein looks blue, even though the blood inside is red.

How does the nose smell things?

You are walking down the street one day and notice a certain faint smell in the air—perhaps a combination of moist earth and cut grass, reminding you of the scent of approaching rain. Suddenly, your brain fires off a memory of you standing sheltered in your open garage while rain pelts the driveway on a hot summer day.

Author Helen Keller, who could neither hear nor see, wrote about this power of smell to recall the past. "Smell is a potent wizard who transports us across thousands of miles and all the years we have lived . . . odors, instantaneous and fleeting, cause my heart to dilate joyously or contract with remembered grief."

The sense of smell is closely linked to memory and emotion.

More than any other sense, the sense of smell is linked to memory and emotion. Seeing a photograph of yourself standing in the garage watching the rain, or feeling rain on your hand, or hearing rain patter on your roof won't evoke the memory of what it felt like a tenth as well as smelling the smell of that long-lost day.

And according to new research, a human nose and brain can discern more than a trillion separate odors, from the different fragrance notes in fresh-ground coffee to the waxy smell of a new box of crayons. We live awash in odors, new ones arriving with each breath.

The sense of smell is so powerful that it plays a central role in survival. Smell enables animals to find mates and—most important—food. A newborn animal searches for its mother's milk through the sense of smell, since its eyes aren't yet sharp enough to see the nipple. Human babies do this, too. On the flip side, spoiled food usually smells bad—rotten or moldy or otherwise stinky—so smell helps us avoid getting sick.

(And smell is crucial to

taste—hold your nose, and an apple tastes no different than a carrot.)

When you smell, say, just-popped popcorn in a movie theater, thank scent molecules, drifting through the air and up your nose. These tiny chemical fragments dissolve in the wet mucus of the epithelium membrane, several inches up from each nostril. There, they make contact with odor receptors.

The smells around us are complex, and we each have some 40 million odor receptors to help decode wafting-in scents. (Dogs, expert smellers, may have 2 billion.) These fiber-studded nerve cells are connected by longer fibers (axons) to the brain's olfactory bulb, located behind the nose.

Scientists say that it's the unique structure of each scent molecule that enables the brain to figure out what, exactly, we're smelling. And as each molecule is mapped by the brain, it files away the information, allowing us to instantly recognize scents ("lemon!" "lilacs!") in the future.

(Some odor molecules, such as those given off by flowers, float right up our nose and lodge in the odor receptors. But some odor molecules from food we're eating take a different route, wafting up from the back of the throat.)

The nerve cells of the odor receptors are connected by tendrils to the olfactory bulbs, whose nerve fibers project directly into the brain. (The part of the brain they extend into, the limbic system, just happens to be the seat of our emotions.)

Odor molecules come in various shapes—wedges, spheres, rods, discs. When a molecule makes contact with an odor receptor, the receptor changes shape—like a flexible lock, altering to fit an intruding key. This shape-changing prompts a nerve cell to fire off a signal, which travels through the olfactory bulbs and into the brain. The brain interprets the signal as a particular smell—say, "wet dog."

Scientists think there are "families" of odors and that each family's molecules have similar shapes. One way to categorize seven "primary odors" is: minty, floral, musky, resinous (like turpentine), acrid (like vinegar), foul/putrid (like rotten eggs), and ethereal (like the smell of a fresh pear).

Different receptors seem to pick up on different parts

Fast Fact

Many objects around us—like those made of glass—don't smell, because they don't evaporate and send off odor molecules at ordinary temperatures and air pressure.

of an incoming smell. Some 275 different components combine to create the scent of a rose, and the smell of fresh-brewed coffee can contain up to 500. Change the components in the smell that the brain labels "popcorn!" and the receptors will cause it to report back "corn on the cob" instead.

How do two nostrils help us smell?

Nostril Count...

Smell what's in front of you—if you are lucky!

Smell what's on either side of you.

Smell what's down the block and in the next state.

If the same scent molecules drift up both nostrils when we take a sniff of roasting turkey or pumpkin pie, why isn't one nostril enough? Just as two ears help us figure out what we're hearing, and where the sounds are coming from, we also smell in stereo.

Unlike our widely separated ears, the nostrils are side by side at the end of the nose. But experiments show that each nostril sniffs in its own sample of air, separated in space by about 1.5 inches (3.8 cm). The brain compares the scents arriving from each nostril, putting together a picture of what's being smelled—and where it's coming from.

Our nostrils also have varying airflows, depending on how nose tissue contracts or expands with blood flow. When one side is slightly swollen, the other is free-breathing. Scent molecules that dissolve slowly in mucus may be whisked quickly through the more open side, with less chance for detection.

But fast-dissolving molecules make their biggest scent impact when swept into contact with a large swath of neurons. Having two nostrils with different airflows allows us to detect both kinds.

In a real-world experiment, researchers at the University of California, Berkeley, found that two nostrils are definitely better than one. The researchers dipped a 33-foot (10.1-m) length of string in chocolate essence, then arranged it on a grassy lawn outside a university building. Like kids on an Easter egg hunt, volunteers tried to pick up the chocolate trail—using only their noses and a zigzag sniffing pattern.

Wearing eye masks, earmuffs, heavy gloves, and knee and elbow pads, volunteers crawled along the ground, trying to detect a chocolaty scent. Out of 32 people, 21—an impressive two-thirds—were able to follow the trail from beginning to end.

But with one nostril taped shut, the volunteers found it harder to pick up the scent. Likewise, when wearing a device that pumped the same air into both nostrils, the human bloodhounds were slower—and only about half as accurate.

Why does our breath smell bad, especially in the morning?

The Smelliest Clouds on Earth...

Help!

ugh!

Oi!

A post-pizza exhalation...

An after-peanut-butter emanation...

Or an early morning "haven't-brushed-yet" aeration.

For thousands of years, people have worried about their breath. More than 3,500 years ago, the ancient Greek physician Hippocrates advised rinsing out the mouth with a mixture of wine and herbs to sweeten the breath. And a cosmetics manufacturer in ancient Rome became a rich man when he started producing breath mints.

Most of us—if not all of us—have bad breath now and then. And we humans aren't the only ones to breathe out smelly air. Dog breath can be pretty foul, too. And if we got close enough, we'd probably discover that there's squirrel breath, giraffe breath, and hippopotamus breath, too.

One cause of smelly breath is the pungent food we eat. For example, after we digest garlic, its odor will perfume air in the lungs (and even seep through the pores in our skin).

Some diseases and conditions can cause bad breath, too—a fruity odor from diabetes, a fishy odor from kidney problems, a cheesy smell from tonsillitis.

But 90 percent of bad breath comes from everyday conditions in the mouth (hint: a lot like a reeking garbage can on a summer afternoon). Tiny particles of food collect between or under teeth, braces, and dentures. And there they sit, rotting—sometimes for days on end. Not surprisingly, this creates a smelly situation.

Bacteria that live in the mouth and feast on the tiny leftovers actually create the bad smell. As they chow down, their waste products emit sulfur gases—the same gases that give rotten eggs their unlovely odor. These bacteria especially like to hang out on the back of the tongue, creating that carpet of white

we sometimes see when we wake up in the morning.

(By the way, it's hard to know whether you have bad breath, unless someone tells you so. A dentist suggests this test, best performed in private: Lick your own wrist, licking from the back of the tongue to the tip. Let dry for 10 seconds, and sniff. If you don't like the smell, neither will anyone else.)

Luckily, the body makes its own antibacterial mouthwash to keep things sweet-smelling: saliva. The mouth bacteria that cause bad breath are anaerobic, which means they like to live where there's little or no oxygen. Saliva, among other ingredients, contains lots of oxygen.

Morning breath, that delightfully foul breath that often follows a full night's sleep, develops when bacteria run wild. The salivary glands slow their production to a trickle during the night, since

Fast Fact

Your mouth can make more than 6 cups (1.4 l) of saliva a day.

you're not awake and eating. The mouth dries out, bacteria multiply, and your breath smells like last night's rotting dinner.

What can you do about bad breath? Brush and floss your teeth, to get all the between-teeth food particles out. Gently brush your tongue, especially the rear part, with your toothbrush. Snack on carrots, apples, and other fiber-full, teeth-scrubbing foods. Drink a lot of water. And have your teeth deep-cleaned at the dentist's office about once or twice a year.

What are our tonsils for?

Once upon a time, getting your tonsils out was almost a rite of passage in childhood. Around age seven or eight or so, usually after a string of strep throat infections, you went into the hospital for an operation and woke up without your tonsils. Afterward, you got to eat lots of ice cream to soothe your painful throat. Like another frequently removed organ, the appendix, tonsils were seen as almost disposable body parts—not very important; won't be missed.

Today, however, opinions about these two little clumps of tissue are changing. Doctors aren't so quick to remove them. And researchers are discovering that the tonsils are actually front-line guards in the defense against bacteria, viruses, and other pathogens making their way into the body.

In fact, there are four different kinds of tonsils ringing the back of the throat, including tonsils at the root of the tongue and tonsils behind the nose (the adenoids). The tonsil collection is part of the body's immune system, the defensive network that includes the lymph nodes, spleen, and all the varieties of disease-fighting white blood cells.

But it's the twin palatine tonsils, situated on either side of the dangly uvula above the back of the tongue, that we know as *the* tonsils. These tonsils are fleshy, olive-shaped pink masses. If you look in a mirror, open your mouth wide, stick your tongue out, and say "aaaahhh," you should be able to see the two spongy-looking tonsils.

The tonsils are made of lymphoid tissue, like the lymph nodes that stud the body in spots like the neck and underarms. Even though tonsils are small, their surface area is large. Cleverly, each tonsil has 10 to 30 deep crypts, or closed caves. So germs from food, air, saliva, or other sources easily come into contact with part of the tonsils' surface as they pass through the back of the throat. Meanwhile, the tonsils are teeming with lymphocytes, white blood cells whose business is to identify incoming bacteria and

> For a long time, tonsils were seen as almost disposable body parts and were often removed.

viruses and direct the immune system's fight against the invaders.

Recent studies show that tonsils may play an important role in stopping lung infections—like flu—before they get a foothold. Besides their local, back-of-the-throat activities, the tonsils also seem to influence how the rest of the immune system targets an infection. The tonsils sit in a strategic position in the body—a key entry point for pathogens, an open doorway. By "sampling" bacteria, viruses, and other intruders that stream their way from mouth and nose, tonsils help the body mount a concerted defense.

Tonsils are most sensitive, researchers say, when we are 3 to 10 years old. During those years, it's common for tonsils to become swollen and inflamed when they get overwhelmed by, say, strep bacteria. Antibiotics are sometimes prescribed to give the immune system a fighting chance to douse the infection. But if recurring infections cause abscesses in the tonsils, or if tonsil size interferes with breathing during sleep, the doctor often will still recommend removal.

How come acids in the stomach don't destroy it?

It's a mystery: Some human beings feast on other animals' organs—liver, kidneys, heart, lungs—and their stomachs oblige by digesting the whole lot. (In fact, the Scottish dish called "haggis" is a sheep's stomach, stuffed with organ meats and oatmeal.) Yet our own stomachs survive the caustic acid bath of each meal. How come?

From the time we take the first bite of breakfast to our last evening snack, the stomach makes about 6 cups (1.4 l) of digestive "juices." A key ingredient: extremely corrosive hydrochloric acid. Drop a piece of zinc into a cup of digestive juice, and the acid would gradually dissolve the metal.

(Which isn't surprising if you've ever been sick and vomited: That burning in your throat is caused by acid ejected from your stomach.)

Only 0.5 percent of the stomach's digestive juices are hydrochloric acid, but that's more than enough to digest dinner. The rest of the digestive liquid is a mix of water, sodium chloride (salt), potassium chloride, and some calcium. The mix activates stomach enzymes called pepsins, which break down proteins. Pepsins are also threats to living cells.

Chew and swallow a bite of food, and a chemical chain reaction begins immediately. The stomach releases gastrin, a hormone that signals cells in the stomach's lining (the parietals) to forge hydrochloric acid from hydrogen and chloride atoms. Food in the stomach—say, bits of that salad or burger you ate—begin to break down in the acidic juice.

Meanwhile, other stomach cells begin churning out a substance called pepsinogen. With the help of hydrochloric acid, water enters pepsinogen, transforming it into protein-chomping pepsin. It's pepsin that severs the bonds between protein's linked-up amino acids.

The stomach's environment is so caustic that it kills or inhibits many microorganisms that might harm us. So why isn't the stomach injured by its own chemicals? Luckily, the stomach has an arsenal of built-in defenses against its own digestive weapons.

One way the stomach protects itself: The stomach's lining of epithelial cells continuously regenerates. In the ongoing acid bath, some 500,000 epithelial cells are shed and replaced each minute. So stomach tissue underneath remains protected from the harsh environment in the churning sac.

Next, there's that all-purpose protective slime the body loves to churn out (say, from your drippy nose): mucus. Mucus is made by the epithelial cells and spreads over the stomach

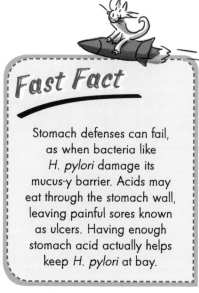

Fast Fact

Stomach defenses can fail, as when bacteria like *H. pylori* damage its mucus-y barrier. Acids may eat through the stomach wall, leaving painful sores known as ulcers. Having enough stomach acid actually helps keep *H. pylori* at bay.

wall as a thick, gooey barrier. Digestive juices eat through the mucus, but more slips out behind it. The lining makes so much of the slimy stuff that nearly 40 percent of an empty stomach's weight is actually mucus. The stomach lining also manufactures its own antacid—the alkaline substance called bicarbonate. Finally, the stomach seems to be able to switch its environment from acid to alkaline, using special pH sensor molecules.

Why do we have an appendix?

The appendix is one of the body's most unobtrusive organs. No painful protests, like the ungrateful stomach after Thanksgiving dinner. No gasping after a sprint to the finish line, courtesy of the overworked lungs. And no ominous rumbling, like intestines encountering an iffy restaurant clam.

We usually notice the appendix only when something goes terribly wrong with it. What are some symptoms of appendicitis? Pain in the lower right abdomen, nausea, vomiting, and a fever. If the ailing appendix is removed, it seems like no great loss.

Did nature simply get sloppy and produce a wormlike cave on the large intestine? Or is the appendix a "vestigial" organ, some small fragment of us that once played a part now long forgotten?

Recently, researchers at Duke University in North Carolina unveiled a new explanation for the appendix's existence. Hint: Rather like the fire extinguisher that usually sits unused on the wall, this tiny organ may be good in a crisis.

The 2- to 4-inch-long appendix juts from the right side of the large intestine like the tail on a dog. Only about a third of an inch in diameter, the narrow appendix has an opening nearly as small as the tip of a mechanical pencil. There's a one-way door at the exit (Gerlach's valve). Mucus, made in the appendix, flows through this valve and on into the bowel.

Trouble starts when something—usually a bit of dried feces—blocks the tiny opening. The result can be raging infection and inflammation, along with pain, vomiting, and fever. The appendix can swell and even burst, causing a deadly infection called peritonitis. Fortunately, appendicitis is usually easily treated. The infected organ is removed, and antibiotics stop infection from spreading.

When an ailing appendix is removed, the digestive

Measure FOR Measure
2 to 4 inches = 5 to 10 cm
a third of an inch = 0.84 cm

Appendix War Stories...

system seems to function just as well without it. So what's it for? Earlier research had suggested that the appendix is part of the immune system, fighting infections by secreting antibodies into the intestines.

The Duke researchers also think that the appendix is a part of the body's defenses. But its main role, they say, may be as a sanctuary for helpful bacteria, a place where friendly organisms can hang out until they're urgently needed.

The intestines run on

"good" bacteria, colonies that break down food and occupy space desired by not-so-friendly microorganisms. But when we come down with a serious intestinal disease involving diarrhea, the supply of good bacteria quickly dwindles. The researchers note that diarrheal diseases like cholera and dysentery still plague much of the underdeveloped world, and were common throughout human history.

The human appendix sits in a relatively protected place, away from infections

raging in the rest of the gut, near the immune system's lymph glands. Inside this safe house, in the mucus behind the one-way door, helpful bacteria can grow and multiply. When diarrhea has run its course, the intestines are depleted of bacteria both good and bad. Researchers think that the appendix can then "re-inoculate" the colon with a ready-made colony. In the developed world, where people are less likely to suffer from diseases like dysentery, the appendix can be removed without apparent harm.

Where does the fat go when you lose weight?

With all the fat lost from eating less and exercising more, it seems as if it should show up somewhere—like in storage in seedy waterfront buildings. The truth is, all that lost fat simply disappears. To see how it happens, we first need to know what fat is doing on our bodies to begin with.

Most body parts are obviously useful. The heart pumps blood from toes to head. The lungs breathe air in and out. The eyes let us see the purple flags of sunset; the ears let us hear the birds' chirping chorus at dawn. The bones hold us up, so we don't collapse into a formless heap. The brain thinks, reasons, remembers—and runs the rest of the body. And fat—well, fat just sits there. . . .

But not really. Fat is actually just as important as every other body part. In fact, we can't live without it. Fat is the body's portable grocery, providing free food when supplies are scarce. Fat insulates us in cold weather, helping keep our internal organs at a steady temperature. It cushions our bones from breaking; it secretes hormones.

When fat disappears from your body, it doesn't retire to a fat farm. The truth is, most of it is burned up in your muscles.

Muscles actually prefer to use sugar for fuel, because it burns easily. Sugar is available from three places: Some is stored right in the muscles, some in the liver, and a little circulates in the blood. But only about 750 calories' worth of sugar fuel is on tap for the muscles at any given time.

So muscles burn a mix of fuel: sugar and fat. The mix varies—the slower you move, the higher the percentage of fat burned. (The greatest percentage of fat is burned when you sleep.) However, the slower you move, the

---

Fat is the body's portable grocery.

smaller the total amount of fat and sugar burned. You may burn less than 60 calories an hour sleeping, but you will burn 450 to 600 in an hour of slow running.

The body's sugar supply is scant. But a mere 30 pounds (13.6 kg) of body fat provides nearly 105,000 calories of energy to a hungry body—enough to survive several months. Having enough body fat was crucial for much of human history, when food was often scarce. It is still critical for the millions of people who face famines on a regular basis.

What happens to burned fat? When sugar is completely burned, all that is left is water and carbon dioxide. The same is true of fat that's burned in muscles. However, some fat may be processed by the liver instead. There, fragments of partially burned fat—called ketones—are left over.

The carbon dioxide is carried by the blood to the lungs and breathed out into the air. (Plants use carbon dioxide, so your burned-up fat makes the world a little greener.) The water is used by the body or excreted through breath, sweat, and urine. Ketones travel from the liver through the blood and get burned in the muscles and the brain for energy. Or they're broken down in the kidneys. The end result (again) is carbon dioxide and water—and disappearing fat.

The SKINNY ON FAT

Fat is our friend...
Until you can't fit in your jeans.

One-half of Americans have way too many fat cells...
But I'll keep you warm!
I'll protect you!
I'll feed you!

Maybe that's why it's so hard to lose weight?
It's hard to say good-bye to friends.
Bye-Bye!

Why are our five fingers different lengths?

ands and fingers aren't unique to human beings; other primates have them, too. Take a look at a gorilla's or chimp's hands and you'll see a set of four fingers, varying in length from index to pinky, along with a real thumb. (While other animals, such as raccoons, have paws that resemble hands, official "hands" belong only to primates.)

Hands are useful for grasping—hanging on to a tree limb (or hanging on to a ladder), picking berries (or picking up groceries), throwing a clod of dirt (or throwing a baseball). If our fingers were the same length,

POLKA-DOT NAILS

At some point, you've probably noticed a white spot or three on your fingernails. Such spots, according to dermatologists, are one of the most common body blemishes, as familiar to most of us as pimples and scars. (In any 100 people, more than 60 will probably have a spotty nail or two.)

The spots are so common—but can seem so mysterious—that people have come up with creative names for them: *fortune spots*, predicting good luck; *sweethearts*, tallying the number of romantic suitors; and even *lies*, the fingernail version of Pinocchio's growing nose. The *Oxford English Dictionary* notes that "gifts" can mean white nail spots (a usage dating to 1708), since each spot supposedly predicted receiving one.

But falling in love or winning the lottery have nothing to do with white spots, unless you happen to hit one of your fingers in all the excitement. Dermatologists say the white marks crop up because we ding our fingers so often. The culprit? Anything from a mis-caught ball to a jabbing cuticle stick.

How does it work? Our fingernails are made of a protein called keratin. The spots are thought to be a mix of keratin and air, places where new nail cells were incompletely formed, or "keratinized." The spots appear because of repeated dings to the nail bed at the base of a fingernail.

The white spots slowly rise as the nail is pushed up by new growth from the nail bed. Since a nail grows about 0.04 inch (1 mm) in 10 days, it can take months for the spotted part to reach the tip for trimming off.

Still, there's a lot researchers don't know about the spots, since not many studies have been done. In the 1970s, Harry Arnold Jr., then a dermatology professor at the University of Hawaii, noted some nail-spot mysteries. If spots were always the result of injuries to the nail bed, he wondered, then why did some seem to make their first appearance nowhere near the nail's lunula (half-moon)? And why, after an injury to one nail, did white spots sometimes appear on fingers of the opposite hand—in a mirror-image pattern? Nail spots, he suggested, might be under the control of the body's nervous system.

---

our hands wouldn't be such flexible tools.

When we hold a spherical object like an orange in the palm of our hand, the fingers actually curve around evenly, giving us a firm grip.

Tapering fingers (and strong thumbs) allowed early humans to use specially shaped stones to smash, scrape, and cut other objects. (A long pinky finger would be more likely to get caught and squashed.)

Besides precision grips, our different-length fingers also provide a balanced support for crawling or leaning on our hands.

Among different species of primates—from baboons

to monkeys—fingers and thumbs vary in shape and length. Long, thin fingers are best for tree swinging. Chimpanzees, who make and use simple tools like termite catchers, have hands that most resemble ours.

Most primates, from chimpanzees, gorillas, and orangutans to Old World monkeys, have opposable thumbs that can bend outward at up to a 90-degree angle from the other fingers. The most developed opposable thumbs are handy for holding small objects between the thumb and index finger.

Thumbs have only one middle joint, rather than the two joints found on the four regular fingers. The

 Our different-length fingers give us a more precise grip and provide a balanced support for leaning on our hands.

four longer fingers can curl further around an object, while powerful muscles allow the thumb to lock in the grip, viselike. Human opposable thumbs are, compared to those of other primates, bigger and stronger. A

chimp can pick up a peanut from the ground but can't open a tightened lid on a jar of peanut butter. Our own powerful thumbs seem to have evolved in tandem with our toolmaking skills.

Among individuals in each primate species, fingers and thumbs vary, too. Compare your hands to those of your friends, and you'll see subtle and not-so-subtle differences. Boys and men often have longer ring than index fingers. Girls and women tend to have similar-length ring and index fingers, or shorter ring fingers. Scientists say the differences are due to the influence of the hormones estrogen and testosterone in the womb.

Why do we have wax in our ears?

Suffering from a little waxy build-up? While not so good for polished wooden furniture, it may actually be a good thing when it comes to ears.

Cerumen is the oily main ingredient, made by thousands of tiny glands hidden in the ear canal's outer walls. As cerumen is secreted from the glands, it collects dead skin cells. The end result: earwax.

While a build-up of too much earwax can muffle incoming sounds, the right amount helps to keep ears healthy. Skin lining the ear canal is very thin, and dries out easily. Earwax coats the skin, helping hold moisture in. Meanwhile, earwax, like the coating on a sheet of wax paper, acts like a handy water repellent. So when water sprays into our ears in the shower, earwax helps it to run out the way it came.

Earwax also protects the body from intruders trying to enter through a side door. Studies show that fresh cerumen is a natural

CONTINENTAL EARWAX DIVIDE

Why do some people have more waxy buildup than others? Part of the answer lies in genes. Some people are born with narrower, clog-prone ear canals, some ear canals are especially hairy, and some just make more wax. Intriguingly, humans from different parts of the world have different earwax. People whose ancestors came from Europe or Africa tend to have "wet" earwax, about half fat by weight. People whose ancestors came from Asia tend to have low-fat "dry" earwax.

germicide that can kill *Staphylococcus*, *Streptococcus*, and *E. coli* bacteria, and even some strains of the flu virus and fungi. Cerumen contains enzymes that damage the cell walls of invading bacteria, and the acidity of earwax also is an effective barrier against unwanted microbes.

Most earwax starts out as pale yellow. But by the time it's ready to fall out, debris-encrusted wax can be a dark, crumbling mass. The tiny-but-mighty balls of wax act as sticky traps for anything that wafts, walks, or flies into the ear. So an old plug of earwax may contain tiny hairs, teensy bugs, dust, soot, soil, and bits of plants. Earwax is the body's flypaper.

How do our ears get rid of used wax? Older, dirt-laden wax slowly migrates to the entrance of the ear, helped along by jaw movements as we talk or chew. The old wax, along with dead skin cells, dries up and drops out of the ear, adding to the dust in the world.

But while our ears are self-cleaning, wax can occasionally lodge stubbornly in place. Clues to a waxy build-up include a feeling of stuffiness in the ears and muffled hearing, as if you were in a car driving up a mountain road. The ear canal may also itch or ache. As the built-up wax presses on nerves in the ear, your throat may feel tickly, and you may even develop a slight cough.

While putting a few drops of mineral oil into the ear may help the plug slip out, other home remedies range from useless to dangerous. Cotton swabs can push wax further into the ear, and other homemade tools can puncture the eardrum. Your family doctor can use ear drops and special tools to remove wax safely.

Do we really use only 10 percent of our brains?

Whether it's half, 10 percent, or "a few percent," we hear the claim every day: At any given moment, most of the brain is just idling, or even turned off, like the lights in a dark room. If we could just wake up the hibernating part of our brain, imagine what we could do . . .

But while the idea that we only use a fraction of our brains can motivate us to achieve more, it's only a (useful) myth. Like those alligator families lurking in the New York City sewer system, the wasted brain idea is just a very old urban legend.

The brain is the body's command center, and, like a souped-up engine, it uses extra fuel. An adult's brain

> The brain can be exercised, like a muscle, and become smarter.

weighs about 3 pounds, or about 2 percent of his or her body weight. But the energy-hog brain can burn up to 70 percent of the body's blood glucose (sugar). Most of that energy is consumed by the brain's 100 billion neurons, firing off signals to other neurons, cells, and glands at up to 200 miles per hour.

Neurologists point out that losing just a little brain tissue in an accident can have

drastic consequences, and injury to even small areas of the brain in a stroke can affect the ability to speak and move. In fact, scientists say, there doesn't seem to be any brain part that, if damaged, doesn't show up in some loss of function.

Electrical stimulation of the brain during brain surgery has also shown that there are no unused back rooms in the brain. Everywhere the electrical probe touches calls up an emotion or memories, or stimulates a body movement.

In fact, when you are sitting quietly in a chair daydreaming, your entire brain is busy, dredging up pleasant memories, controlling your heart rate,

100.0% Brain Workouts!

Learn to read and sing Chinese folk songs...

Practice your balance beam routine...

Paint your toenails in a crossword puzzle chat room, while finishing your homework.

keeping your body warm, your eyes blinking, your lunchtime sandwich digesting, and you from falling over sideways. The major parts of the brain—front, mid, hind, and their subsections and glands—are silently humming with activity.

Not surprisingly, PET scans, which use a radioactive element to visualize the activity of the working brain, have found no part that is idle. Which is why you can write a paper for school while also listening to music, tapping your foot, and continuing to breathe. Most of the brain is active at any given moment, and neurologists say we use 100 percent of our brain over the course of a day.

But that doesn't mean that some regions aren't more active than others, depending on the job at hand. And it doesn't mean that your brain has no room for improvement. Research shows that when you learn something new—how to play the piano, speak French, throw a curveball, solve a calculus problem— you actually grow new connections between brain neurons. (Their size, shape, and function may change, too.)

Based on brain imaging studies, scientists say that vigorous physical exercise, like running, can also stimulate the growth of new neurons and connections. Giving us even more brain cells to use 100 percent.

Measure FOR Measure
3 pounds = 1.4 kg
200 miles per hour = 322 km/h

Why does bright sunlight make you sneeze?

Bright Lights 'N' Big Sneezes

Trigeminal Tickle — "Hey I'm going to..."

Solar Sneeze — "AH-AH-AH"

Triple Ah-choo! — "Gesundheit!" "Choo!"

No one knows when the first human being emerged from a dark cave into bright sunlight . . . and began sneezing uncontrollably. But English scientist and philosopher Francis Bacon wrote about the phenomenon in 1635:

Looking against the Sunne,
doth induce Sneezing. The
Cause is not the Heating of the
Nosthrils [nostrils]; For then
the Holding up of the Nosthrils
against the Sunne, though one
Winke, would doe it.

In other words, the nose can't be the culprit in sun sneezing, since if you close your eyes, walk out into the sun, and expose your nose, you probably won't sneeze. What, then, is the cause? Bacon speculated about moisture descending from the brain into the eyes and nose, but had no real answer for the phenomenon. And nearly 400 years later, scientists are still trying to figure it out.

Bright sunlight can set off a volley of sneezes.

Ophthalmologists note that many patients sneeze during eye exams, when physicians shine very bright light into their eyes in a darkened room. So "ye olde Sunne" doesn't need to be out for the sneezing fits to commence.

When scientists look into an unexplained phenomenon, it usually gets a formal-sounding name. So sneezing in bright light has been dubbed the photic sneeze reflex (light is made of particles called photons), solar sneezing, and even ACHOO (for autosomal dominant compelling helio-ophthalmic outburst)—a cute way of

saying that when you sneeze in the sun, your genes made you do it.

Photic sneezing does seem to run in families, and scientists think that we inherit the tendency to sneeze in the sun from our parents. No one knows exactly how it works, but the stimulus seems to start in the eye's optic nerve. The optic nerve runs near the face's trigeminal nerve and into the same nerve hub in the brain. (And in photic sneezers, these wires may be, in some sense, crossed.) Part of the trigeminal nerve branches into the nose. So when the optic nerve reacts to very bright light after a period of darkness, neurons in the nerves leading into the nose may fire off, too. Presto: a volley of sneezes.

According to one study, the majority of photic sneezers sneeze three times in a row. Scientists say that the number of sneezes—2, 3, or even 40—may be genetically

Fast Fact

Up to 35 percent of us occasionally sneeze when we emerge from a dark place (like a movie theater) into brilliant sunlight.

determined, too. One mystery: why photic sneezers don't sneeze every time they encounter bright light after a period of darkness. Scientists speculate that there may be a certain brightness threshold required to trigger the response.

While sun sneezing is usually annoying, it can actually be hazardous for drivers emerging from long tunnels or pilots in dim cockpits turning their planes into the sun's glare. But sunlight isn't the only odd sneeze-promoter. Some people sneeze each time they pluck their eyebrows.

Are identical twins really identical?

Twins, the oh-so-subtle difference...

Nobody can tell us apart...

We're exactly alike...

Hey, how'd you do that?

Identical twins may look alike, laugh alike, and sometimes be dressed alike. But when it comes to twins, new research shows that "identical" doesn't mean "exactly alike." In fact, "identical" twins can have differences in their genes—or in how those genes are expressed—that predispose one to develop a disease like Type 1 diabetes or Parkinson's, while the other twin remains healthy.

Identical twins result when an egg, already fertilized by a sperm, splits in half. Each half contains the same gene lineup as the original embryo. Identical twins are the same sex, share the same blood type, and often look almost exactly alike as children.

But just after conception, changes can occur. Scientists have known for many years that twins who start out "identical" develop differences due to the environment, and the first environment is the womb. For example, one twin may receive a better supply of nutrients from the placenta than the other (and up to 30 percent of identicals actually have separate placentas).

And as they grow up, identical twins also diverge over time. Genetics accounts for most of how twins turn out, but can't account for everything. Studies have shown that changes are most obvious in twins separated at birth and raised by different parents. But even among those who grew up together, everything from diet and exercise to sun exposure can have an effect on appearance. Twins can also have different friends, opportunities, and experiences.

The result can be "identical" twins who look and act increasingly less alike over their lifetimes.

Now, research has shown that identical twins may be much less similar from the outset than scientists had believed, perhaps accounting for differences in developing illnesses from cancer to schizophrenia.

Even before birth, epigenetic factors—chemical markers attached to a gene that increase, slow, or shut off its activity—can vary between twins. And epigenetic changes increase over a lifetime, affected by diet, smoking, and other environmental influences. Then there are chance mutations in one embryo's DNA, as is thought to occur in some cases of cleft palate (a split in the upper mouth).

In 2008, researchers found that one twin sometimes had extra copies of DNA segments, or was missing DNA coding letters. In one case, a missing set of genes pointed to an increased risk of leukemia. That twin had leukemia; his brother didn't.

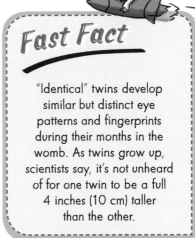

Dividing body cells also lose or acquire DNA as they develop, scientists note. In 2011, researchers found that about 12 percent of DNA can vary between identical twins. And in one study, researchers found that the average "identical" twin pair has about 359 genetic differences that appear by early in their development. So no matter how alike twins look on the outside, each is as different as a February snowflake.

Why do songs get stuck in your head?

It could be a classic rock song you heard on the car radio ("Welcome to the Hotel California . . ."). It could be the jingle from a commercial you saw last night ("Break me off a piece of that Kit Kat bar . . ."). Or it could be from the boat ride you went on at Disney World ("It's a small world after all . . ."). Whatever the trigger, you've got a snippet of music playing over and over in your mind. And it's driving you a little crazy.

Like yawning, catchy tunes—especially those with words—seem to be contagious. Just mention a song like "Dancing Queen" (or nearly any ABBA tune, for that matter), and someone within hearing distance will

Tunes that get stuck in your head are known as earworms.

get it stuck in his or her head. Others can't hear the words "My Sharona" without enduring hours of relentless repetition, thanks to The Knack.

So why does the brain act like a broken jukebox, the same piece of music clicking on again and again? The last several years have seen a small flurry of research into the viral brain tunes known as earworms. Like the "real"

earworms in an old Star Trek movie, musical worms enter our ears and burrow straight into our brains. The reason seems to involve the human brain's love of patterns, and its dogged compulsion to fill in musical blanks.

A survey of college students by James Kellaris, a marketing professor at the University of Cincinnati, found that nearly everyone experiences stuck songs. While certain songs turn up again and again on earworm lists, Kellaris says that each of us tends to be bedeviled by our own do-over ditties.

Researchers say that the music most likely to get lodged in the brain has a simple, catchy, repeating tune and/or lyrics (or even an unexpected musical twist), and has been heard frequently on radio or TV. The brain seems to dip into its repeating repertoire most often when we're tired or anxious.

Dartmouth University researchers used MRIs to image the brains of volunteers as they listened to music, including the earworm-worthy theme from the 1963 movie *The Pink Panther*. The catch: Bits and pieces of the tunes were missing. Researchers found that the auditory cortex in the listeners' brains remained active during the gaps in familiar tunes, automatically filling in the musical blanks. In effect, people couldn't stop their brains from continuing a well-known tune. It's in the auditory cortex, researchers think, where songs become memories.

In our music-heavy environment, with tunes playing in stores, restaurants, elevators, and in every earphoned ear, stuck songs are a fact of life. How to switch off the inner music? If it's July but your brain is playing endless loops of "The Little Drummer Boy," try turning on the radio for a musical change. But if "The Lion Sleeps Tonight" comes on, it's time for a new strategy. Getting involved in an attention-grabbing activity, from reading to playing a sport, may, at least temporarily, reset your compulsive brain.

Escape From an Earworm?

REPEAT YOUR NAME BACKWARDS... / PLAY THE RADIO LOUD!!! / SING A SONG YOU HATE MORE THAN THE EARWORM!

INDEX

Acknowledgments

Thanks to *Newsday* people, past and present, who've had a hand in the How Come? column, especially B. D. Colen, Anthony Marro, Michael Muskal, Marci Kemen, Liz Bass, Maryann Skinner, Dotty Beekman, Reg Gale, Jayme Wolfson, Sandra Miller, Judy Cartwright, Ted Scala, Jackie Segal, Robin Topping, Mary Burke, Larry Striegal, Jimmy Smith, Judi Yuen, Goodwin Anim, Ylka Reyes, Alberto Ortez, Lourdes Fernandez, and Sophie Williams. Thanks also to Priscilla Lundine, Willy Schwartz, and Debby Lee Cohen and family.

For answering many puzzling physics questions over the years, many thanks to Jearl Walker. We are also grateful to our literary agent for the first *How Come?* book, Meg Ruley.

At Workman, we are grateful to the late Peter Workman and his enthusiasm for *How Come?*, and to Suzanne Rafer. Many thanks go to Margot Herrera, our ace editor for the first three books. Thanks to Justin Krasner, Danny Cooper, copy editor Joan Giurdanella, production editor Carol White, and our inspired book designer, Ariana Abud. And a round of thanks to everyone else at Workman who's contributed to creating and getting the word out about *How Come?*

A million thanks to our wonderful editor, Maisie Tivnan, for her insightful editing, done with grace and good humor.

As always, huge thanks to our literary agent, Janis Donnaud. And special thanks to our readers, who keep sending us the best questions.

—Kathy Wollard and Debra Solomon

About the Authors

KATHY WOLLARD is the author of *Newsday*'s popular How Come? column. She has physics and journalism degrees from New York University, and has written about science and health for *Self, Scholastic, Popular Science,* and *Family Fun* magazines. A former New Yorker, she and her husband, author Evan Morris, now live in Ohio.

DEBRA SOLOMON is an animator working in NYC. She worked on the How Come? column for 18 years and loved every column Kathy Wollard wrote. Her films have aired on HBO and won awards in festivals worldwide. She created the animated Lizzie for the Disney Channel hit show *Lizzie McGuire*.